AMERICAN EPOCH

A HISTORY
OF THE UNITED STATES
SINCE 1900

Volume I

AMERICAN EPOCH

AMERICAN EPOCH

A HISTORY OF
THE UNITED STATES
SINCE 1900

Volume I: The Progressive Era
and the First World War   1900–1920

Arthur S. Link

Edwards Professor of American History
and Director of the Woodrow Wilson Papers
Princeton University

William B. Catton

Charles A. Dana Professor of History
and Chairman, Division of the Social Sciences
Middlebury College

Fourth Edition

Alfred A. Knopf ![running dog] New York

THIS IS A BORZOI BOOK
PUBLISHED BY ALFRED A. KNOPF, INC.

Copyright © 1955 by Arthur S. Link
Copyright © 1963, 1967, 1973 by Arthur S. Link and William B. Catton
All rights reserved under International and Pan-American Copyright Conventions. No part of
this book may be reproduced in any form or by any means, electronic or mechanical,
including photocopying, without permission in writing from the publisher. All inquiries
should be addressed to Alfred A. Knopf, Inc., 201 East 50th Street, New York, N.Y. 10022.
Published in the United States by Alfred A. Knopf, Inc., New York, and simultaneously in
Canada by Random House of Canada Limited, Toronto. Distributed by Random House, Inc.,
New York.

Library of Congress Cataloging in Publication Data

Link, Arthur Stanley.
  The progressive era and the First World War, 1900–1920.

  (His American epoch, v. 1)
  Bibliography: p.
  1. United States—History—1901–1953.
2. Progressivism (United States politics)
3. United States—History—1913–1921. I. Catton, William Bruce, 1926–   joint author.
II. Title. III. Series.
E741.L56 vol. 1   973.9'1   72-14125
ISBN 0-394-31727-0

Maps and charts by Theodore R. Miller

Manufactured in the United States of America

Design by Karin Gurski Batten

First Printing
98765432

Published 1955
Second edition 1963
Third edition 1967
Fourth edition 1973

For Our Wives
Margaret Douglas Link
and
Mina Sweeney Catton

Preface

As the reader will soon discover, this is no routine revision of *American Epoch,* with the addition of a new final chapter and an updating of the bibliography. On the contrary, we have had an opportunity to make a thoroughgoing revision. Large portions of Volume III are completely new, and new sections have been added in the other volumes. Some sections have been combined and others omitted. The material in the previous edition has been considerably shortened by the elimination of excessive detail and a tightening of the prose style, so that even with the addition of sections on the final years of the Johnson administration and an entire new chapter on the Nixon years, the present edition is slightly shorter than its predecessor.

Throughout, every sentence and paragraph have been closely scrutinized with two main objectives in mind: to bring the text into accord with the latest historical interpretations and research, and to achieve a more compact and readable prose. The result, we hope, is a book that is not only fresh and up-to-date from the point of view of scholarship, but also one which is faster moving and more readable.

We should perhaps say a special word about our treatment of the Cold War. We have read the recent so-called revisionist works on the subject with great interest, and we have learned a great deal from them, for example, concerning Russia's own legitimate security needs and America's overreaction to what seemed to be aggressive Russian moves. We have tried to relate the events of this subject without prejudice to either side, and we hope that we have achieved some kind of reasonable balance. We also believe that it is much too early and that the available materials on the Russian side are much too sparse to enable us to come to any definitive judgment concerning responsibility for particular controversies and the general mutual distrust that characterized relations between the United States and Russia from 1945 to 1962.

Readers will also find a somewhat revised view of Warren G. Harding and new accounts of the dynamics of progressivism and the struggle for women's rights.

American Epoch was originally conceived in the hope that its readers might gain some insight into the struggles and achievements of the American people during the period of the greatest change in their institutions, economy, and ways of life. It is our hope that this fourth edition will further enlarge this understanding.

The dedication very inadequately expresses our indebtedness to the two people who have helped us most in our professional careers. We would particularly like to thank Professors Travis B. Jacobs and Peter A. Stitt of Middlebury College for their advice and critical comments concerning certain portions of Volume III. In addition we are grateful to the following editors at Alfred A. Knopf, Inc., who have been unfailingly helpful through all stages of this revision: Arthur Strimling, David C. Follmer, Suzanne Thibodeau, Barbara Wrubel, Zivile Rawson, and Susan Rothstein. Finally we continue to be grateful to Theodore R. Miller for his splendid maps and graphs.

ARTHUR S. LINK
WILLIAM B. CATTON

Princeton, New Jersey
Middlebury, Vermont
January 10, 1973

Contents

Maps

Charts

∾

The Progressive Era and the First World War 1900-1920

In which the American people
surmount the depression of the
1890s, find prosperity and peace at
home, launch the progressive
movement in city, state, and nation
to restore representative government
and subject organized wealth to their
control, and, withal, become a world
power with dominions beyond the
seas and play a decisive role in the
reshaping of a new military balance
in the world.

Chapter 1

The American People during the Progressive Era

The years from 1900 to 1920 were a golden period of American development. They were usually prosperous years, marked by solid progress in living standards for all classes. They were, moreover, hopeful years. Americans, confident that they had the ability to set aright the social and economic injustices inherited from the nineteenth century, launched a virtual crusade on all levels of government to revitalize democracy, bring economic institutions under public control, and find an answer to the twin evils of special privilege and poverty.

The progressive generation was, finally, a period when Christian moralism subdued the crass materialism of the Gilded Age, and morality and righteousness became the keynotes of politics.[1] The YMCA movement swept through colleges and universities, and social Christianity triumphed over Calvinism, as man's first duty became love of man instead of God. Drunkenness, prostitution, the exploitation of women and children, stock watering—these and other evils were bound to fall before the reformer's trumpet blast. It did not even seem rash during this heady season to think that Americans, by participating in a world war and reconstruction, might help to usher in a new age of democracy, peace, and progress everywhere.

[1]For a general definition of progressivism and a description of the various progressive movements, see pp. 50–52.

3

POPULATION CHANGE, 1900–1920

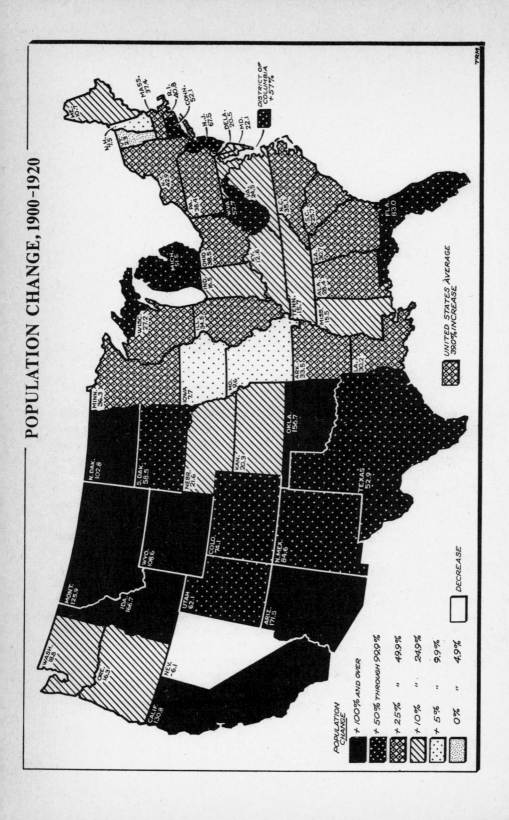

TRM

WASH. 18.8
ORE. 16.3
CALIF. 130.8
NEV. -6.1
IDA. 166.7
MONT. 125.9
UTAH 62.1
ARIZ. 171.5
WYO. 108.6
COLO. 74.1
N.MEX. 84.6
N.DAK. 102.8
S.DAK. 58.5
NEBR. 21.6
KAN. 20.3
OKLA. 156.7
TEXAS 52.9
MINN. 36.3
IOWA 7.7
MO. 9.6
ARK. 33.5
LA. 30.2
WIS. 27.2
MICH. 51.5
ILL. 34.5
IND. 16.5
OHIO 38.5
KY. 2.6
TENN. 15.7
MISS. 15.5
ALA. 28.4
GA. 20.7
FLA. 83.0
S.C. 25.7
N.C. 35.3
VA. 24.5
W.VA. 52.7
PA. 38.4
N.Y. 40.9
ME. 10.7
N.H. 15
MASS. 37.4
R.I. 40.8
CONN. 52.1
N.J. 67.5
DELA. 20.5
MD. 22.1

DISTRICT OF COLUMBIA + 57%

UNITED STATES AVERAGE 390% INCREASE

POPULATION CHANGE
+ 100% AND OVER
+ 50% THROUGH 99.9%
+ 25% " 49.9%
+ 10% " 24.9%
+ 5% " 9.9%
0% " 4.9%
DECREASE

1. The American People, 1900–1920: A Demographic View

From 1900 to 1920 the population of the United States increased nearly 40 percent, from 75,994,575 to 105,710,620. Although 70 percent of the people still lived east of the Mississippi River in 1920, the most spectacular growth had occurred in the West. The Pacific states, for example, more than doubled in numbers over the two decades, as contrasted with a growth of 43 percent among the Middle Atlantic states.

The most striking trend in American population from 1900 to 1920 was the steadily increasing migration of people from the countryside to cities. Urban population grew nearly 80 percent, a rate of increase six and a half times that of the rural areas. More than 40 percent of the people lived in towns and cities over 2,500 in 1900. The percentage of town and city dwellers was 51.4 two decades later; if we include persons living in towns under 2,500, the percentage of urban population in 1920 was actually 60. As cities grew larger they began to acquire a different character, more and more becoming centers of commerce and industry, where people from outlying areas went to work and then returned to suburban homes. This trend was evidenced in the 26.5 percent growth between 1910 and 1920 of the so-called metropolitan districts, that is, cities of 200,000 or over with a number of outlying suburbs. By 1920 there were thirty-two such metropolitan districts in which 30,-188,543 people, or more than 28 percent of the total population, resided.

Most Americans—88 percent, to be exact—were white in 1920. There were over 400,000 Indians and Orientals and 10,463,131 Negroes in the United States, but blacks were a smaller proportion of the population in 1920 than they had been in 1900. Most Americans in 1920 were also native-born. But the numbers of the foreign-born had increased, under the impact of the tremendous immigration of the past two decades, from 10,341,276, or 13.6 percent of the total population in 1900, to 13,920,692, or 13.2 percent of the total in 1920. Nearly 83 percent of the foreign-born lived either in the North or Middle West, but 85 percent of the Negroes lived in the South, with the highest concentration in South Carolina, Georgia, Florida, Alabama, Mississippi, and Louisiana.

As medical knowledge expanded through experience and research, Americans grew healthier every year during this period. Indeed, the progress of medicine was spectacular in overcoming the ancient ravagers of mankind. The death rate in areas where reliable statistics were kept declined between 1900 and 1920 from 17 to 12.6 per thousand for whites and from 25 to 17.7 per thousand for nonwhites. This progress was made possible in part by a sharp decline in deaths from typhoid fever and tuberculosis, and in part by the practical elimination of smallpox and malaria.

In spite of great progress accomplished through utilization of new techniques, drugs, and a broadening knowledge of the causes of disease, much

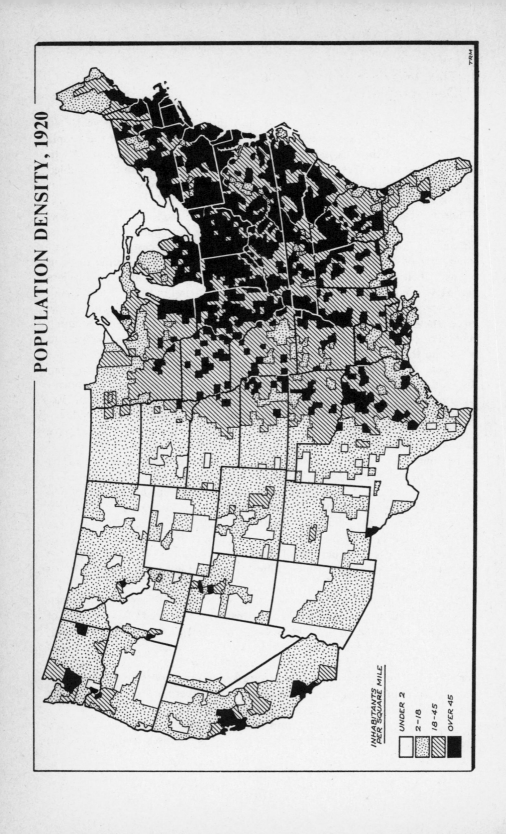

POPULATION DENSITY, 1920

INHABITANTS
PER SQUARE MILE

UNDER 2
2 - 18
18 - 45
OVER 45

remained to be done in this field by the end of the First World War. For example, one authority concluded in 1909 that the death rate could be reduced one-fourth by the partial elimination of preventable diseases. Hundreds of thousands of workers were needlessly killed, maimed, or disabled each year. At the same time, a committee on the physical welfare of New York City's school children found that 66 percent of these children needed medical care or better nourishment, 40 percent needed dental care, 31 percent had defective vision, and 6 percent suffered from malnutrition.

2. The American People: Income, Wealth, and Industry

The most striking economic phenomenon of the first years of the twentieth century was the steady increase in the wealth and income of the people of the United States. Adjusted to fluctuations in the cost of living, the total national income increased from $36,557,000,000, or $480 per capita, at the turn of the century, to $60,401,000,000, or $567 per capita, in 1920. The economic progress of the period can also be read in the steadily increasing volume of industrial production. To state the matter briefly, while population increased by about 40 percent during the decades between 1899 and 1919, the number of manufacturing establishments increased 32 percent; capital invested, more than 250 percent; average number of wage earners, nearly 100 percent; and value of products, 222 percent.

The major manufacturing industries at the turn of the century were still the enterprises that furnished the basic necessities—meat packing, iron and steel, foundries and machine shops, lumbering, milling, clothing, textiles, and tobacco. By the time the Census of Manufacturers of 1919 was taken, however, there were abundant signs that a new technology, with all its implications for social life, was in process of coming into being. Industries that were either small or in their infancy in 1900—paper and printing, chemicals, and petroleum products—had burgeoned into lusty giants by 1919. The automobile industry, which had scarcely existed in 1900, now ranked second only to steel among the manufacturing industries and turned out a product valued at nearly $4 billion.

Slightly less than 33,800,000 men and an additional 8,637,000 women, or a total of about 42,437,000 persons, were gainfully employed in the United States in 1920. Generally speaking, the prewar years were marked by full employment and a rising material standard of living for all classes. Yet the benefits of prosperity were not always distributed evenly, and the share of the national income received by the wealthy few was only slightly diminished on account of the high tax policies of the second administration of Woodrow Wilson. According to the best but still unreliable estimates, the richest fami-

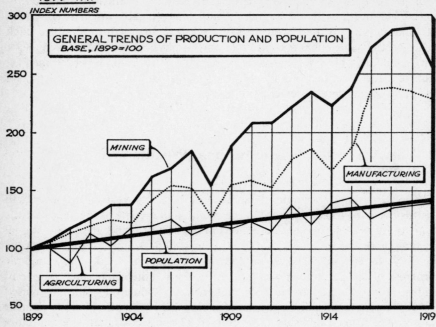

ECONOMIC GROWTH OF THE UNITED STATES
1899–1919

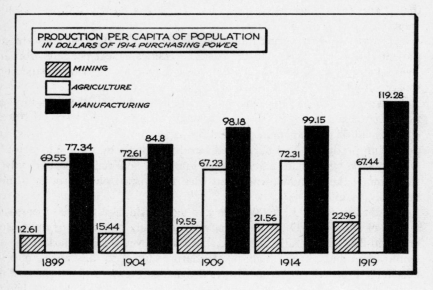

THE NATIONAL INCOME, 1909-1926

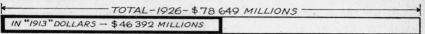

TOTAL-1926- $78 649 MILLIONS

IN "1913" DOLLARS — $46 392 MILLIONS

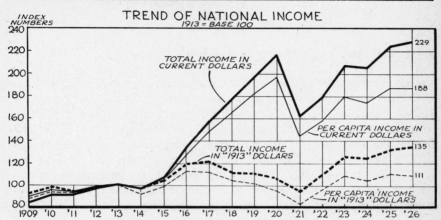

TREND OF NATIONAL INCOME
1913 = BASE 100

INDEX NUMBERS

TOTAL INCOME IN CURRENT DOLLARS

TOTAL INCOME IN "1913" DOLLARS

PER CAPITA INCOME IN CURRENT DOLLARS

PER CAPITA INCOME IN "1913" DOLLARS

229

188

135

111

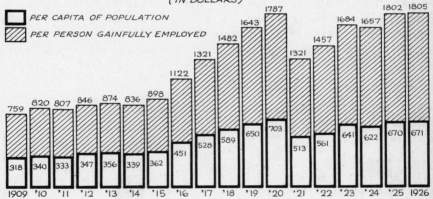

NATIONAL INCOME PER CAPITA AND PER WORKER
(IN DOLLARS)

☐ PER CAPITA OF POPULATION
▨ PER PERSON GAINFULLY EMPLOYED

759 820 807 846 874 836 898 1122 1321 1482 1643 1787 1321 1457 1684 1657 1802 1805

318 340 333 347 356 339 362 451 528 589 650 703 513 561 641 622 670 671

1909 '10 '11 '12 '13 '14 '15 '16 '17 '18 '19 '20 '21 '22 '23 '24 '25 1926

lies, constituting 1.6 percent of the population, received 10.8 percent of the national income in 1896. More accurate figures taken from income tax returns reveal that the wealthiest 5 percent received 14.98 percent of the national income in 1913 and 12.34 percent in 1920.

3. American Agriculture Finds Stability

American agriculture enjoyed such stability and prosperity during this period of industrial expansion as it had not known since 1865. As a result of the technological revolution, which was already beginning to make its impact felt, farm population decreased from 32,077,000 in 1910 to 31,556,000 in 1920. During the same decade, however, land under cultivation increased from 878,792,000 acres to 955,878,000 acres, and gross farm income rose from $7,477,000,000 to $15,907,000,000. One result of this phenomenal increase was not only unparalleled prosperity for farmers, but also a general increase of nearly 400 percent in the value of farm property.

This spectacular increase in the value of farm property made the acquisition of land more difficult at the very time when the supply of free arable land was being exhausted. Thus, while the number of farm owners increased only slightly (from 3,201,947 to 3,366,510) from 1900 to 1920, the number of tenants increased by 21 percent. More than 38 percent of all farms were operated by tenants in 1920, as contrasted with 35.3 in 1900 and 25.6 percent in 1880. Farm tenancy, especially sharecropping, was so common in the

THE GROWTH OF AMERICAN MANUFACTURES
1899 – 1921

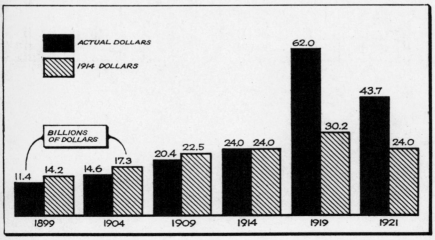

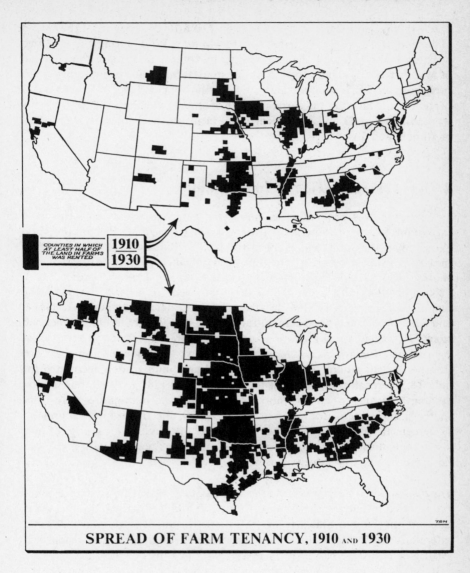

COUNTIES IN WHICH AT LEAST HALF OF THE LAND IN FARMS WAS RENTED

1910
1930

SPREAD OF FARM TENANCY, 1910 AND 1930

South that its prevalence in that region evoked little comment. But the spread of tenancy through the heartland of the Middle West during the first two decades of the twentieth century was so inexorable as to raise the question of whether a large minority of midwestern farmers were not rapidly approaching a condition of peasantry. One authority concluded in 1914 that 40 percent of the farms in the corn belt were operated by tenants. In 1920 tenants worked between 42 and 43 percent of all farms in the immensely rich states of Illinois and Iowa.

4. The Changing Tide of Immigration

Immigration was not only the most persistent but also one of the most important forces in American history down to the outbreak of the First World War, for the development of the United States was governed in large measure by the ebbing and onrushing tide of alien peoples to the Atlantic shores. Almost 14 million immigrants came to the United States between 1860 and 1900, and over 14.5 million followed from 1900 to 1915. The majority of immigrants after 1860 came from England, Ireland, Germany, and Scandinavia and were akin culturally and historically to older American stock. However, an immigration of peoples heretofore unfamiliar to most Americans—Italians, Slavs, Magyars, and Jews from southern and eastern Europe—began around 1880. This so-called new immigration accounted for only 18.3 percent of the total in the decade from 1881 to 1890, but it soon became a rushing stream. Almost 52 percent of the immigrants were from southern and eastern Europe from 1891 to 1900, and the proportion grew to 72 percent from 1901 to 1910. Let us examine the three major groups of new immigrants and see the causes for their coming to a country with a civilization so different from their own.

The Italians. Italian emigration to the United States began slowly in the 1880s and reached important proportions about 1900. More than 2 million Italians came to the United States from 1901 to 1910, and an additional 889,000 entered during the four years before the war. The high mark was reached in 1907, when 286,000 passed through the gates at Ellis Island.

Italy alone among the western nations deliberately encouraged emigration and used it as an instrument of national policy to rid herself of surplus population and increase the supply of gold from abroad. The great majority of Italian immigrants came from Sicily and the southern provinces, where estates were largest and living standards were lowest. The Italian peasant, moreover, faced the unpleasant prospect of serving two years in the army as a conscript. Finally, the Italian birth rate was one of the highest in Europe, so that only an extraordinary death rate kept population from increasing to the point of disaster. To escape starvation and the lash of the landlord and the army officer, millions of Italians fled to the United States, Argentina, Brazil, and Uruguay.

The Slavs. The migration of the Slavic peoples of eastern Europe to the United States exceeded even the outpouring of the Italians and constituted the major element in the new immigration. From Austria-Hungary and Russia, which governed most of the Slavic peoples before the First World War, there came 619,000 immigrants from 1881 to 1890, 1,191,000 from 1891 to 1900, and over 1.5 million from 1900 to 1914. As these figures include about 1.5 million Jews, we must reckon the total Slavic immigration to the United States from 1881 to 1914 at about 6 million. Ranked in order of numerical importance, they were Poles, Slovaks, Croatians, Ruthenes, Czechs, Bulgarians, Serbians, Russians, and Dalmatians. Except for the Russians, they were all oppressed subjects of a dominant nationality; 95 percent of them were peasants only a generation or two removed from serfdom. Exploited by landlords, they were poor, ignorant, and, like the Italians, were one-fourth to one-half illiterate.

The Jews. Nearly 2 million Jews entered the United States from 1881 to 1915. The great bulk of them came from Russian Poland or Russia, about one-fourth from Austria-Hungary, and a few from Rumania. The reasons for this great exodus, paralleled only by the movement of the Jewish people at the time of the destruction of Jerusalem and the great dispersion, are not hard to find.

Most of the Jews had congregated in Poland during the Middle Ages because tolerant Polish kings welcomed them. Russia acquired the provinces in which the Jews were concentrated when Poland was partitioned in the eighteenth century, and the czarist government embarked upon a long and deliberate policy of persecution after 1881. Jews were forbidden to live beyond the "pale of settlement," that is to say, their original area of domicile in the western provinces. Exceptions were made in favor of those in certain occupations, but educational and other forms of discrimination reduced the numbers who could avail themselves of this privilege. Although forced to serve in the army, they could not become officers. Subjected to numerous and heavy taxes, they could never aspire to political office.

Thus the four scourges—poverty, militarism, religious persecution, and political tyranny—were in varying degrees responsible for the willingness of Italians, Slavs, and Jews to embark upon the long journey to the New World. All authorities agree, however, that the forces drawing immigrants to America—the lure of new opportunities, propaganda of steamship companies, and tall tales of recruiting agents—were more powerful than the forces driving them from their homelands. Moreover, most of the new immigration was made in direct response to the need for unskilled labor in the United States and was stimulated by agents of employment bureaus working closely with railroad and industrial employers.

Irish immigrants had supplied a large proportion of the unskilled laborers

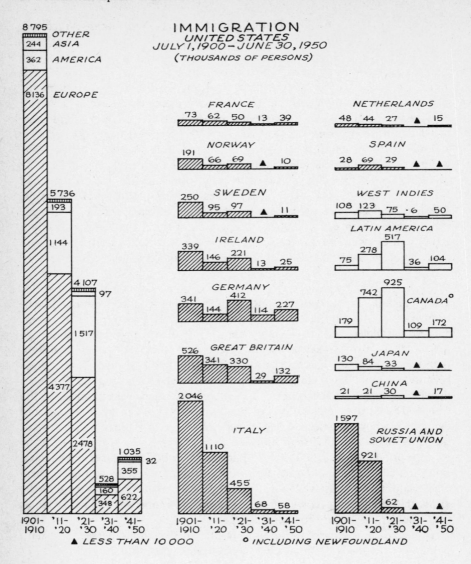

IMMIGRATION
UNITED STATES
JULY 1, 1900 – JUNE 30, 1950
(THOUSANDS OF PERSONS)

▲ LESS THAN 10 000   ° INCLUDING NEWFOUNDLAND

from 1846 to about 1890. As the Irish gradually moved up the economic and social ladder and the numbers of Irish immigrants declined, the Slavs and Italians followed in their footsteps and did the work that they had previously done. Only 16 to 17 percent of the Italians, 3 to 5 percent of the Ruthenes, Croatians, Rumanians, and Slovaks, and 8 to 10 percent of the Magyars and Poles were skilled workers when they came to the United States. Invariably they went to the industrial areas of the East and Middle West and found employment on railroads, in textile factories in New England, steel mills in Pittsburgh and Chicago, midwestern stockyards, and coal mines from Pennsylvania to Colorado. By 1914 they constituted the bulk of the working force in the basic industries. The Jews were as poor as other eastern European immigrants, but they brought with them a high degree of skill and experience in the trades. They congregated in the garment sweatshops of New York, Chicago, and other large cities mainly because they found Jewish employers in the clothing industry.

5. The Social Impact of the New Immigration

The fact that the American society absorbed this transfusion of different national strains without violent reactions was testimony to its growing maturity and adaptability. Yet it was everywhere evident that the processes of social assimilation, which had on the whole worked admirably among the Germans, Irish, and Scandinavians, practically ceased to operate among the newer immigrants. Older Americans viewed them suspiciously and thought that they were an inferior people, incapable of understanding American ideals.

This hostility was evidenced in the formation in 1887 of the American Protective Association, an anti-Catholic organization much like the Know-Nothing party of the 1850s, and in the spreading fear that the new immigration would undermine Anglo-American institutions and eventually dilute the old American racial stock. It was reflected, also, in the absence of any governmental effort to protect the immigrant from exploitation and thievery. But the worst aspect of the record was the exploitation of these immigrants by the railroads and industries. Surveying the American scene in 1915, the Commission on Industrial Relations noted that two-thirds of immigrant families lived at a subsistence level or below.

All foreigners, regardless of race, nationality, or physical and moral condition, could enter the United States before 1882. In that year the first general federal immigration act was passed, and the process of restriction was begun when, at the insistence of Californians, Chinese were excluded for ten years. The Chinese Exclusion Act was reenacted from time to time and made permanent in 1902. No sooner had the fears of Californians been quieted regarding the prospect of a Chinese inundation than another and more alarming prospect arose—the specter of an invasion of the state by Japanese workers and farmers. There were only 2,000 Japanese subjects in the United States in 1890, but two decades later their number had increased to 110,000. A powerful and well-organized agitation for exclusion of the Japanese led in 1907-1908 to the negotiation of an agreement between the American and Japanese governments that virtually ended Japanese immigration to the continental United States (see p. 141).

Thus almost complete exclusion of Orientals had been accomplished by 1908. Moreover, the doors had been shut against paupers, the sick and diseased, polygamists, prostitutes, contract laborers, anarchists, and convicts. By this time, however, the demand for a severe restriction, if not outright exclusion, of most European immigrants was mounting on all sides. The weapon that the exclusionists advocated at this time was a literacy test. President Cleveland had vetoed a bill imposing such a test in 1897. Such a measure passed Congress in 1913 and again in 1915 only to be nullified by the vetoes of President Taft and President Wilson. The exclusionists in Congress finally mustered sufficient strength in January 1917 to pass an immigration bill imposing the literacy test over Wilson's veto. Thus the open door to America—for centuries the gateway of opportunity for countless millions—was partially closed.

6. American Negroes during the Progressive Era

The gloomiest aspect of the American social scene during the first two decades of the twentieth century was the condition of Negroes. Foreign observers could never cease to wonder how Americans could boast of democracy while denying essential democratic privileges to one-tenth of the population. The great paradox was not resolved during the Progressive period. In fact, the social and political status of blacks worsened by and large, while their economic status only slightly improved.

Optimists, to be sure, could point to a few signs of progress since 1865. Demonstrating a passion for education in the face of incredible obstacles, Negroes had reduced their illiteracy rate from 95 percent in 1865 to 44.5 percent in 1900. And even greater progress was made during the decades between 1900 and 1920. The illiteracy rate among Negroes ten years of age and over declined from 30.4 percent in 1910 to 22.9 percent in 1920.

The Negro's progress toward education had been accomplished before 1900 with the help of northern philanthropists and churches and only slightly with the aid of the southern states. After 1900, however, there was an increasing awareness throughout the white South, especially in the border states, of the need for greater public aid to Negro education. Even so, no southern state by the end of the First World War was making a serious effort to provide anywhere near equal or even adequate educational opportunities for its Negro youth. In 1910, for example, there were only 141 Negro high schools, with a total of 8,251 pupils, in all the states from Maryland to Texas.

Meanwhile, social and political forces had been at work in the South to make the Progressive era a time of profound discouragement for Negroes. For one thing, the Civil War and Reconstruction had not altered southern racial concepts or southern determination to keep blacks in a subordinate status. For another, slavery had given way to sharecropping, so that the vast majority of Negroes found, not economic freedom, but merely another form of bondage after 1865. As a substitute for the social controls of slavery, which went by the board in 1865, the southern whites after Reconstruction had substituted a legal caste system that prohibited intermarriage and established a severe pattern of segregation for schools, public places, and transportation facilities. Informal race controls were tightened, and many a Negro suffered the extreme penalty for violating the rules of racial etiquette. Finally, many southern states in the late 1870s and early 1880s began gradually to make voting by Negroes difficult. The southern legislatures acted cautiously in this regard, however, and large numbers of Negroes voted in many southern states as late as the 1890s.

A genuine political division among southern white voters occurred for the first time since 1860 during the Populist revolt, and both Democrats and Populists bid for Negro votes. This resurgence of Negro political activity frightened both agrarian and conservative southerners and led them to conclude that the Negro must be removed forever as a participant in southern political life. Mississippi had shown the way to disfranchise the great mass of Negro voters in 1890—by use of a literacy test, poll tax, provisions requiring an understanding of the Constitution, and long residence requirements for registration—without openly violating the Fifteenth Amendment. Then, as an aftermath of the revival of Negro political activity during the Populist upsurge, all southern states except Maryland, Tennessee, and Kentucky disfranchised Negro voters from 1895 to 1907.

The one man who, more than any other person, brought peace between the races in the South after this bloody decade of conflict was Booker T. Washington. His rise to leadership of the Negro people was one of the most dramatic episodes in the history of the United States. Born a slave in Franklin County, Virginia, in 1856 and educated at Hampton Institute in his native state, Washington founded Tuskegee Institute in Alabama in 1881 as a school where Negro boys and girls might learn to become useful members of southern communities as teachers, farmers, and tradesmen. Washington was recognized as the preeminent spokesman of American blacks by 1895. Therefore, it came as something of an official pronouncement when, at the height of the disfranchisement movement, he counseled southern Negroes to eschew politics and learn to become good citizens. Whites all over the country quickly seized upon his program of vocational education and political quiescence for southern blacks as a formula for racial peace.

This so-called Washington Compromise found favor especially among conservative southerners and won their limited support for Negro education. But it did not operate to diminish the anti-Negro passions of the southern masses. The Populist revolt brought to the fore a new leadership of violent men. Some, like Cole L. Blease of South Carolina, were sheer demagogues; others, like James K. Vardaman of Mississippi, had many qualities of statesmanship. All these new leaders, however, rose to power on a wave of racism that found expression in violence in many forms. The last sixteen years of the nineteenth century had witnessed more than 2,500 lynchings, and the century had ended with a race riot in Wilmington, North Carolina, the climax of the disfranchisement campaign in that state. This was followed in the twentieth century by other riots, the worst of which occurred in Atlanta in September 1906. Moreover, lynching continued in the twentieth century to be an important aspect of race control, as more than 1,100 blacks fell victims, from 1900 to 1914, to mobs that often discarded the rope for the faggot.

To Negroes, however, the most frightening development of this period was the spread of southern racial concepts and techniques of violence to the North and Middle West. Southern orators like Benjamin R. Tillman of South Carolina carried the message of white supremacy to northern audiences and stimulated latent prejudices. The most effective southern propagandist was Thomas Dixon, an erstwhile Baptist minister of North Carolina, whose novels, *The Leopard's Spots* (1902) and *The Clansman* (1905), were calculated to arouse the basest racial prejudices of white readers and sold by the hundreds of thousands. *The Clansman* was made into a motion picture, *The Birth of a Nation,* in 1915, which was a powerful factor in stimulating race riots in the North and Middle West during and after the First World War. These will be related in a later chapter.

It is small wonder, then, that the progressive era was a dreary period for Negroes ambitious for the advancement of their race. There was, however, one ray of hope: the development of an aggressive and advanced leadership among both races. Foremost among the militant Negroes was a young scholar, William E. B. Du Bois, a native of Massachusetts with a doctor's degree in history from Harvard University. Du Bois and a small group of Negro intellectuals met at Niagara Falls, Canada, in June 1905, adopted a platform demanding political and economic equality for black men, and announced their determination to begin a new war for emancipation. Meeting the following year at Harpers Ferry, West Virginia, the site of John Brown's raid, the Niagara movement, as the Du Bois group was called, reiterated its resolves and renewed its courage.

Progressives and champions of social justice in the North at first paid scant attention to the Niagara rebels. Then, an anti-Negro riot occurred in Springfield, Illinois, in August 1908, within half a mile of Lincoln's home, and humanitarians in the North at last awoke to the imminent threat of the southernizing of their section. The young black rebels and a distinguished group of white educators, clergymen, editors, and social workers met in New York City on Lincoln's birthday in 1909 to consider the crisis in race relations. A year later they organized the National Association for the Advancement of Colored People. It was pledged to work for the abolition of all forced segregation, equal justice for Negroes, and enlarged educational opportunities for Negro children. The only black official of the NAACP during its formative period was Du Bois, who was director of publicity and research and editor of the association's monthly magazine, *The Crisis.* But the selection of Du Bois as official spokesman signified that the revolt against the Washington Compromise had at last found powerful support among progressives in the North and held promise for the day when the northern people would rediscover their equalitarian heritage.

7. The Growth of American Education

The federal commissioner of education could boast at the turn of the century of the steady development of educational institutions since 1890 and of an increase of 19.2 percent in the number of children enrolled in public and private schools and institutions of higher learning. These general national statistics, however, obscure the details of the educational picture in the various regions. Progress in the North and Midwest, for example, had been even more substantial than they would indicate. On the other hand, the situation in the South in 1900 was so gloomy that leaders of the region wondered if there were any hope at all. Southern children on an average received three years of public schooling, as compared with the average of nearly seven years for children in the North. Southern states spent an average of $9.72 per pupil in 1900, as compared with an expenditure of $20.85 per pupil in the north central states.

The general educational picture had improved perceptibiy by the end of the First World War, but the most significant advances are not revealed by general statistics. To begin with, the growth of kindergartens since 1900 had evidenced the expanding influence in America of the champions of the child of preschool age. Only about 250 cities had established kindergartens in 1900. By 1920, on the other hand, there were almost 8,000 separate kindergartens, with 511,000 children enrolled. Even more important was the remarkable expansion of public high schools from 1900 to 1920. There were about 6,000 public high schools in the United States, with 500,000 pupils, in 1900. Twenty years later there were over 14,000, with some 2 million students enrolled.

The most important educational revolution in this period occurred in the

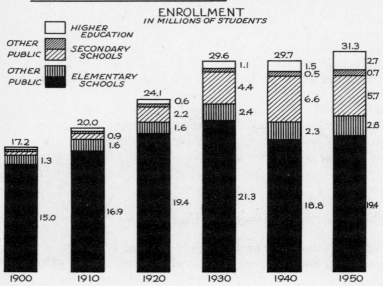

South. Under the spur of publicists like Walter H. Page and philanthropic agencies like the Southern Education Board, political leaders launched virtual crusades for education in the southern states. The result was a mass awakening from 1902 to about 1910, comparable to the educational revival that swept through the North and Middle West before the Civil War. In the short span of a decade, appropriations for school purposes by the southern states doubled, enrollment of white children increased almost a third, and the average length of the school term lengthened from five to six months. Southern illiteracy, moreover, declined from 11.8 percent of the native whites in 1900 to about 5.5 percent in 1920 and from 44.5 percent of the Negroes ten years of age or older to about 22.9 percent.

A revolution in the theory and practice of education was also getting under way at this same time. Educational psychologists and experimentalists were already beginning to undermine older pedagogical theories and were stimulating a new scientific attitude toward children even as the twentieth century opened. The new so-called progressive theories gained wider acceptance in the years before the war, especially after the philosopher John Dewey, a Vermonter teaching first at the University of Chicago and afterward at Columbia University, assumed leadership of the movement.

Dewey set out to fulfill the American dream of a public school system that was the chief training ground for democracy. Repudiating the classical tradition that emphasized formal and polite learning, he advocated a curriculum that had meaning for an urban age and prepared the child to live in a democratic society. He taught, moreover, that curriculum and subject matter should be adapted to the needs and capabilities of children, not of adults; that the learning process should be centered around the child's own experiences; and that "learning by doing" should supplant memorization of data that had no meaning to the child. His theories were assailed by traditionalists and sometimes violently abused by his own disciples. Even so, Dewey left such a deep imprint on American educational theory and practice that he can be said to have accomplished, almost single-handed, one of the significant cultural revolutions of his time.

Important developments were also taking place in higher education in the United States. For one thing, the formation of the Association of American Universities in 1900 and of regional associations soon afterward marked the beginning of a concerted campaign to raise academic standards all over the country. As a result, the number of colleges and universities increased only slightly between 1900 and 1920, from 977 to 1,041; at the same time, their enrollment more than doubled from 238,000 to 598,000. Other important changes were taking place in this field: enormous improvement in facilities for graduate and specialized training; a significant development of technical education and growth of private institutions, like the Massachusetts Institute of Technology, and state engineering and agricultural colleges; new methods of teaching; expansion of state aid to public universities, colleges, and junior colleges; and the beginning of an important adult education movement.

8. Religious Institutions and Movements

The most important social phenomenon of the prewar period was the survival of religion after the violent storms of the last quarter of the nineteenth century. The growth of skepticism, the war between Darwinists and fundamentalists, and the spread of new philosophies like Marxian scientific materialism and social Darwinism had so promoted the growth of secularism that probably a large majority of American intellectuals by 1920 would have disavowed Christian faith. Yet Christian ethics not only survived but found wider acceptance and fuller meaning. American Protestantism largely abandoned fundamentalism and rediscovered the ancient Christian message of social justice, while the Roman Catholic church expanded its ministry to the poor.

The years before the taking of the religious census in 1916 were a period of substantial growth in numbers, influence, and wealth for all religious groups. All told, Protestant bodies enrolled 26,205,039 members in 1916, as compared with 20,857,303 in 1906; and among Protestant denominations the Baptist and Methodist bodies were easily the most numerous and powerful.

But the most spectacular religious development during the period 1890–1916 was the tremendous growth of the Roman Catholic church in the United States, the result chiefly of the new immigration. This church grew from 7,343,186 members in 1890 to 15,721,815 in 1916, a gain of 114.1 percent. During its period of rapid growth the Roman Catholic church was neither torn by internal dissensions nor concerned with theological disputes. There was a movement in the late nineteenth century to "Americanize" the Catholic church in the United States by bringing it into close cooperation with other religious groups. This effort was ended by Pope Leo XIII's firm stand in 1899 in behalf of traditional practice. Any trend toward modernism in the church, moreover, was firmly suppressed by Pope Pius X in 1907. Thereafter, modernism simply did not exist in American Catholicism.

The decision to adhere to traditional Catholic doctrines and practices did not, however, signify any diminution of the social conscience of the Catholic church. Catholic bishops and priests were shepherds of most of the new immigrants and a large portion of the submerged urban masses; they well knew what poverty and suffering were. James Cardinal Gibbons of Baltimore had been one of the leading champions of the Knights of Labor during the 1880s. His attitude was probably decisive in the issuance in 1891 of Pope Leo XIII's encyclical *Rerum Novarum,* one of the most important assertions of the rights of labor. Catholic laymen and priests like Father John A. Ryan of the Catholic University of America figured prominently in the twentieth-century movement for adoption of social and economic legislation.

For American Protestantism, on the other hand, the progressive era was a time of change on all sides. The old divisive forces that had kept Protestant groups separated were still at work, evidenced by the steady offshooting of new sects from parent bodies. The most notable of these new movements was Christian Science, founded around the turn of the century by a remarkable Bostonian, Mrs. Mary Baker Eddy. She denied the existence of death, evil, or the material world and worked out a new science from the Scriptures by asserting that disease did not exist. Christian Science had gained almost 100,000 adherents by the First World War and was growing rapidly. The most numerous of the new sects, however, were the various holiness, or pentecostal, bodies, most of which came out of Methodism and taught a primitive fundamentalism.

Furthermore, Protestantism was still suffering the effects of the profound division in its ranks between traditionalists, who adhered steadfastly to ancient creeds and confessions, and modernists, who ranged theologically all the way from liberal orthodoxy to outright humanism, but who usually emphasized the social mission of the church at the expense of doctrine. There could be no doubt that modernists were in the ascendancy from 1900 to 1920. The northern Presbyterian church preserved the purity of its doctrines at the cost of expelling several of its most distinguished ministers and of losing control of its leading school, Union Seminary in New York City. The Lutherans generally remained impervious to the new intellectual currents. But northern Methodists, northern Baptists, and Congregationalists were by and large captured by the modernist clergy.

In spite of these divisive forces, there were numerous signs during the first years of the twentieth century that forces drawing Protestant bodies together were at last beginning to prevail. Even the great division between traditionalists and modernists was a cohesive force, since it cut across denominational barriers and drew men together on one side or the other. Within the denominations, too, unifying forces gathered strength. The union of the northern Presbyterian and Cumberland Presbyterian bodies in 1906, for example, healed an old wound in the ecclesiastical body. Northern Baptist groups gradually came together in close cooperation, while the three principal Methodist bodies set under way a movement for unification that would come to fruition years later.

Among the denominations, moreover, subordination of minor theological differences and cooperation on various levels of church activity became the prime objective of Protestant leaders after 1900. Unity came first on the local level, in the formation of city, county, and state federations of churches, and in older organizations like the Young Men's Christian Association, the Young Women's Christian Association, the International Sunday School Association, and the American Bible Society. The dream of the champions of Protestant unity was finally realized in 1908 with the formation of the Federal Council of Churches of Christ in America. Spokesmen of thirty-three evangelical bodies and 17 million members sharing common beliefs and purposes united to proclaim their faith in the ecumenical church.

The launching of the Federal Council of Churches in 1908 also signified the triumph in American Protestantism of the social gospel, a movement to revitalize the church and proclaim Christianity's message to an industrial society. There had always been a strong socially minded left wing of Protestantism in America, at least since the advent of Methodism in the eighteenth century. By 1865 the church had tamed the older frontier areas and overcome slavery, only to be confronted afterward by a host of new and less obvious challenges—social Darwinism, aggressive materialism, and new forms of bondage.

Perhaps a majority of urban Protestant churches during the Gilded Age fell under the control of businessmen concerned mainly with laying up treasures on earth. Perhaps their ministers glorified the captains of industry as fervently as did the college professors and editors of the day. Yet the years from 1870 to 1890 were a time also of the awakening of the social consciousness of Protestantism. An increasing number of clergymen began to measure the competitive, exploitative *Zeitgeist* by the Christian standard and found the new values wanting. Some of these pioneers found an answer in Christian Socialism; others rejected socialism but sought to resurrect the old Christian doctrine of brotherhood. In any event, a significant articulation of social

Christianity emerged out of the widespread discussion of the 1870s and 1880s. It was evident by 1890 that Protestantism was changing, that it was becoming less otherworldly in outlook and beginning to view salvation in social and ethical, as well as in theological, terms.

The years from 1890 to 1920 saw the social gospel come of age. The 1890s witnessed wholesale acceptance of the theory of evolution by liberal theologians. The consequent accommodation of religion to Darwinism was accompanied by the elevation of three ancient Christian beliefs to new prominence in American religious thought. They were, first, the conviction that God is everywhere present and works through human institutions; second, belief in the fatherhood of God and the brotherhood of man; third, the view that the Kingdom of God is here now and that the chief duty of the church is the extension of that Kingdom. Together, these beliefs constituted a frame of reference and a point of departure for the proponents of social Christianity.

The host of social gospel preachers increased, and their good works multiplied from 1890 to the end of the First World War until it seemed that urban Protestantism had truly been transformed. At the same time, Christian Socialism became respectable and commanded the sympathy, if not the allegiance, of an increasing number of clergymen. The Salvation Army, founded by William Booth in London in 1878, spread to the United States in 1880 and, after 1890, expanded its relief and rehabilitation work among the outcasts of society. So-called institutional churches, which sponsored hospitals, missions, social and relief agencies, and boys' and girls' clubs, spread through the great cities. Finally, most of the major denominations officially recognized their social mission around 1900 by establishing commissions of social service.

Among the champions of the social gospel one man emerged as leader and spokesman—Walter Rauschenbusch, for many years professor of church history at Rochester Theological Seminary. A socialist, Rauschenbusch reserved his severest criticism for industrial capitalism, a "mammonistic organization with which Christianity can never be content." For the law of competition he proposed to substitute cooperation, collectivism, and democracy, and thus to hasten the consummation of the Kingdom of God on earth. The publication of Rauschenbusch's eloquent *Christianity and the Social Crisis* in 1907 immediately established him as the major prophet of the social gospel movement.

A year after the publication of *Christianity and the Social Crisis* the social gospel achieved fulfillment in the formation of the Federal Council of Churches, for the movement for Protestant unity had from the beginning stemmed more from social action impulses than from any desire to achieve doctrinal accord. At its first meeting in Philadelphia the council adopted a ringing manifesto, "The Church and Modern Industry," placing official Protestantism squarely behind the movement to end exploitative capitalism through social welfare legislation and the strengthening of labor unions.

For all its power and commanding influence, the social gospel movement was a development in urban Protestantism. It was in the campaign to end the liquor traffic that urban and rural Protestants found a common outlet for mutual social energies and impulses. The later excesses of the prohibitionists and their failure to change the habits of a nation should not obscure the fact that in the beginning, at least, the temperance and prohibition movements were responses to one of the major social challenges of the time. The liquor problem grew to menacing proportions between 1860 and 1880, as investment in the liquor business increased 700 percent, saloons multiplied in the cities, and intemperance increased everywhere. Moreover, liquor interests cooperated with vice rings and corrupt politicians, so that saloons were often fronts for houses of prostitution, and liquor dealers' associations and brewers worked hand in glove with city bosses.

The answer of the aroused church membership to this, as they thought, dire threat to home and family was immediate and emphatic. The Protestant churches, containing most of the nondrinking population, went directly into politics in the 1880s and 1890s. On the local level they smashed saloons and elected city councils opposed to the liquor dealers. On the county and state levels they organized alliances and leagues to work for local option and statewide prohibition. Leadership in the temperance agitation in the North and Middle West was taken by the Methodists, often more socially alert than other Protestant groups. In the South, Methodists and Baptists joined hands in the movement.

The Women's Christian Temperance Union, founded by Frances Willard in 1874, was the first successful attempt to marshal the ranks of Protestantism against the liquor traffic. But effective organization of church forces on a national scale came only in 1895 with the formation of the Anti-saloon League at Washington, D.C. Methodist, Baptist, Presbyterian, and Congregational churches went into politics under the league's aegis with such determination that the division between church and state almost ceased to exist in many southern and midwestern states. The leagues—with their general superintendents, organizers, and hosts of speakers—became the most powerful factors in politics in many states.

The goal of Anti-saloon leaders was at first local option or statewide prohibition. Three-fourths of the American people lived in dry counties by 1917, while two-thirds of the states had adopted prohibition. As the movement gained power, however, it assumed more and more the character of a religious crusade. The Anti-saloon leaders lost sight of their original objective after 1913 and began to agitate for national prohibition by constitutional amendment. The powerful Anti-saloon lobby in Washington obtained passage in 1913 of the Webb-Kenyon Act, which prohibited transportation of alcoholic beverages into dry states. Three years later a prohibition amendment received a majority vote, though not the necessary two-thirds, in both houses

of Congress. When Congress imposed prohibition on the District of Columbia
in 1917, it was evident that the day was not far distant when Protestantism's
crusade would culminate in nationwide prohibition by federal amendment.

9. Main Trends in Literature

Regenerative forces combined between 1900 and the First World War to
produce a literary flowering in the United States and to lay foundations for
new trends in American creative writing. It was a productive and fertile
period. Traditionalism survived under new forms; a new literary genre, naturalism, reached its apogee; and literary preeminence passed from the East to
the Middle West and, to a lesser degree, to the South.

The Victorian giants were either dead or dying by the turn of the century.
Henry James, who had discovered reality in the drawing room, had escaped
to the more congenial British milieu. His creative energies were almost spent
by 1900. William Dean Howells lived on until 1920, but while he remained
a friend of many young authors his great work was also done. Mark Twain,
the novelist of American boyhood, survived like a ghost from the nineteenth-
century past until 1910. His only significant work after 1900 was *The Mysterious Stranger,* published posthumously.

For all their realism, authors like James and Howells lived in a moral
universe. Realism to them meant probing into human character and mirror-
ing life as they found it. Their subjects may have been drab or driven by greed,
but they were above all else human beings with will, spirit, and purpose. Their
work was taken up in the early twentieth century by a goodly company—
Ellen Glasgow of Virginia, Willa Cather of Nebraska, Dorothy Canfield of
Kansas and Vermont, Ole Rölvaag of Minnesota, and Edith Wharton of New
York. They depicted life in the new South, the Middle West, or New York
drawing-room society in all its stark drabness, irony and tragedy. As realists,
however, they also knew the other side of the picture. And in the end they
glorified the human spirit, magnified the struggle against evil, and thus carried
on the humane tradition.

Meanwhile, a new literary movement, naturalism, was beginning in the
1890s to make its first impression on American writers. The leading French
naturalist, Emile Zola, enunciated the philosophy of the new school. The
writer, he said, must study human nature as the biologist studies the animal
world and describe sheerly natural phenomena without compassion and without applying moral criteria. It was a discipline too strong for most Americans,
and early so-called naturalists like Jack London, Frank Norris, Hamlin Gar-
land, Ambrose Bierce, and Stephen Crane were more harsh realists than true
disciples of Zola.

The publication in 1900 of Theodore Dreiser's *Sister Carrie,* however, marked a real turning point in American literary history. Here was a genuine effort to discover a new view of humanity based upon the findings of science and to discern a theory of existence divorced from religious beliefs. Dreiser found an answer to the search for truth in biology. Man is an animal driven by instincts to struggle for survival in an impersonal universe. In his striving for wealth, power, or sexual satisfaction, he reverts to his true animal nature, and the façade of civilization falls away. Social forces, moreover, are impersonal and drive the weak, who cannot outwardly defy social conventions, to crime and violence.

The American public was not yet ready for such strong literary fare, and Dreiser bided his time without compromising his integrity. When he published *Jennie Gerhardt* in 1911 he won, not popular acclaim, but acceptance by a wide circle of intellectuals. Dreiser's leadership of the naturalistic school was firmly secured in his publication of *The Financier* in 1912 and *The Titan* in 1914. Although naturalism had not become an obsession among American writers by 1914, it clearly commanded the allegiance of a majority of serious young writers. The day could not be far distant when it would dominate the ethos of American literature.

The years before the First World War witnessed, too, a remarkable outburst of poetic creativity. As the Victorian era gave way to the modern age, the genteel tradition survived in a simpler form; new poetic forms emerged, and poetic themes varied from the very abstruse to the homely and common aspect of life. But, withal, a real renaissance occurred, and America recovered her poetic voice.

The two poetic giants of the early years of the twentieth century, William Vaughn Moody and Edwin Arlington Robinson, were both traditionalists who wrote in the genteel manner. Moody, a professor at the University of Chicago, was an idealist outraged by the social and economic injustices of his time and by his country's venture into imperialism. His "Ode in Time of Hesitation" (1900) and "Gloucester Moors" and "On a Soldier Fallen in the Philippines," both published in 1901, were prophetic expressions of American social consciousness. Robinson, however, dealt with a simpler and more abiding theme—the individual's search for God and truth in darkness and suffering. Life and human destiny remained mysterious to Robinson; he could not fathom their secrets. Yet in the "black and awful chaos of the night," he felt "the coming glory of the Light." His first collected works, *The Children of the Night,* appeared in 1897. *The Town Down the River* (1910), and *The Man Against the Sky* (1916) established him as the preeminent man of letters among a remarkable generation of poets and novelists.

Robinson was in some respects a latter-day Puritan, in others a transcendentalist. Such could not, however, be said of a new school of poets of the people. They came upon the literary horizon in 1912 with the publication in Chicago of *The Lyric Years,* an anthology of contemporary verse, and the printing of the first issue of *Poetry: A Magazine of Verse.* The editor of

Poetry, Harriet Monroe, was certain that traditionalism was passing, and so she urged poets to write about contemporary life. The Chicago poets, Vachel Lindsay, Edgar Lee Masters, and Carl Sandburg, replied enthusiastically. Lindsay's "General William Booth Enters into Heaven," published in the first issue of *Poetry,* marked the beginning of his ecstatic glorification of the common people and their destiny. Masters, a Chicago lawyer who wrote poetry as an avocation, laid bare the alleged sham and moral shabbiness of small-town America in *Spoon River Anthology* (1915). On the other hand, Sandburg, whose first volume appeared in 1916, magnified Chicago: the roaring, brawling hog butcher and steelmaker of the world. Another poet of the common people, Robert Frost, was not a Chicagoan. He was the bard of the farmers and workers of New England, and his quiet verse mirrored the staid New Hampshire countryside. The publication of his *A Boy's Will* in 1913 and *North of Boston* a year later immediately established his eminence among the new poets.

At the same time another revolt against the genteel tradition was brewing far to the east, among a group of American and English poets in London. These were so-called imagists, led by Ezra Pound, Amy Lowell, and later T. S. Eliot. They were striving toward a new verse form and new artistic standards. Asserting that the poet's purpose was to re-create impressions caught in the fleeting image, they rejected metrical form and rhyming as artificial devices that posed obstacles to the creation of the pure image. Rejecting also romanticism as being the literary expression of a decadent humanistic culture, the imagists sought merely to re-create the impressions of everyday life.

These novelists and poets raised American literature to new eminence and gave it such standing in the western world as it had not enjoyed since the 1840s and 1850s. But none of the truly creative writers of the early twentieth century enjoyed material success or popular acclaim. Except for the few who had independent incomes or other professions, they lived in obscure poverty, like Edwin Arlington Robinson, who was rescued by Theodore Roosevelt and given a sinecure in the New York Customs House, or Vachel Lindsay, who earned his bread by touring the country as a vagabond minstrel. Americans were actually reading and buying more books than ever before by the First World War; but the reading public rewarded sentimentalists and romanticists who amused and entertained them without questioning their virtue.

Chapter 2

Aspects of Economic Development

Pride in the nation's economic growth since the end of the depression of the 1890s had in large measure given way by the end of the progressive period to foreboding among many thoughtful Americans. Along with growth had come a steady movement toward concentration of economic power in fewer and fewer hands. This movement in industry, finance, and transportation was one of the most powerful and significant forces in recent American history. For one thing, it completely transformed an economy of relatively small competitive producers into one dominated, and to a degree controlled, by an oligarchy of giant corporations. For another, many of the domestic problems of this century, at least before 1917, arose from the obvious necessity either of halting the movement toward monopoly or oligopoly—that is, domination of an industry by a few large producers—or else of bringing the great corporations, banks, railroads, and public service monopolies under effective public control.

No other question received as much attention or stimulated as many investigations and proposals for amelioration. Journalists, publicists, and politicians described the changes taking place: big business was becoming monopolistic, or nearly so, while the few men who dominated Wall Street were also extending their control into industry and transportation. As the statistics were plain enough for all to read, the people reluctantly agreed that the old promise of American life—the promise of equality of opportunity and a fair field for all comers—was rapidly becoming an anachronism. How to revitalize this promise—in brief, how to bring the great new aggregations of economic power under social control—constituted progressivism's greatest challenge and dilemma.

This question, which perplexed the progressive mind and agitated the American people, is beyond the scope of the present chapter. Here we are concerned only with the development and progress of the concentration movement—how it came about and where it seemed to be heading.

10. The Emergence of the Modern Corporation

The most obvious and the most important development in American industry after the Civil War was the rise of the corporation as the dominant type of industrial organization. The corporate form was used extensively before 1865 only in transportation, insurance, banking, and, to a lesser degree, in textiles. However, with the enlargement of industrial units, the spread of mass-production techniques, and the growth of the trust movement after 1865 (see below), the corporation rapidly displaced the proprietorship and partnership as the chief agency for combining capital and labor. Corporations turned out 66 percent of all manufactured products by 1899. Ten years later the proportion had increased to 79 percent.

The men who managed American corporations and made important decisions during the latter part of the nineteenth century usually owned the properties that they controlled. However, the domination of corporations by the men who owned them gradually gave way from 1900 to 1920 in the face of a new trend: the emergence of the giant supercorporation, ownership of which was so widely dispersed that there could be no real correlation between ownership and management. In other words, one consequence of the emergence of the large corporation was the establishment in power of a professional managerial class who were only theoretically accountable to stockholders.

The most important factor stimulating the growth of the supercorporation was the movement of bankers into the transportation and industrial fields. The process first began on a large scale during and after the Panic of 1893, when J. P. Morgan & Company and Kuhn, Loeb & Company, the two leading Wall Street investment firms, set about reorganizing and consolidating bankrupt railroad properties. Morgan was so successful in rehabilitating insolvent railroads that he began to seek an opportunity to extend his control into industry. His chance came when a bitter rivalry between Andrew Carnegie and certain producers of finished steel products, with whom Morgan was associated, threatened to plunge the entire steel industry into a chaotic price war. Morgan came forward at this juncture with a plan to combine 60 percent of the iron and steel producers into one giant corporation. This resulted in the creation in 1901 of the United States Steel Corporation, the retirement of Carnegie, the great freewheeling entrepreneur, and the establishment of the House of Morgan as the dominant power in the industry. This event was a turning point in modern American history, but it was only a beginning. As Morgan combined more and more industries and railroads after 1901, his power grew almost by geometric ratio. He was not merely the organizer and consolidator. He also underwrote the floating of securities that launched the new corporations on their way. And through his representatives on boards of directors, and because he controlled the sources of credit, he was able to exercise a decisive voice in the corporations' policies.

The process of banker consolidation and control did not culminate until the 1920s, but the effects of this revolution in the character, ownership, and control of large corporations was already apparent by the outbreak of the First World War. By this date supercorporations dominated many fields of American enterprise: steel and iron, railroads, anthracite coal, agricultural machinery, copper, the telephone and telegraph, and public utilities. Hundreds of thousands of shareholders now owned these properties, but control had passed from owners to a managerial class responsible to a board of directors, who in turn were often beholden to investment bankers.

11. The Consolidation Movement in Industry, 1879–1903

The movement toward concentration of control in industry went through two major phases before the First World War: first, the trust movement, which began in 1879 and ended about 1890; second, the consolidation movement from 1897 to 1903, in which combinations were mainly constructed by using the holding-company form, under which a parent company owned the stock of its subsidiaries.

Most of the trusts of the first period of combination were organized by the manufacturers and businessmen directly involved, without the intervention of professional promoters or underwriting bankers. The trust was simply an extralegal arrangement by which competing manufacturers pooled properties to achieve monopoly. The Standard Oil Trust of 1879, superseded by the Trust Agreement of 1882, engineered by the dominant refiner, John D. Rockefeller, affords a good example of how this was done. First, the Trust Agreement was approved by the stockholders and owners of forty-odd oil companies, which together controlled over 90 percent of the refining industry and an almost equal proportion of the pipe lines. Second, a valuation of the properties and assets of the member corporations was made, and trust certificates with a par value of $100 each were issued in exchange for the property on the basis of this valuation. Finally, the combined properties were managed by nine trustees elected on a basis of stock ownership. Following Standard Oil's lead, similar trusts were organized in other important branches of industry; other combinations, organized by purchase or as holding companies, were also launched in the late 1880s and early 1890s.

The use of the trust form to achieve monopoly was abandoned in the 1890s, and the combination movement came almost to a standstill for a time. The Panic of 1893 was in part responsible, but even more important were the sweeping laws against conspiracies in restraint of trade that were enacted by Congress and many state legislatures. Few manufacturers were willing to risk heavy damages and dissolution by federal and state courts. The situation changed drastically in 1895, however, when the Supreme Court decreed that the federal antitrust law, the Sherman Antitrust Act of 1890, did not apply to combinations in the field of manufacturing.

The apparent removal of the formidable federal barrier to industrial combinations, the election of McKinley in 1896, and the return of prosperity in 1897 all combined to clear the way for a second consolidation movement that lasted until 1903. So great was this movement that in comparison the consolidations of the earlier period pale into insignificance. All told, not more than twelve important combinations, with a total capitalization of under $1 billion, had been organized from 1879 to 1897. Yet the Census of Manufactures in 1899 reported some 185 combinations with a total capital of over $3 billion. They accounted for nearly one-third of the entire capitalization of all manufacturing industries in the country. A comprehensive survey of American corporations in 1904 listed 305 industrial combinations, with an aggregate capital of nearly $7 billion, in operation. In addition, thirteen important combinations, with a capital of $500 million, were in process of reorganization; and combinations controlled fully two-fifths of the manufacturing capital of the United States. With 95 percent of the nation's mileage under the control of six groups, concentration in railroads had reached an even more spectacular level than had been achieved in industry. Moreover, some 1,330 public service corporations had been consolidated into a few holding companies that had a combined capitalization of $3.75 billion.

The reasons for this tremendous number of consolidations are not hard to find. Having acquired an understandable dislike of severe competition during the depression of the 1890s, manufacturers were easily persuaded that combination offered a sure means of controlling the price of their products and maintaining an orderly market. The fact that the three most important monopolies—Standard Oil, American Sugar, and American Tobacco—had prospered and paid dividends while the rest of industry struggled through destructive price wars was not lost upon the business community. Manufacturers, moreover, anticipated increased profits through the vertical integration of plants to achieve a continuous industrial process, large-scale production, the exploitation of the national market, and the utilization of by-products. In other words, large-scale enterprises would have capital to invest in labor-saving machinery and research, and they could assure control of raw materials and engage in nationwide marketing.

The consolidation movement came to a halt in 1904, chiefly because almost every branch of industry susceptible to combination had already been combined. But the activation of the federal antitrust law by Theodore Roosevelt and his successor, William H. Taft, was also an important factor in bringing the movement to an end. In fact, from 1904 to 1914 the federal government on the whole succeeded in compelling the great corporations to comply with the antitrust law. Most of the genuine monopolies were dissolved. Other combinations, like the International Harvester Company, the New Haven Railroad, and American Telephone and Telegraph, voluntarily acquiesced in reorganization plans approved by the attorney general. By 1914 the era of monopoly in American industry had passed, and a new economic structure was emerging. It was an oligopolistic structure, in which a few giant corporations dominated their branches of industry and usually determined price and wage policies. We will examine this new development in greater detail in a future chapter.

12. The Emergence of Financial Empires

The savings of the middle and upper classes began to flow into banks and insurance companies as the wealth of the United States increased during the two decades before American intervention in the First World War. All American financial institutions combined had assets and resources of only $9 billion in 1899. Only twelve years later the country could boast of savings and liquid capital of nearly $28 billion. As a result, the entrepreneurs of the money market, the investment bankers, assumed leadership after 1897 in marshaling and allocating capital for industrial, railroad, public utility, and other forms of expansion. As we have seen, they were also the chief agents in promoting and financing the new consolidations. But the portentous fact was not the growth of American wealth, for that reflected an expanding and healthy economy; it was the startling concentration of control that took place among banks and insurance companies and the transformation of leading investment bankers from entrepreneurs of capital into dominant forces in the American economy.

So swift were these processes of concentration that there were by 1904 two financial empires in Wall Street: the House of Morgan and the Rockefeller group. Using its profits from railroad reorganization and promotion of large corporations, the Morgan firm bought control of the National Bank of Commerce and partial ownership of the great First National Bank of New York City. From this vantage point Morgan rapidly extended his control or influence over other banks and trust companies in New York, Philadelphia, and Chicago. Moreover, the House of Morgan was represented in the counsels of United States Steel, International Mercantile Marine, International Harvester, General Electric, and other large corporations. By 1904 it controlled, besides, the Southern, Reading, Northern Pacific, Great Northern, New Haven, Erie, and other railroads, whose total mileage was over 47,000 and whose combined capital amounted to nearly one-fourth of the group railroad capital in the United States. Such an empire might have satisfied a man of modest ambition. However, Morgan set out around 1900 to win the richest prize of all—the large New York insurance companies. Control of their huge resources would open an almost unlimited market for securities. Morgan won the New York Life and Mutual Life by interlocking their directors into his own system. Finally, he bought a controlling interest in the Equitable Life in 1910. These three companies had assets of nearly $2 billion by 1913 and some $70 million of new money every year for investment.

On the other side of Wall Street was the far-flung Rockefeller group with its allies: the National City Bank, Hanover National Bank, Farmers Loan and Trust Company, and lesser banks; the Standard Oil Company; the Union Pacific, Southern Pacific, and nine other major railroads; and Morgan's rival in the investment and promotion fields, Kuhn, Loeb & Company, headed by Jacob H. Schiff. The normal process of concentration had been reversed to construct this financial imperium. Industrialists in the Standard Oil monopoly had channeled their excess profits into investment and promotion.

Around the Morgan and Rockefeller empires clustered a number of smaller kingdoms. "These two mammoth groups jointly . . . constitute the heart of the business and commercial life of the nation," one financial expert wrote in 1904, "the others all being the arteries which permeate in a thousand ways our whole national life, making their influence felt in every home and hamlet, yet all connected and dependent on this great central source, the influence and policy of which dominates them all."

The two groups did not always live in peace before 1907. Their rivalry for control of railroads, corporations, and insurance companies was sometimes bitter and on one memorable occasion reached the point of open war. The stakes of this battle were nothing less than control of most of the western transcontinental railroads. Morgan and his ally, James J. Hill, controlled the two northern transcontinental systems, the Northern Pacific and the Great Northern, in 1901. On the other hand, Edward H. Harriman and Kuhn, Loeb & Company controlled the central and southern systems, the Union Pacific and Southern Pacific. Neither group controlled the Burlington, the outlet to Chicago used by the Hill lines. Hill persuaded the owners of the Burlington to sell their railroad to the Northern Pacific and Great Northern in 1901, and

Harriman and Schiff executed a daring flank attack by attempting to buy control of the Northern Pacific. The ensuing battle in the New York Stock Exchange drove the price of Northern Pacific common from $100 to over $1,000 a share. When the smoke had cleared it was discovered that Harriman and Schiff owned a majority of the shares of Northern Pacific, but that Hill and Morgan still controlled a majority of the voting stock. The rivals agreed to terms of peace to avert further conflict. They formed the Northern Securities Company, a holding company to control the Northern Pacific and Great Northern lines, and Harriman and Schiff were given minority representation on the board of directors. In addition, Harriman was awarded a seat on the board of the Burlington.

Morgan's preeminence was spectacularly revealed during the Panic of 1907, when he dramatically marshaled Wall Street's resources to prevent total demoralization of the securities markets. After this demonstration of personal power, the Rockefeller–Kuhn, Loeb group concluded that further opposition to the Morgan combination was futile. Thus, the Morgan and Rockefeller groups were merged from 1907 to 1913 into one confederated association by interlocking directorates and purchases of one another's stocks.

This confederation's power was dramatically highlighted by the careful investigation of a House subcommittee—the Pujo Committee—in the early months of 1913. This committee found that the Morgan-Rockefeller community of interest had achieved a very considerable control of the credit resources of the nation by consolidating bank and trust companies, gaining control over insurance companies, and interlocking their directorates among the boards of railroads and industrial and public utility corporations. How widely this influence extended was illustrated by the fact that the Morgan-Rockefeller group had 118 directorships in 34 banks and trust companies, with total resources of over $2.5 billion; 30 directorships in 10 insurance companies, with total assets of over $2 billion; 105 directorships in 32 transportation systems, with a total capitalization of more than $11 billion; 63 directorships in 24 producing and trading corporations, with a total capitalization of over $3 billion; and 25 directorships in 12 public utility corporations, with a combined capitalization of over $2 billion. In brief, the House of Morgan and its allies on January 1, 1913, had 341 directorships in 112 banks, railroads, industries, and other corporations with aggregate resources or capitalization of more than $20 billion.

The question whether a "money trust" existed as a result of the aggrandizement of power by the Wall Street bankers was hotly debated before the Pujo Committee. The committee did not claim that the Morgan empire had established an absolute monopoly of credit. It revealed beyond cavil, however, the vast and growing concentration of control of money and credit in the hands of a few men. The significance of the committee's findings was not lost upon the American people. How could genuine economic freedom and equality of

FOREIGN TRADE
1900–1956

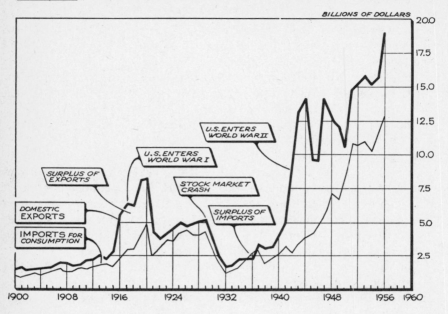

opportunity exist in such circumstances? "This is the greatest question of all," Woodrow Wilson observed, "and to this statesmen must address themselves with an earnest determination to serve the long future and the true liberties of men."

13. The United States and the World Economy, 1897–1914

Foreign trade had been the lifeblood of the American economy since colonial times. Reflecting the profound changes taking place in the domestic economy, the volume and character of foreign trade underwent important changes from 1897 to 1914. First, foreign trade expanded at a faster pace during this period than at any time since the Civil War. Exports increased from almost $1.4 billion in 1900 to nearly $2.5 billion by 1914, while imports rose from $850 million to $1.8 billion during the same period. Second, an important shift in the character of exports and imports took place. In 1900 agricultural products constituted 60 percent of the nation's exports, manufactured products only 35 percent. By 1914 manufactured products accounted for nearly 49 percent of American exports. At the same time, development of new industries at home lessened American demand for manufactured goods from abroad and stimulated increased demand for raw materials like rubber, tin, and manganese.

The rapid growth of American exports of manufactured goods and capital before 1914 foretold the coming of the day when the United States would occupy a commanding position in the world economy. However, London was still the center of international exchange before 1915, and the United States continued to occupy its traditional status as debtor to Europe. In 1897 Europeans held American securities, over half of them in railroads, valued at nearly $3.5 billion. By the eve of the First World War, European investments in the United States, direct and indirect, had more than doubled. In part this was offset by American investments abroad, but the balance of payments still ran heavily against the United States.

Nonetheless, the two most significant trends during the period 1897–1914 were the growth of American exports of manufactured goods and the rapid increase in the export of American capital abroad. The first was achieved in spite of the lack of a sizable American merchant marine, experience in doing business in foreign countries, or a well-organized governmental program to support foreign trade. The growth of American investments abroad, on the other hand, took place under the guidance of experienced bankers and often with the support of the State Department.

The United States was the richest and industrially the most powerful nation in the world when it went to war with Spain in 1898. But up to this time practically every available dollar had gone into building railroads, opening the West, and constructing industries at home. American investments abroad totaled only $684,500,000 on the eve of the Spanish-American War. Yet this figure stood at $3,513,800,000 in 1914. Except for $692,000,000 invested in Europe and $246,000,000 in the Far East, American capital had not ventured far from home. American capitalists had invested $867,200,000 in Canadian mines, industries, and railroads. The encouragement given foreign investors by the seemingly stable Díaz government of Mexico from 1877 to 1911 had attracted $854,000,000 from the United States, most of which went into railroads, mines, ranches, and oil. American investments in Cuba, which was a quasi-protectorate of the United States after 1898, grew from $50,000,000 in 1897 to $200,000,000 by 1914. By the latter date Americans had also invested $136,000,000 in the other Caribbean islands, $93,000,000 in Central America, and $366,000,000 in the more stable countries of South America.

14. The Conditions and Hazards of Labor, 1897–1914

The period 1897–1914, generally speaking, was a time of relative stability and steady economic progress for labor. Except for a brief interlude in 1908, full employment prevailed during most of the period. Real earnings of all workers in manufacturing, the only group for whom we have reliable statistics, increased at the rate of 1.3 percent annually from 1890 to 1914, for a total increase of 37 percent for this entire period. It would have increased more had there not been a rise of 39 percent in the cost of living for workers during the period 1897–1914.

This picture of increasing and steadier employment accompanied by a substantial increase in real wages did not encourage the friends of labor. Surveying the industrial scene in 1915, the majority members of the Commission on Industrial Relations, appointed by President Wilson to ascertain the causes of industrial unrest, observed that "a large part of our industrial population are . . . living in a condition of actual poverty. How large this proportion is can not be exactly determined, but it is certain that at least one-third and possibly one-half of the families of wage earners employed in manufacturing and mining earn in the course of the year less than enough to support them in anything like a comfortable and decent condition." The social consequences of this state of affairs were ominous: children of the poor died at three times the rate of children of the middle classes; 12 to 20 percent of the children in six large cities were underfed and undernourished; only one-third of all children enrolled finished elementary schools; less than 10 percent of the children in public schools were graduated from high schools.

There were, even so, encouraging developments that offered hope for the future. To begin with, some progress had been made since 1897 toward reducing the hours of labor in industry and transportation. Average hours in industry fell from 59.1 a week in 1897 to 55.2 in 1914. These general averages, however, obscure the important differential in hours worked between organized and unorganized labor. The movement for shorter hours had begun in the building, printing, and other skilled and organized trades and was most successful among them. One survey, for example, revealed that in six unionized industries average weekly hours declined from 53.4 in 1897 to 48.8 in 1914. In contrast, average weekly hours in eight unorganized industries declined from 61.9 to 58.2 during the same period.

Secondly, the first real progress was made during the years from 1907 to 1914 toward reducing the hazards of labor. Statistics of industrial accidents are unreliable for this period, but an incomplete survey in 1907 revealed that at least 500,000 American workers were either killed, crippled, or seriously injured while at work. As late as 1913, according to a more reliable survey, 25,000 workers were killed on their jobs, and another 700,000 were seriously injured.

The sporadic efforts made by several states to reduce the industrial accident rate had been unproductive before 1907. Between 1907 and 1914, however, the public awakened to the great wastage of human resources by industrial deaths and accidents. The safety movement began in 1907, when the United States Steel Corporation inaugurated a comprehensive campaign to reduce the accident toll. So successful was this program that a few other leading corporations and railroads, notably the International Harvester Company and the Chicago & North Western Railroad, instituted safety campaigns before 1914.

Thirdly, the reports of social workers and factory inspectors in many states also focused public attention on the social necessity of healthful working conditions in industry. The problem was most acute in textile mills and garment sweatshops where large numbers of women and children were employed. In fact, nowhere in the country were working conditions so incredibly bad as in the garment sweatshops of New York City, most of which were located in tenements that were literally firetraps. The Triangle Shirtwaist Factory fire on the East Side in 1911, in which 148 women lost their lives, led to the appointment of a Factory Investigating Commission and a thorough revision of New York's factory code between 1912 and 1914.

Finally, the urgency of eliminating occupational diseases like phosphorus and lead poisoning was brought home to employers and the public in a number of ways from 1900 to 1914. Medical research provided the essential knowledge, while state and national reform groups, like the American Association for Labor Legislation, carried on the necessary propaganda work. A campaign against phosphorus matches, for example, resulted in the enactment in 1912 of a federal statute forbidding their manufacture. Lead poisoning in its various forms was partially eliminated. But the greatest progress came when the American Medical Association joined hands with the American Association for Labor Legislation to begin a comprehensive campaign against industrial diseases.

15. The Rise of the American Federation of Labor

Nothing better illustrates the precarious position that workers occupied in American society during the half century between the Civil War and the First World War than the story of labor's attempts to achieve some measure of protection through organization. Organized labor passed through several phases during this long period and was confronted at times with almost insurmountable obstacles. Nonetheless, labor organizations won a larger degree of recognition than ever before in American history. And although labor's great goal—unionization of all workers—was unrealized by 1914, the foundations of a strong labor movement had been well laid.

There were two initial attempts at labor organization on a national scale between 1865 and the late 1880s before the dominant pattern of unionization was established. The first, the National Labor Union, founded in 1866, was a loose aggregation of trade unions and assorted reform groups. It was practically defunct by 1872. More important was the Knights of Labor, organized in Philadelphia in 1869. It attempted to organize workers along industrial rather than craft lines, without regard to sex or race. The union won a few spectacular strike victories and attained a membership of over 700,000 by early 1886, but it rapidly disintegrated after newspapers and employers charged it with responsibility for a serious riot in Chicago in May 1886.

While the Knights of Labor was enjoying momentary success, the leaders of the Cigar Makers' Union, Samuel Gompers and Adolph Strasser, were building the first powerful trade union in American history. Other unions federated with the cigar makers in a Federation of Organized Trades in 1881, and the union was reorganized as the American Federation of Labor in 1886. The AF of L under Samuel Gompers, who dominated the organization until his death in 1924, for the most part spurned industrial unionism (that is, unionism that groups all workers in a single industry into a single organization) and built upon the foundation of craft and trade unions. From its beginning, moreover, the AF of L eschewed utopianism and was avowedly opportunistic and practical in its objectives.

The AF of L's lasting power was demonstrated when it weathered the defeat of the steelworkers' and miners' unions in major strikes in 1892 and 1894 and came out of the depression in 1897 with 265,000 members. From this point it soon fought its way to dominance in the American labor movement. Its membership had climbed to 548,000 by 1900. There were spectacular gains until 1904, when membership reached 1,676,000. Then membership declined under the hammer blows of an organized employer campaign until 1911, when it began slowly to mount again. It stood at a little over 2,000,000 in 1914.

Standing apart from the AF of L were the four railroad brotherhoods—the conductors, engineers, trainmen, and firemen—who since the 1880s had been the best-paid workers in the country, a labor aristocracy conscious of their power and privileged position. They had won the ten-hour day throughout the country by 1910. Then in 1916 the four unions, 400,000 strong, combined to do battle for their next objective, the eight-hour day. This they won with the adoption by Congress of the Adamson Act, establishing the eight-hour day as the standard for all workers engaged in interstate railway transportation.

16. The Progress of Unionization in the Coal Industry

The period from the end of the Panic of 1893 to the First World War was a time of labor's first concerted striving toward the goal of industrial democracy. Many factors combined to give the AF of L opportunities and advantages that its predecessors had not enjoyed: superb esprit de corps accompanied by a feeling of solidarity, wise leadership, and a public opinion that was growing less hostile to the labor movement. Building largely on foundations already laid, Gompers and his colleagues from 1897 to 1914 succeeded in expanding membership and winning collective bargaining, higher wages, and shorter hours in most of the building trades and the skilled crafts. On the other hand, labor's new militancy was matched by an equally aggressive determination on management's side to prevent unionization in the mass industries. This, therefore, was the crucial question: Could the AF of L carry the fight into the basic industries and triumph over great aggregations of power?

The first test came in the effort of the United Mine Workers of America, an industrial union affiliated with the AF of L, to organize the coal industry. Decisively beaten in a general coal strike in 1894, the UMW had only 10,000 members and seemed dead by 1897. Leaders of the union nonetheless demanded increased wages and recognition, and the operators' refusal set off a general strike in the bituminous fields that began on July 4, 1897. The strikers were well organized and magnificently led, and operators in western Pennsylvania, Ohio, Indiana, and Illinois surrendered in the following September. It was a notable victory, not merely because the miners won recognition, higher wages, and other demands, but also because it was a spur and inspiration to the entire labor movement.

Emerging from this strike well organized and over 100,000 strong, the UMW now turned its sights on the anthracite coal industry centered in five counties of northeastern Pennsylvania and controlled by nine railroad companies. The president of the UMW, John Mitchell, authorized a strike on September 12, 1900, and 150,000 anthracite miners walked out of the pits. The union had demanded recognition, establishment of labor-management committees to settle petty disputes, a wage increase, and the right to employ checkweighmen. Before the strike was over, Mitchell waived the demand for recognition and suggested that the remaining issues be arbitrated. And when the operators granted a 10 percent wage increase and made other concessions in October 1900, Mitchell gladly called off the strike. Although the UMW won only part of its demands, it had succeeded in accomplishing its major objective—thorough organization of the anthracite industry.

The anthracite operators refused even to discuss wage rates with UMW officials in 1902, and Mitchell called a second strike that began on May 14. Public opinion strongly favored the miners and veered even more sharply in their favor as the result of an incident that occurred in August. A citizen of Wilkes-Barre appealed in the name of Christianity to George F. Baer, president of the Reading Railroad, to end the strike by giving it to the union. Baer replied in a letter, which was subsequently published, that the interests of the miners would be protected, "not by the labor agitators, but by the Christian men to whom God, in His infinite wisdom, has given control of the property interests of the country."

As the strike dragged on into the autumn of 1902 coal prices skyrocketed, and people in the eastern cities thought they faced a serious coal famine. President Roosevelt summoned Mitchell and leading operators to a White House conference on October 3, 1902. While Mitchell agreed to submit the issues to arbitration and to end the strike, the operators denounced the UMW as a lawless body and declared that they would never arbitrate. This was too much for Roosevelt. He issued secret orders to the army to move 10,000 troops into the anthracite region, seize the mines, and operate them as receiver for the government. Next he sent Secretary of War Elihu Root to New York City to warn J. P. Morgan, who had close financial ties with the operators, of the impending seizure. Morgan and Root at once sketched out a plan of mediation, and the operators accepted it with the reservation that no labor official should be appointed to the arbitration commission. Mitchell approved the plan, insisting only that the president be given complete freedom in naming arbiters. Roosevelt added a humorous touch, which he greatly enjoyed, by appointing the former grand chief of the Railway Conductors' Brotherhood to the commission in the capacity of "sociologist."

Roosevelt's intervention and the subsequent arbitration of the dispute was a landmark in American labor history. For the first time the federal government had looked at an industrial dispute on its merits, without automatically taking management's side. From the commission's award the miners won the nine-hour day, a 10 percent wage increase, the right to select checkweighmen, and a permanent board of conciliation. Not until 1916 did the UMW finally win recognition from the anthracite operators. Even so, the gains from the victory of 1902 were significant indeed.

Thus, the UMW had organized the eastern and midwestern bituminous areas and the entire anthracite industry by 1903. On the troubled frontiers of coal, however, they met fierce resistance and defeat that spelled eventual disaster. West Virginia was the key to long-range success or failure; for so long as the West Virginia fields were unorganized, the UMW and northern operators could never be protected from the competition of this low-wage and low-cost area. The UMW executed full-scale campaigns in 1900 and again in 1902 to organize the state, but all their efforts failed. Meanwhile, the task of organizing the southern area became increasingly important and difficult as new coal fields were opened in Virginia, Kentucky, Tennessee, and Alabama. The UMW launched a third great strike in West Virginia in 1912 and 1913 but was only partially successful. So long as West Virginia and other southern fields remained unorganized there could be neither stability in the coal industry nor security for the UMW.

In the meantime, the miners suffered bloodier defeats on another frontier, Colorado. A UMW strike against John D. Rockefeller's Colorado Fuel and Iron Company and other operators in 1903–1904 ended in rout for the union and deportation of many of the strikers. Ten years later, in September 1913, the UMW again attempted to overcome the Colorado coal companies. This time the state was torn by violent civil war, set off when National Guard troops attacked and burned a strikers' tent colony at Ludlow on April 20, 1914, killing eleven women and two children.

The Ludlow Massacre and civil war in Colorado horrified the nation, provoked investigations by a congressional committee and the Industrial Relations Commission, and set off a wave of sympathy for the strikers. But John D. Rockefeller, Jr., who now controlled the Colorado Fuel and Iron Company, refused to surrender to the UMW. Rejecting President Wilson's plan of settlement, he instituted a labor relations program, the chief feature of which was the formation of a company union, which retained for management full power over policies affecting the workers. Nonetheless, the American people (and young Rockefeller as well) had been taught a tragic lesson in the consequences of industrial despotism and absentee capitalism.

17. "As Steel Goes"

Socialists and other left wing elements in the labor movement often charged that Gompers and the AF of L represented only the aristocracy of labor and that they were indifferent to the necessity of organizing the basic industries that employed the mass of workers. These critics ignored some important facts. This was a period when organized labor progressed from impotence to a position of considerable power, in spite of the absence of any favorable legislation or any effective public support in behalf of the labor movement. To say that Gompers and his leaders did not recognize the importance of unionizing the basic industries, like iron and steel, textiles, and lumber, is simply not true. But Gompers knew the AF of L's weakness as well as its strength, and he knew that the time had not yet come for an all-out campaign against mass industries.

The wisdom of Gompers's view was confirmed many times during the progressive period. The AF of L's most discouraging and significant reversal was its failure to organize the steel industry. All during the period under discussion steel stood as an antiunion bastion, setting an open-shop pattern for other mass industries and providing antiunion leadership for thousands of small manufacturers.

Carnegie had defeated the Amalgamated Iron, Steel and Tin workers, which then included only skilled workers, during the violent Homestead strike of 1892. When the Carnegie plants were merged into the United States Steel Corporation in 1901, union officials decided that they now had no alternative but to attempt to organize all steel workers, skilled and unskilled. First, however, the Amalgamated demanded that the union scale of wages be paid in all plants of the American Sheet Steel, American Steel Hoop, and American Tin Plate companies, all subsidiaries of United States Steel. The directors of the corporation offered a compromise that would have halted the progress of unionization. The union officials refused and then, on August 10, 1901, called a general strike against all plants of the steel corporation. A majority of workers walked out, but the strike for a number of reasons was doomed from the beginning. In the end the Amalgamated surrendered unconditionally. The corporation agreed to pay union wages, but the wage rate was no longer an important issue. In return, the union withdrew from fourteen mills, agreed neither to seek to extend its influence nor even to welcome new members, and conceded the corporation's right to discharge workers for union activities.

Officials of United States Steel made no direct assaults upon the carcass of the Amalgamated for a time after their victory of 1901. Instead, they instituted measures to win the loyalty of the workers: profit sharing was begun in December 1902; an employee-safety program was launched in 1906–1907; and finally a workmen's compensation and old-age pension program was inaugurated in 1910. Meanwhile, the American Sheet and Tin Plate Company, the last of the unionized subsidiaries of the corporation, posted notices in June 1909 announcing that it would begin an open-shop policy on July 1. The protests of the Amalgamated were not even acknowledged, and the union called a second general strike against the corporation. Although the workers responded en masse throughout the far-flung steel empire and the AF of L joined the struggle with financial support, the strikers never had a chance. After holding out for fourteen months they surrendered on August 23, 1910.

Thus, after 1909 the United States Steel Corporation boasted an open shop throughout its vast domain. Moreover, the Lake Carriers' Association, an ally of United States Steel, destroyed the Lake Seamen's Union during a long and bitter strike from 1909 to 1912. The establishment of management's absolute authority in all branches of the steel corporation had been accomplished by relentless warfare against the union, use of spies and blacklisting of strike leaders, domination of local governments, and a welfare program that undermined the union's appeal. United States Steel remained the citadel of antiunionism in the mass industries until 1937.

18. Left Wing Unionism and the Rise of Socialism

Left wing unionism first developed on an important scale, not in the teeming cities of the East, but in the mining regions of the western slope of the Rockies. Here raw industrial absolutism provoked brutal retaliation by frontier miners. The result was class warfare on a grand and violent scale without ideological overtones. Out of this morass of class conflict an organization emerged in 1905. It was the Industrial Workers of the World, a coalition of the Western Federation of Miners, the socialistic American Labor Union, and the Socialist Trade and Labor Alliance. Organized along industrial lines, the IWW was frankly revolutionary. Its weapons were revolutionary rhetoric, organization of the mass of workers, and strikes; its objectives were abolition of the wage system and establishment of a proletarian commonwealth.

The IWW showed signs of coming apart at the seams within a year after its formation. The basic difficulty was dissension between leaders of the Western Federation of Miners, who were more interested in promoting labor's immediate goals than in building the socialistic state, and the head of the Socialist Trade and Labor Alliance, Daniel De Leon, a dogmatic Marxian theorist. De Leon was unceremoniously expelled in 1908, and from this time on the IWW was a champion of lower-class workers without concern for pure revolutionary dogma. In the West it fought the battles of the lumbermen, migratory workers, and frontier miners. Its emphasis on the militant strike brought it into collision with employers, the police, and the courts, and prevented any systematic organizational campaigns. In the East the IWW provided leadership for unskilled workers whom the AF of L had ignored. It led a strike in Lawrence, Massachusetts, against the American Woolen Company in 1912 and won a wage increase. It took command of rebellious silk workers in Paterson and Passaic, New Jersey, and led them in a successful strike in 1912 and 1913.

While the IWW was careening from one bloody conflict to another, the political counterpart of left wing unionism, socialism, was struggling for a program and a means of expression. The Socialists were united during the 1890s in the Socialist Labor party, which De Leon ruled until his inflexible Marxist dogma provoked a rebellion by a moderate element in 1899–1900. Meanwhile, in 1897 the midwestern labor leader, Eugene V. Debs, had founded a potential rival, the Social Democratic party, dedicated to advancing public ownership of railroads, utilities, and industrial monopolies. The anti-De Leon faction in the Socialist Labor party, headed by Morris Hillquit of New York and Victor Berger of Milwaukee, joined the Debs group in Indianapolis in 1901 to launch the Socialist Party of America.

The Socialist party included visionaries and dogmatic Marxians, but it was so completely dominated by the moderates—Debs, Hillquit, and Berger— that it was more the left wing of progressivism than a revolutionary workers' party. The party had a membership of over 58,000 by 1908; four years later the figure stood at nearly 126,000. The party's influence during this period, however, was far greater than its small membership would indicate. Socialist administrations by 1912 governed Berkeley, California, Milwaukee, and Schenectady. One of the party's leaders, Victor Berger, sat in the House of Representatives and was soon joined by another Socialist from New York City's East Side, Meyer London. And the Socialist presidential candidate, Debs, polled over 897,000 votes in the election of 1912.

19. The Counteroffensive of the Employers, Injunctions, and the AF of L in Politics

For a time at the turn of the century it seemed that the lion and the lamb might lie down together. The sign of impending industrial peace was the organization in 1900 of the National Civic Federation, founded to prove that "organized labor cannot be destroyed without debasement of the masses." The federation's leaders included industrialists like Mark Hanna and George W. Perkins, bankers like J. P. Morgan, and labor spokesmen like Samuel Gompers and John Mitchell. For a few years the federation rendered service to the labor movement by lending a sort of respectability to the AF of L.

That the federation represented only a minority of employers, however, was demonstrated by a significant movement that was already on foot when the federation was organized. It was a mass offensive of employers to destroy unionism altogether and to establish an open-shop pattern throughout American industry. This counterattack began in 1900 in Dayton, Ohio, where the union movement had made considerable progress. Within two years the local employers' association had driven the unions out of town. Flushed with victory, propagandists went from Dayton to arouse employers in other cities to the defense of what they called "the American Plan"—that is, the open shop. So successful were responding employers' associations in Beloit, Wisconsin, Sedalia, Missouri, and Chicago, that the leaders of the open-shop crusade received appeals for assistance from employers' groups all over the country.

Obviously, what most industrialists and businessmen wanted was destruction of the labor movement. The National Association of Manufacturers took command of the open-shop campaign in 1903 and formed the Citizens' Industrial Association for the purpose of forming employers' associations throughout the country. The Citizen's Industrial Association also executed a broad campaign to rally public opinion behind the American Plan. Appealing to the average citizen's individualism and prejudices, this propaganda defended the right of Americans to work when and where they pleased, depicted labor organizers as agitators and Socialists, and portrayed employers as champions of free enterprise and ancient American liberties. This counteroffensive did not destroy unionism, but it struck such a heavy blow that the AF of L not only failed to grow but actually lost membership between 1904 and 1910.

Gompers had managed to fight off those idealists who advocated aligning the AF of L with the Socialist Labor party, the Populists in 1892, and the Democrats during the great battle of 1896. It would have been difficult for Gompers to maintain this policy of nonpartisanship in any event, given the momentum and attraction of the progressive movement. But one event, more than any other, was responsible for the AF of L going into the political arena. It was the entrance of the federal courts into labor disputes in a decisive way. It began during the Chicago railroad strike of 1894, when the attorney general of the United States obtained an injunction against Eugene V. Debs and other leaders of the American Railway Union for conspiring to restrain trade and obstruct the movement of mail. The theory upon which this and later injunctions were issued was that the prohibitions against restraint of trade embodied in the Sherman Antitrust Act of 1890 applied as much to labor and farm unions as to corporations. The effect of this doctrine, which was confirmed by the Supreme Court in 1895, was not to outlaw unions, per se, as illegal conspiracies, but to forbid union practices that might be construed to be unreasonable, or illegal, restraints upon trade.

The Sherman Act was used before 1901 less against illegal industrial combinations than against labor's allegedly illegal weapons—mass picketing, the sympathetic strike, the secondary boycott, and blacklisting of goods manufactured by antiunion employers. It was the continued intervention of the federal courts after 1901 that finally compelled Gompers and the AF of L to take an active role in national politics. The immediate provocation arose out of two cases involving the boycott of nonunion products—the *Danbury Hatters'* case and the *Buck's Stove and Range Company* case.

The United Hatters of North America in 1902 called a strike against a hatmaker of Danbury, Connecticut, D. E. Loewe and Company, and declared a nationwide boycott of Loewe's products. Officials of the company struck back by organizing the American Anti-Boycott Association and by suing the United Hatters in 1903 for triple damages of $240,000 under the Sherman Act. The Supreme Court five years later confirmed the judgment of the lower courts that the boycott was a conspiracy in restraint of trade. The district court thereupon awarded the company full damages and made members of the union personally responsible for payment of the claim. In the second case, the Buck's Stove and Range Company in 1907 obtained an injunction in a federal court ordering officials of the AF of L to end a boycott against the company's products. Gompers and the executive committee of the AF of L ignored the injunction, and a federal court sentenced them all to jail for terms ranging from six months to one year. The Supreme Court in 1914 upheld the injunction but removed the penalties on a technicality.

The effect of the rulings in these two test cases was to confirm that all of labor's strike activities fell within the purview of the federal courts, and that union leaders and members were liable to jail terms and loss of property if they defied injunctions. In short, labor might wage industrial warfare only if the federal courts approved. Obviously, the AF of L's surest means of protection against such judicial interference was to obtain amendment of the Sherman law to give labor unions immunity from its prohibitions.

The leaders of the AF of L tried in various indirect ways from 1900 to 1906 to force the desired changes in the Sherman Act, but their pressure, as contrasted with the growing political power of the NAM, was pitifully weak. Gompers and his associates decided in 1906 that the time had come to begin an all-out political campaign. First they presented to President Roosevelt and Congress a bill of grievances, demanding, among other things, amendment of the Sherman law and relief from judicial interference. Next, they entered the congressional campaign of 1906 and helped to elect six union members to the House of Representatives. Two years later Gompers presented the AF of L's demands to the platform committees of the Republican and Democratic national conventions. The Republicans refused to make any concessions or promises, while the Democrats adopted a disingenuous platform plank that seemed to promise substantial relief. Taking what they could get, Gompers and his colleagues openly campaigned in behalf of the Democratic ticket headed by Bryan.

The Republican victory in 1908 was only a momentary reversal, for the political situation from 1910 to 1912 seemed to offer the AF of L an opportunity finally to achieve its goal. Internal warfare split the Republican party and made certain a Democratic victory in 1912. And when the Democrats nominated a progressive, Woodrow Wilson, and reaffirmed the promises that they had made to labor four years before, Gompers and his executive committee campaigned openly and effectively for the Democratic ticket. Wilson won a sweeping victory in the electoral college, the Democrats won control of both houses of Congress, and it seemed that labor's friends were finally in control of the federal government.

In large measure labor's hopes were realized during the period of Wilson's first administration, from 1913 to 1917. The new secretary of labor, William B. Wilson, was a former secretary-treasurer of the UMW; some fifteen union members sat in the House of Representatives; and the new president was considerably more susceptible to labor pressure than Roosevelt or Taft had been. The changed climate was everywhere evident in Washington—in the exposure of an NAM lobby by a congressional committee in 1913; in the forthright investigation of the Colorado coal strike in 1914 by the House labor committee and the Industrial Relations Commission; in adoption in 1915 of the Seaman's Act, sponsored by Gompers and Andrew Furuseth of the International Seamen's Union, which freed sailors from bondage to their labor contracts; in passage of the Smith-Hughes Act in 1916 (approved in 1917), providing for federal aid to state vocational education; and in passage of the Burnett immigration bill, which established a literacy test for immigrants, over Wilson's veto in 1917.

Even so, the AF of L's chief objective was still amendment of the Sherman

Act to give unions immunity from prosecution for using illegal strike weapons. In this campaign Gompers and the AF of L lobby ran head on into the stubborn opposition of President Wilson and the Democratic majority in Congress. The issue first arose decisively during the preparation of new antitrust legislation, the Clayton bill, in 1914. This measure as it emerged from the House judiciary committee included no provisions for labor's benefit. Gompers and his now powerful lobby at once descended upon Congress and the White House. Labor spokesmen in the House threatened to oppose the Clayton bill, and there were many stormy conferences between the labor leaders and administration spokesmen. So firmly did the administration maintain its stand, however, that Gompers had to accept a compromise that denied the AF of L its supreme objective. The House committee added sections to the Clayton bill providing for jury trials in criminal contempt cases and circumscribing the issuance of injunctions in labor disputes. Another provision declared that neither farm nor labor unions should be construed to be illegal combinations, per se, in restraint of trade. But as the courts had repeatedly declared that labor unions were not unlawful combinations, this declaration by Congress conferred no new benefits. A final provision legalized strike activities that the courts had heretofore approved.

President Wilson and the chairman of the House committee that framed the labor sections of the Clayton bill frankly declared that the bill did not give labor unions immunity from prosecution for violating the antitrust law. But Gompers hailed the Clayton Act as labor's "Magna Charta" and announced that the AF of L had finally won freedom from judicial interference under the Sherman law. As we shall see in a later chapter, the Supreme Court thought otherwise.

Chapter 3

A Variety of
Progressive Movements

When an assassin's bullet catapulted Theodore Roosevelt into the presidency in 1901, the United States was already in the first stages of the political convulsion that historians, perhaps somewhat loosely, call the progressive movement. Basically, progressivism was the response of the great majority of Americans to the problems generated by recent industrialization and urbanization. Most disturbing were the breakdown of responsible government in city, state, and nation; the spread of slums, crime, and poverty in the large cities; the exploitation of labor, particularly women and children; the growth of industrial and financial concentration; and, above all, the emergence of great economic concentrations—railroads, large corporations, and banking empires—that could profoundly affect the destinies of the people while remaining beyond their control.

In actual fact, there was no such thing as *a* progressive movement. That is, there was no organized campaign uniting all diverse efforts at political, social, and economic reform. On the contrary, there were numerous progressive movements operating in different areas simultaneously. For example, there was the effort of social workers and students of the labor question to bring state and national governments to the side of women, children, and other unprotected groups. This movement for social justice was often, but not always, independent of the movement for political reform. There was the far-reaching campaign, getting under way in the 1890s, to end the reign of corruption in, and to restore representative government to, the cities. Next came a movement to bring state governments out of their subservience to railroads and corporations and to make them instruments for advancing social welfare. Finally, there was a progressive movement on the national level, the main thrust of which was the attempt to subject railroads, industrial corporations, and banks to effective public control.

There were two broad currents in progressivism during its early years— reform and reconstruction. Many Americans were reformers because they worked for honest and efficient government, but some of them had no desire for any important reconstruction to take place in the areas of political or economic life. They might, for example, believe strongly in the businesslike administration of government while at the same time they regarded income tax or plans to aid farmers as pernicious class measures. Other Americans believed in both reform and reconstruction. To achieve the latter, they came to rely more and more upon concerted, purposeful, and democratic governmental action. The political and economic reconstructionists were the growing, dominant element among progressives after the Panic of 1893. It is these champions of the expansion of governmental power that will hereafter be referred to as "progressives."

It is important to be very clear about one central fact: progressives were not Socialists. To be sure, progressives generally desired expansion of governmental power in order to substitute collective for individual decisions in broad matters of social and economic policy. However, they sought the reform and reconstruction of capitalism, not its destruction; their great goal was not the establishment of a socialistic commonwealth, but rather the achievement of a humane and democratic capitalistic system that would benefit all people.

It was inevitable that this should have been true because progressivism, particularly in its political manifestations, was primarily a revolt of the middle classes—small businessmen and bankers, the more prosperous farmers, and editors, professors, clergymen, and other professional groups—against a state of affairs that seemed to guarantee perpetual control to the privileged few who owned the wealth of the United States. Although progressives from time to time worked creatively and effectively with the leaders of organized labor on all levels of government, progressivism had no solid basis of popular support among the masses of workers and cannot be said to have been truly labor oriented. Moreover, while leadership in the reform movements of the 1890s was to a significant extent agrarian, extreme farm unrest subsided after the return of prosperity in 1897. Leadership in the revolt against the status quo passed, therefore, to the cities and towns.

It does no gross harm to historical truth to say that something like a general progressive reform movement was beginning to take shape by the early 1900s. To a significant degree, progressives were united by a common ideology. Social justice reformers were organized in state and national associations and united behind common programs. City reformers united in the

National Municipal League in 1894. In the arena of national politics, moreover, progressives in both the Republican and Democratic parties sought the same objectives and often worked together to achieve them.

20. The Dynamics of Progressivism

Progressivism's major components had their origins as recognizable movements in the 1890s. They were among the immediate responses to the economic distress caused by both the agrarian depression of that period and the Panic of 1893. It is more difficult to explain why the movement gained its greatest momentum and achieved its most important triumphs between 1897 and 1917, a time of expanding prosperity and national contentment. Some recent authorities have suggested that the prime dynamic forces were the resentment that older established classes felt toward the *nouveaux riches* and the general fear of the middle classes that they were being ground between the rising upper and lower classes. This is what is called the "status revolution" theory of progressivism's causation. The theory has been tested in particular situations many times, but in no instance have scholars been able to substantiate it. Invariably, they have found that progressives and their conservative opponents came from the same classes and ethnic and religious backgrounds. The moving forces in progressivism were as complex and varied as the movement itself, and they are to be found only in the details of historical record.

Progressivism's roots lay deep in American evangelical Christian and democratic traditions, but it had its immediate origins in a series of disconnected movements for reform and reconstruction during the 1890s. The first of these was the agrarian revolt, which culminated in populism and a Populist -Democratic fusion in 1896. The Populists and then the Democratic-Populist candidate in 1896, William Jennings Bryan, failed to win national power because they remained essentially agrarian spokesmen and never won the support of either industrial labor or the urban middle classes. However, populism and Bryanism did shake the political foundations and cause a certain realignment of the two major parties. More important, the propaganda spread by the Populists publicized widespread distress and at the same time revived the concept of governmental action to ensure economic well-being. In addition, the Populists' emphasis upon greater popular participation in, and control of, political and financial institutions paved the way for sweeping reforms in the near future.

The sharp intensification of human distress during the Panic of 1893 dramatized for increasing numbers of urban Americans the wide contrast between the privileged position of the well-to-do and the plight of the poor. The impact was heaviest on ministers, priests, and social workers in the slums of the great cities. As Walter Rauschenbusch, the social gospel leader, said about

the poor whom he saw in New York during the depression of the 1890s:
"They wore down our threshold, and they wore away our hearts. ... One
could hear human virtue cracking and crumbling all around." The suffering
that resulted from the depression stimulated enormously the two movements
that furnished much of the moral zeal for progressivism—the social gospel
and the movement for social justice.

Americans in the 1890s, already convulsed by the indictments of the Populists and Bryan, were further agitated by a burgeoning literature of exposure.
It started with Henry George's *Progress and Poverty* (1879); gained momentum with the publication of Edward Bellamy's utopian socialist novel, *Looking Backward* (1888); and came to fully developed form in Henry Demarest
Lloyd's scathing indictment of the Standard Oil Trust, *Wealth Against Commonwealth* (1894). From this time onward, arraignment and exposure were
the order of the day in American journalism. Moreover, by the 1890s econo-
mists, political scientists, sociologists, and other publicists were beginning to
challenge successfully the philosophical foundations of the laissez-faire state
—social Darwinism and classical economics—and the whole cluster of ideals
associated with rugged individualism. Leading this revolt were young econo-
mists like Richard T. Ely, sociologists like Lester F. Ward, political scientists
like Woodrow Wilson, and iconoclasts like Thorstein Veblen. Their ranks
would swell mightily in the early 1900s.

A final generative force was the rapid growth of the urban middle classes
in the United States between the Civil War and the First World War. Three
profoundly important things happened to these classes in the 1890s and early
1900s. First, they grew so rapidly in numbers because of business expansion
that they were able to wield the balance of political power in many sections
of the country by 1900. Second, influential segments of these groups, molded
by their specialized training and professional standards and affiliations, joined
in insisting upon rationality and efficient administration in public affairs.
Finally, because they were the best educated and most idealistic segment of
the population, they were deeply affected by the exposures of corruption and
the accounts of economic and social distress. By the late 1890s they were
building up a full head of steam of moral indignation. The boiler would soon
explode with very significant political repercussions.

With these observations by way of introduction, let us examine one of the
most significant and fruitful reform movements in American history.

21. The Social Justice Movement

The social justice movement was the first large-scale attempt to palliate the
grosser aspects of American life—the miserable living conditions of city
masses, the exploitation of women and children in industry, and the degradation of submerged, unprotected workers. The vanguard in the movement were

priests and ministers who worked in the slums. However, a separate class of social workers, usually employed by charity organizations and settlement houses—community centers that began to spring up in the late 1880s—emerged in the 1890s. They constituted a growing and vociferous element in the American society after 1900. They made intensive surveys of labor conditions, causes of poverty, and means of alleviating social distress. As time passed, moreover, they became departmentalized, some concerned with care of immigrants, some with problems of labor, some with juvenile delinquency. As one authority has said, "By the latter part of the 1890s a start had been made toward the accumulation of social facts; after the turn of the century the study of mankind was to be carried forward with a vigor and zest that imparted a characteristic tone to the intellectual climate of the Progressive era."[1]

The leaders of the social justice movement by 1900 had gone far beyond the concept of private amelioration and were beginning to evolve ambitious new schemes of social salvation. What they now envisaged was nothing less than systematic use of state police power to accomplish rearrangement of economic relationships. In other words, state governments, and later the federal government, should enter the battle to protect the weak—first by legislation based upon investigations of social workers, next by employing social workers as agents of enforcement.

First to come under the concerted attack of the social justice forces was the old problem of child labor. It posed the most poignant challenge, for by 1900 probably 1.7 million children under sixteen were employed in the cotton mills of New England and the South, in the berry fields of New Jersey, and on farms. The problem grew even worse as the textile industry advanced in the South during the early years of the twentieth century.

The attack on child labor opened simultaneously on two fronts—in the Southeast in 1901, with the introduction of child labor bills in the legislatures of the Carolinas, Georgia, and Alabama; in the North, with adoption of pioneer legislation by New Jersey, New York, and Illinois in 1903–1904. The southern and northern wings of the movement came together in 1904 in the National Child Labor Committee, which had twenty-five branch committees in twenty-two states by 1910.

The accomplishments of this dedicated band constituted perhaps the greatest single triumph of the social justice movement before the First World War. In 1900 twenty-four states and the District of Columbia made no provision for a minimum age for workers. But by 1914 every state but one had established a minimum age limit, usually fourteen, while many states had prohibited children between fourteen and sixteen from working at night and in dangerous occupations.

[1]Robert H. Bremner, *From the Depths: The Discovery of Poverty in the United States* (New York, 1956), p. 85.

The movement for a federal child labor law did not reach serious proportions until near the end of the progressive period. Senator Albert J. Beveridge of Indiana introduced the first federal bill in 1906, but the National Child Labor Committee refused to endorse it on the ground that it was best to work for a while longer in the states. However, conditions seemed ripe for federal action in 1914, and the committee sponsored the introduction of a bill in Congress that year. It prohibited the shipment in interstate commerce of goods manufactured in whole or in part by children under fourteen and of products of mines or quarries where children under sixteen were employed. The measure passed the House of Representatives in 1914 but languished in the Senate while spokesmen of the NAM and southern textile interests denounced it as an unconstitutional invasion of the police power of the states. Then President Wilson pushed the bill, now called the Keating-Owen bill, through the Senate in the summer of 1916. It was the most significant victory of the social justice movement before the New Deal.

A second major objective of the social justice crusade was protection of women in industry by limiting the number of hours they might work. Illinois enacted the first enforceable eight-hour law for women in 1893—the result of the labors of Florence Kelley of Chicago's Hull House, the settlement house founded by Jane Addams. However, the state supreme court nullified the Illinois statute two years later, and leadership in this campaign passed to the East. There the standard was carried by consumers' leagues, which were organizations of socially minded women. Beginning with the enactment of statutes by New York in 1896 and Massachusetts in 1900 limiting women's hours to sixty a week, the movement spread slowly to Nebraska, Michigan, Colorado, Oregon, Washington, and Tennessee. Once the United States Supreme Court ended doubt about the constitutionality of women's hours legislation, the movement gained enormous momentum. Thirty-nine states enacted hours legislation for the first time or strengthened existing laws between 1909 and 1917.

A third, and perhaps the most ambitious, social justice objective was minimum wage legislation for women workers. By enacting the first statutes of this kind from 1896 to 1909, Australia and Great Britain provided inspiration to American reformers. An even more important impetus came from governmental and private investigations in the United States from 1911 to 1914. They revealed that large numbers of women received wages entirely inadequate to maintain a decent standard of living. The National Consumers' League made minimum wage legislation part of its long-range program in 1910, and the Women's Trade Union League joined the fight in the following year. The campaign had begun.

This feminine coalition scored its first victory in 1912, when the Massachusetts legislature established a wage commission empowered to recommend minimum wages for women and to expose employers who refused to conform. The following year saw the adoption by eight midwestern and western states of statutes that went the whole way and empowered wage commissions to establish binding minimum wage rates. However, the movement lost most of its strength after 1913. During the following decade only six additional states, the District of Columbia, and Puerto Rico joined the states that sought to protect the living standard, health, and morality of women workers.

The last major objective of the champions of social welfare was establishment of public systems of industrial accident insurance. Western European nations had long since demonstrated the excellence and feasibility of such systems. In the United States, however, the common law rules relating to industrial accidents still governed the payment of damages.[2] The obvious injustice of throwing practically the entire financial burden of industrial accidents and deaths on workers and their families—for that was usually the result of the application of the common law rules—led to an early movement to abrogate or modify these doctrines. Most states by 1910 had modified the common law rules in favor of the injured worker; even so, he was little better off than before because he still had to sue to recover damages. Maryland, Montana, and the federal government experimented from 1902 to 1909 with crude and limited systems of accident insurance, but this represented all that had been accomplished to this date. A brief period of intense official investigation into the entire subject ensued between 1909 and 1913. All commissions concluded that the prevailing compensation system had collapsed and recommended enactment of accident insurance laws. A wave of protest and legislation swept over the country as the people learned the facts. Ten states established insurance systems in 1911, and twenty states, three territories, and the federal government followed suit from 1912 to 1916.

Thus it was that professional social workers, students of the labor problem, and leaders of advanced social opinion grew strong during the progressive era, emerged as a redemptive element in the American democracy, and banded together in crusades to transform an individualistic and competitive society into something approximating the welfare state. There were dozens of organizations and more campaigns for social reforms than we have space to relate. Some social justice advocates, going far beyond the objectives we have described, set on foot discussions of social security, unemployment relief, and laws designed to advance the interests of organized labor. These pioneers on the advanced social frontier failed to obtain the legislation that they advocated. They were, however, blazing trails for a new social justice movement that would come to fruition in the 1930s. The line of descent from the social justice movement of the early 1900s to the New Deal is clear and straight.

---

[2]Briefly stated, under these common law rules the injured employee was not entitled to compensation if he had willingly assumed the risks of his job, if he was himself negligent, or if his injury had been caused by a fellow worker's negligence. Moreover, in most cases the injured employee had to sue for damages and prove that he had suffered as a direct result of his employer's negligence.

22. The Supreme Court and Social Legislation

Social justice reformers were not only beset by the opposition of employers and other representatives of selfish economic interests, but they also faced even more formidable opposition from yet another source—the bench and bar of the United States. The great majority of American lawyers and judges at the turn of the century had been reared on the Anglo-American legal tradition, which often valued liberty above justice and the rights of property above humanity. They believed firmly in the automatic operation of economic laws, cultivated strong hostility to the concept of public control, and were usually ranged on the side of railroads and large corporations.

The implications of this fact for the social justice movement become at once apparent when one recalls the peculiar power of judges in the American constitutional system. Unlike their counterparts elsewhere in the western world, American judges had established the privilege of determining whether legislation violated the provisions of written state and federal constitutions. As judges nowhere rendered decisions in an intellectual vacuum, their own preconceived notions of the proper functions of government invariably affected their legal judgments. In rendering decisions in cases involving social legislation, therefore, judges often unconsciously permitted inherited prejudices, instead of sound legal precepts, to control decisions that they made.

Proponents of social welfare legislation occasionally ran afoul of the verdicts of state judges, but federal courts, and eventually the United States Supreme Court, posed the greatest threat. This was true during the progressive period, not because federal courts always nullified state efforts at social amelioration, but because the Supreme Court in the 1880s had established the doctrine that corporations were persons within the meaning of the Fourteenth Amendment. (For this development, see p. 103.) Corporations were therefore at liberty to appeal to federal courts for protection; and federal judges insisted upon reviewing state regulatory legislation to determine whether it violated the Fourteenth Amendment's dictum that no state should deprive a person of life, liberty, or property without due process of law.

It was not, however, until 1898 that the Supreme Court rendered its first important decision involving state labor legislation. In *Holden* v. *Hardy* the court upheld a Utah statute establishing the eight-hour day for miners. The decision also expounded in forceful language the legal theories underlying all social legislation by the states, namely, that it was the duty of the state to protect the health and morals of its citizens; that this protection could be afforded by proper use of police power; and, finally, that such use of police power did not unlawfully infringe the freedom of contract guaranteed by the Fourteenth Amendment. While this decision clearly established the right of the states to limit the hours of labor in dangerous occupations, it did not affirm the constitutionality of hours legislation for any and all occupations.

In fact, no one was quite sure how far the states might go in this respect until the Supreme Court set one limitation in its decision in *Lochner* v. *New York* in 1905.

The *Lochner* case involved the constitutionality of a New York statute that limited the hours bakers could work to ten a day and sixty a week. Counsel for the state argued that the bakers' law protected the public's food supply. Lochner's counsel, on the other hand, replied that the law unduly violated the freedom of employer and employee to make a labor contract. A bare majority of the court decided that the time had come to call a halt to improper use of state police power. Asserting that the bakers' trade was not particularly unhealthy, the majority concluded that "Statutes of the nature of that under review, limiting the hours in which grown and intelligent men may labor to earn their living, are mere meddlesome interferences with the rights of the individual." In other words, a state could not contravene the freedom of contract unless there were obvious and compelling reasons for exercising police power.

Worse still for the social justice reformers, the *Lochner* decision created grave doubt about the constitutionality of legislation restricting hours of labor merely on the basis of sex. This issue arose in 1907, when an employer challenged an Oregon ten-hour law for women. Perceiving that this was a supreme crisis in the life of the social justice movement, Florence Kelley, chief factory inspector of Illinois, and Josephine Goldmark, the driving spirit in the National Consumers' League, turned to Louis D. Brandeis of Boston, nationally known as "the people's attorney," to defend the law; Brandeis gladly agreed.

Brandeis had long argued that the law had not been altered to fit the new conditions of American economic and social life. The trouble was, he said, that neither lawyers nor judges knew anything about the economic and social conditions out of which cases arose. He proposed to substitute a sociological jurisprudence in the place of a myopic legal traditionalism. As Brandeis put it, "A lawyer who has not studied economics and sociology is very apt to become a public enemy." The Oregon case gave Brandeis an opportunity to put his sociological jurisprudence to practical use and, even better, to demonstrate it before the whole legal profession. In preparing his brief he gave only two pages to conventional legal reasoning and citation of precedents. In contrast, he used more than one hundred pages to demonstrate the economic and social consequences of long hours of work by women. By citing evidence drawn from hundreds of sources he proved that long hours were dangerous to women's health and morals and that reasonable hours produced tangible social benefits.

The case, *Muller* v. *Oregon,* was argued before the Supreme Court in January 1908. Plaintiff's counsel asserted that women, equally with men, were endowed with a freedom of contract that no legislature could impair. To this Brandeis again responded with a masterful array of facts. Brandeis's argument won the day even though the court was dominated by traditionalists. In upholding the constitutionality of the Oregon ten-hour law, the court for the first time admitted the need for facts to establish the reasonableness or unreasonableness of social legislation.

It was an epochal victory for the social justice movement; even more important was the fact that Brandeis's technique of marshaling economic and social data in defense of social legislation soon became ordinary legal practice. Four additional cases involving women's hours legislation reached the Supreme Court from 1908 to 1915. In each case the court adhered to the principle set forth in *Muller* v. *Oregon,* approving even a comprehensive California eight-hour law for women.

The Supreme Court during the period 1898–1915 also reviewed a number of state child labor laws. In no field of social legislation were reformers on surer constitutional ground, and the court consistently affirmed the right of the states to protect their children by prohibiting them from working in hazardous occupations or at an age that was prejudicial to their health and morals. However, it was still a moot question before 1918 whether Congress could use its control over commerce to regulate the labor of children.

Obviously, the court had been profoundly influenced by the progressive upheaval. The extent of that influence was demonstrated in 1917, when the court passed on almost all forms of labor legislation. In *Bunting* v. *Oregon,* the justices tacitly reversed their decision in *Lochner* v. *New York* by approving an Oregon ten-hour law for men in industry. In *Wilson* v. *New* the court narrowly sustained the Adamson Act, which established the eight-hour day for railway workers engaged in interstate commerce. In *Stettler* v. *O'Hara* an evenly divided court upheld an Oregon statute establishing minimum wages for women. Finally, the court upheld the constitutionality of the three systems of industrial accident insurance then in effect in various states. Indeed, it seemed beyond doubt that sociological jurisprudence had at last found acceptance by the highest court of the land.

23. The Struggle for Women's Rights

As the reader has undoubtedly inferred, much of the forward thrust of the social justice, temperance, and other reform movements of the late nineteenth and early twentieth centuries came from women. The same great social and economic developments that generated progressivism were also at work to produce what was perhaps the most remarkable generation of women in American history. Urban middle-class women, freed from age-old slavery to household routine by the introduction of various domestic conveniences and especially by the abundance of cheap servants, began to go to college and professional schools in significant numbers in the 1880s. In 1890 some 2,500 women graduated from college; their number increased to nearly 8,500 in 1910. They were too well educated and imbued with a desire to be socially useful to be content to be mere adornments or sheerly homemakers. Several hundred thousand of them went to work, principally as teachers and office workers. Others moved into the mainstream of social reform, founding and staffing settlement houses, leading the fight against the saloon, working for child labor legislation and the regulation of the hours and wages for women, and helping to organize female workers in the garment sweatshops. To mention only a few among a multitude, there was Jane Addams, who founded Hull House in 1889 and became in the eyes of many the greatest woman of her generation; Lillian D. Wald, who opened the Henry Street Settlement in New York in 1895; Margaret Dreier Robins and Mary McDowell, who were driving forces in the National Women's Trade Union League, founded in 1903; Josephine Shaw Lowell, Florence Kelley, and Josephine Goldmark, who were leaders in the National Consumers' League, organized in 1899; and Julia Lathrop, who was appointed first head of the United States Children's Bureau in 1912.

It was inevitable that such a generation of women would not be content to be second-class citizens, wards of fathers and husbands and deprived of the ballot. Women argued that the United States could never be a true democracy so long as it denied the vote to half its citizens. They pointed to the increase in the number of women in the labor force from 4 million in 1890 to nearly 7.5 million in 1910 as proof that women desperately needed the ballot in order to protect their economic interests. However, they wanted suffrage above all because, as one authority has written, it would be "a vital step toward winning human dignity, and the recognition that they too were endowed with the faculty of reason, the power of judgment, the capacity for social responsibility."

The movement for woman suffrage had in fact begun in 1848 and did not lack devoted leaders during the following half century in Lucretia Mott, Elizabeth Cady Stanton, and Susan B. Anthony. However, the real power and momentum of the movement awaited the emergence of the new middle-class generation and the awakening of a large group among the male population to the indignity and injustice of denying the vote on account of sex. In fact, by 1900 only the territory of Wyoming in 1869 and the state of Wyoming in 1890, Colorado in 1893, and Idaho and Utah in 1896 had granted suffrage to women.

What had been a somewhat desultory campaign turned into a crusade in 1900 with the election of Carrie Chapman Catt as president of the National American Woman Suffrage Association, which had been founded in 1890 by the merger of two hitherto rival organizations. The fight for women's rights now spread from the West to the East and became a significant part of the general progressive upheaval of the time. Women not only spoke and organized indefatigably, but they also mounted suffrage parades in all the large cities. More militant groups—like the Equality League (later the Women's Political Union), the Congressional Union for Woman Suffrage, and the National Woman's Party—demonstrated, picketed, heckled political candidates, and occasionally went to jail, where they carried on hunger strikes in imitation of their British counterparts.

It was evident by 1910–1911, when the states of Washington and California adopted woman suffrage, that the movement was becoming irresistible. Arizona, Kansas, and Oregon fell in line in 1912. In 1913 Illinois granted women the right to vote in presidential elections; Montana and Nevada joined the suffrage ranks in 1914; and the key state of New York fell to women crusaders in 1917. By this date pressure for a federal suffrage amendment was also virtually irresistible. Under the prodding of President Woodrow Wilson, the House of Representatives, on January 10, 1918, approved an amendment forbidding the states to deny suffrage on account of sex; and the Senate, in response to a personal appeal from Wilson, concurred on June 4, 1919. The suffrage amendment, the Nineteenth Amendment, became a part of the Constitution on August 26, 1920, soon after Tennessee completed the thirty-sixth ratification.

Meanwhile, along with political equality had come a comprehensive revision of state laws permitting women to own, inherit, and bequeath property and a revision of divorce statutes protecting women's economic rights and their right to custody of children.

The millennium had not come for American women by 1920. They were still grossly discriminated against in employment and wages, particularly in the professions. Many of them still lived in semislavery to fathers and husbands. However, the first great goal of general political equality had been won, and that must be counted as one of the most important milestones in the progress of American democracy toward equality for all.

24. The Muckrakers

While social workers were beginning their investigations and formulating their programs, a revolution in the field of journalism was also slowly taking form. Its principal aspect was the emergence of a group of reporters, called muckrakers, who trumpeted dire warnings of changes portentous for the future of democracy. These publicists who probed all the dark corners of American life did not make the progressive movement. The social justice movement and the campaign to clean up the cities and states, for example, were well on foot when they entered the battle. However, by exposing the shame and corruption of American public life the muckrakers fired the righ-

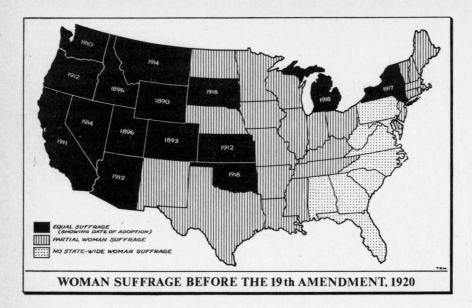

EQUAL SUFFRAGE
(SHOWING DATE OF ADOPTION)
PARTIAL WOMAN SUFFRAGE
NO STATE-WIDE WOMAN SUFFRAGE

WOMAN SUFFRAGE BEFORE THE 19th AMENDMENT, 1920

teous indignation of the middle classes. In so doing, they helped to make the progressive movement a national uprising instead of a series of sporadic campaigns.

A medium for the muckrakers came in the 1890s with the cheap magazine. *Cosmopolitan, Munsey's,* and *McClure's* were already in the field by 1900, catering to the reading habits of the middle classes. The leader of the three, *McClure's,* was the creature of S. S. McClure, an ebullient but erratic Irishman who was evolving a novel concept of the cheap magazine as the nineteenth century ended. Understanding the public excitement over the growth of railroad and industrial combinations, he decided to publish articles of contemporary economic and social significance. Giving complete freedom and generous finanical support to his writers, McClure imposed only two standards—accuracy and readability.

To Ida M. Tarbell, a young writer on his staff, McClure in 1896 assigned the task of writing a history of the Standard Oil Company. He expected that her series would begin the following February. Miss Tarbell, however, spent five years in hard research and writing before her work was completed. Her *History of the Standard Oil Company,* which began in *McClure's* in November 1902 and ran for the following fifteen months, virtually took the country by storm. Although she was coldly objective and a master of the evidence, Miss Tarbell fully revealed the methods that Rockefeller and his partners had used to build the oil monopoly.

At about the time that Miss Tarbell was completing her study, a courageous circuit attorney in St. Louis, Joseph W. Folk, was exposing the corruption of the local Democratic boss. *McClure's* managing editor, Lincoln Steffens, went to investigate, and that was how one of the best reporters of the twentieth century began his remarkable career as a muckraker. From the Missouri city Steffens went on to investigate political conditions in Minneapolis, Cleveland, New York, Chicago, Philadelphia, and Pittsburgh. He found everywhere essentially the same government by corrupt alliances of politicians and businessmen. He returned to write about them in *McClure's*, and to publish his articles in book form in 1904 as *The Shame of the Cities*. Steffens next studied political affairs in several states, and his findings were embodied in a second series in *McClure's* in 1905 and 1906, published in book form in the latter year under the title *The Struggle for Self-Government*.

The third of the trinity of *McClure's* great muckrakers was Ray Stannard Baker, a young journalist from the Middle West, who investigated social and economic problems. He explored the labor situation, for example, and wrote for *McClure's* a revealing account of the Colorado coal strike of 1903–1904. His scholarly and convincing indictment of railroad malpractices, *The Railroads on Trial*, strengthened President Roosevelt's hand in the battle to enlarge the powers of the Interstate Commerce Commission. His *Following the Colour Line* was a pioneer study of prevailing white racist attitudes in the North and South.

Among other writers on the staff of *McClure's*, two were notable. Burton J. Hendrick in 1906 publicized the revelations of corruption and mismanagement among the New York insurance companies, which a commission headed by Charles Evans Hughes had brought to light the year before. George Kibbe Turner's articles in 1909 on the alliance between the Chicago police and organized prostitution led to a famous vice commission's report on the midwestern city in 1911.

McClure's experiment soon proved that the public would buy a magazine devoted to serious discussions of contemporary problems, and other publishers were not long in following his example. *Collier's*, under the editorship of Norman Hapgood, led crusades against twin evils: the patent medicine fraud and the fraud of William Randolph Hearst, the yellow journalist who owned *Cosmopolitan* and a string of daily newspapers. Charles Edward Russell's exposure of the beef trust, published in *Everybody's* in 1905, was another notable contribution.

It was inevitable, however, that the muckraking technique would be adopted by publishers and writers of dubious integrity and exploited merely for financial gain. The first of the yellow muckrakers was Thomas W. Lawson, a stock market gambler and former president of the Amalgamated Copper Company, whose series, "Frenzied Finance," in *Everybody's* in 1905, allegedly exposed the insides of the monster, high finance. His revelations of financial corruption were lurid and highly exaggerated, but they had a tremendous impact. The circulation of *Everybody's* jumped in one year from 150,000 to over 750,000; and there can be no doubt that Lawson contributed to the public demand for control of the stock market that culminated in the Pujo Committee's investigation of 1913.

It was a sure sign that muckraking was heading for the gutter when William Randolph Hearst announced in 1906 that his *Cosmopolitan* would soon publish exposures that would be "the most vascular and virile" of them all. What Hearst had in mind was a series entitled "The Treason of the Senate," which the novelist David Graham Phillips was then writing. As it turned out, Phillips combined truth, fiction, and outright prevarication. But his indictment of the Senate added a powerful impetus to the movement for direct election of senators.

25. The Literature of Revolt

Contemporaneous with muckraking in magazine journalism was the proliferation of a fictional literature dedicated to the cause of democracy. Social and economic criticism ran the gamut from harsh exposés to frank appeals for a proletarian revolution. Frank Norris's *The Octopus* (1901) and *The Pit* (1903) told of the Southern Pacific Railroad's domination of the politics of California and the grain speculators' control of the wheat market. The naturalist Theodore Dreiser contributed two powerful socioeconomic studies, *The Financier* (1912) and *The Titan* (1914), based on the career of Charles T. Yerkes, a traction magnate of Chicago in the 1890s. David Graham Phillips exploited the theme of the corrupting power of money in *The Great God Success* (1901) and *The Second Generation* (1907), while his *Susan Lenox, Her Fall and Rise,* (1917) analyzed the social forces that drove a country girl in the city to prostitution. Robert Herrick's *The Memoirs of an American Citizen* (1905) and *Clark's Field* (1914) were impressive portrayals of the rise of men of wealth in an acquisitive society.

Socialist literary critiques of the shortcomings of American democracy were, if anything, even harsher than the works already cited. Robert Hunter's *Poverty* (1904) and Ben B. Lindsey's *The Beast* (1910), for example, indicated capitalism for making greed, exploitation, poverty, and corruption inevitable. In *The Bitter Cry of the Children* (1906) John Spargo offered a moving plea for child labor reform and a damning indictment of a system that consumed its young. Jack London, like Spargo, a leader in the Socialist party, was easily the most violent literary radical of his time. His *The Iron Heel* (1907) portrayed the capitalistic system at its alleged worst. In *The War of the Classes* (1905) and *Revolution* (1910) London affirmed his faith in the ultimate triumph of the workers.

Foremost in influence among the Socialist critics was Upton Sinclair, whose most important work during the progessive period was *The Jungle* (1906). It was a story of a Lithuanian immigrant working in the Chicago packing houses. Intended as a plea for socialism, *The Jungle* was a moving indictment of an economic system that allegedly brought hunger and misery to great masses of people. As Sinclair later lamented, *The Jungle* appealed to the stomachs rather than the hearts of the American people. They ignored what he said about socialism but were revolted by his descriptions of the filthy conditions of the slaughtering houses. The novel was, therefore, a powerful factor in compelling passage of the Pure Food and Drug Act in 1906.

The political novelists of the first decade of the twentieth century were more prolific, if less critical of American institutions, than the socioeconomic writers. Alfred Henry Lewis' *The Boss* (1903), based upon the career of Richard Croker of Tammany Hall, and Elliott Flower's *The Spoilsman* (1903) portrayed in fictional form the political corruption that Lincoln Steffens knew so well. Brand Whitlock, from his experiences in the government of Toledo, Ohio, added two powerful novels to the literature of exposure— *The Thirteenth District* (1902) and *The Turn of the Balance* (1907). Booth Tarkington, in *The Gentleman from Indiana* (1899), *In the Arena* (1905), and other novels, exploited the theme of corruption of the political life of a state by railroad and business interests.

The most popular of these political novelists was Winston Churchill of New Hampshire, whose *Coniston* (1906) and *Mr. Crewe's Career* (1908) sold by the hundreds of thousands. Churchill seemed to think that a regeneration of American politics would occur if only the sturdy, plain people turned the rascals out and elected honest men. Equally naive was William Allen White's *A Certain Rich Man* (1909), a collection of platitudes with an incredible ending. If Churchill and White illustrated the shallowness of many of the political writers, David Graham Phillips exemplified in fictional form the strenuosity of this literary movement. In *The Plum Tree* (1905) he attempted to expose the system of corruption and special privilege everywhere in the United States.

Whether profound or shallow, these leaders of the literary revolt against the status quo made a considerable contribution to the progressive movement. They wrote on subjects ranging from child labor to the use of state troops to break strikes. Their achievement in highlighting corruption in politics and in revealing the darker phases of American society furnished a basis in conviction for the national effort to achieve government representative of the people and responsive to their social and economic needs.

26. Intellectual Progressivism

Every movement of vitality eventually reaches a point where it spawns philosophers who attempt to systematize its thought and formulate a philosophy to justify its practical program. Although the progressive movement was no exception to this rule, its intellectuals had to do more than merely construct a new philosophy. They first had to overturn the whole structure of ideas upon which the defenders of status quo rested their arguments: social Darwinism and individualism; the cult of hostility to government; the belief that the Constitution was an inspired document and that the Supreme Court was the interpreter of divine judgment; and, finally, the idea that railroad builders, financiers, and captains of industry had contributed to the nation's economic progress. These concepts had become so firmly embedded in the popular mind by 1900 that together they constituted the American creed. They had to be destroyed before progressive concepts could find wholesale acceptance.

Inherent in practically every aspect of the progressive offensive, furthermore, was the ultimate objective of planting faith in the efficacy of public measures of amelioration and control. Students of labor legislation, champions of social justice measures, and expounders of the new sociological jurisprudence, for example, were all trying to build a basis in economic and social fact for the necessity of positive government. So also were social gospel leaders, when they preached doctrines of social salvation, and sociologists, when they urged the necessity of thinking of wrongdoing in social as well as individual terms.

The most significant formulation of progressive political theory came from the pen of Herbert Croly, a New York journalist, whose major works, *The Promise of American Life* (1909) and *Progressive Democracy* (1914), at once established him as the chief philosopher of progressivism. Moreover, as editor of the *New Republic,* which he founded in 1914, Croly gathered around him most of the leading young social and economic thinkers of the time. Croly's writings provided progressives with their most cogent arguments in behalf of positive legislation.

He began by arguing that the most widely accepted American political tradition was the Jeffersonian tradition of distrust of government and extreme individualism in economic affairs. This tradition, Croly said, had become identified with democracy because Jefferson was in fact the first American democratic philosopher and leader. In contrast, the Hamiltonian tradition of strong government had been closely identified in the popular mind with special privileges for the upper classes, because Hamilton was an ardent champion of these classes. Most Americans still believed that the promise of American life could be realized only if the golden age of competition could be restored by withdrawing all special privileges to the business classes. The fact was, Croly warned, that such a policy of laissez faire and drift in an age of inevitable big industry and big finance could only carry the nation to an equally inevitable ruin—to aggrandizement of power by the special interests and the degradation of the masses.

Who could save the nation from such peril? How could the American dream of democracy and equality of opportunity be fulfilled? The answer,

Croly said, was clear. Progressives must abandon their romantic Jeffersonian concepts and support a program of positive and comprehensive state and federal intervention on all economic fronts. This would mean, for one thing, that progressives would have to abandon opposition to class or special-interest legislation. Such a program had perhaps served a useful purpose at one time, but it was now the chief intellectual stumbling block.

The important task ahead, Croly declared, was first to define the national interest and then to achieve its fulfillment by careful planning and legislation. The important question, of course, was, who would define the national interest? Croly answered by calling for a new nationalism that would attract the leadership of the "best minds" in the task of reconciling planning and positive government with the democratic tradition.

The year 1912 saw the publication of a second significant plea for a new political positivism—Walter Weyl's *The New Democracy.* Weyl did not share Croly's mystical faith in the "national interest" and the "best minds." He was much more concerned with facts and figures, and he made self-interest the motivation for his program of social and industrial democracy. In brief, he said, a democracy could not allow large groups to be degraded and exploited because these same groups would in the end resort to violence and perhaps destroy society. Walter Lippmann's *Preface to Politics* (1913), and *Drift and Mastery* (1914), supplemented Croly's and particularly Weyl's arguments. Lippmann, then a young socialist in process of shedding his parlor radicalism, assumed the necessity of democratic collectivism. His major argument was for a pragmatic approach to politics, one based on science and unencumbered by so-called moral criteria.

Another important component of the intellectual attack on the conservative ideology was the discrediting of the divine-origin theory of the Constitution, which was often invoked by opponents of the direct election of senators and other neodemocratic proposals. Discontent over the undemocratic features of the Constitution was as old as the document itself, but not until the progressive period did scholars and politicians evolve the thesis that the Constitution had been written deliberately to frustrate the democratic movement.

This thesis was first systematically developed by Walter Clark, chief justice of North Carolina, in an address at the University of Pennsylvania Law School in 1906. The following year, in *The Spirit of American Government,* Professor J. Allen Smith of the University of Washington repeated Clark's assertion that a minority had conceived the Constitution in class interest and imposed it upon the majority in order to thwart their aspirations. Charles A. Beard, a young historian at Columbia University who had discovered Marx and Engels in England around the turn of the century, went to work to prove that the Constitution had been written to protect merchants, great landowners, moneylenders, and speculators. His findings were embodied in 1913 in *An Economic Interpretation of the Constitution.* Progressives could now say that the Constitution, which had so often stood in the way of their reforms, was no more sacrosanct than any other part of the American past.

As a final blow, intellectual progressives applied the full weight of scholarship and sarcasm toward discrediting the belief that railroad builders, financiers, and captains of industry were heroes and contributors to American progress. The most trenchant of the critics of the moneyed classes was Thorstein Veblen, a strange quondam economics professor, whose economic theory had much greater impact in the 1930s than during his own day. His most widely read work, *The Theory of the Leisure Class* (1899) was a biting attack against the standards and practices of contemporary American business civilization. The most prolific of the debunkers of the plutocracy was Gustavus Myers, a socialist, who grimly set to work to discover how great fortunes in the United States had been accumulated. His *History of the Great American Fortunes,* published in three volumes in 1909–1910, confirmed the old charge that large American fortunes had been made through plunder and preemption of natural resources.

There were, of course, many other leaders equally prominent in this extraordinary and far-reaching revolt of the intellectuals. While we cannot measure their contribution precisely, we can surely say that their part in making the progressive movement a permanent force in American life was not small. Their great contribution lay in discrediting a conservative ideology that had strongly buttressed the status quo and in formulating a philosophy for the social-welfare state. In this respect and for this reason, therefore, the intellectuals were the true leaveners of progressivism.

27. The Shame of the Cities

Through the agitation of political leaders and the exposures of muckrakers, the American people, from the 1890s to about 1910, discovered that representative political institutions in their cities had broken down almost completely. Instead of being governed by representatives impartially chosen, most American cities were ruled by political machines that resembled the modern corporation in their hierarchical structure. The head of the machine was known as the "boss," "big man," or "leader." Because of his generally unsavory reputation, he usually held no office. Almost invariably he had risen from the ranks after years of service. The boss operated like a general in charge of field forces. His orders were commands, passed down from the "ring" to its hundreds or thousands of workers. Machines, usually superbly organized and smoothly run, were the invisible governments of great cities, affecting the well-being of millions of people.

Woodrow Wilson once declared that the prevailing form of American city government had been constructed as if to make the usurpation of power by an extraconstitutional organization inevitable. Wilson's statement was essentially correct. When city charters were granted or rewritten during the high tide of Jacksonian Democracy, their framers deliberately dispersed power and responsibility among numerous agencies—the mayor, a two-house council, and sometimes independent boards and commissions. The result was not democratic government. It was a form under which responsible government was nearly impossible because the agencies for achieving it did not exist. Into the power vacuum created by this sytem of checks and balances and division of authority moved the kind of political machine just described. For all its sins, it did have enough cohesion and concentration of authority to govern.

The machine survived even when forms of government were changed. A more important reason for its existence and power, therefore, was the fact that it rendered service to large numbers of people. The majority of voters in 1900 did not ask whether the organization was corrupt but whether it did something for them. The machine made it a point to do things for them. Its agents met the friendless immigrant at the dock and helped him to find shelter and work. Precinct captains provided coal and food for Widow Flanagan or Mrs. Moskowitz when they were in need. There was nothing scientific about the machine's charity, to be sure. But the submerged third of the people cared little about honesty and efficiency so long as they lived in poverty and slums. They wanted social services that the machines knew how to give and that progressives had not yet developed.

The machine survived also because it was held together by the twin codes of patronage and loyalty. The chief source of livelihood of lesser dignitaries was petty office and graft, and the boss could command a host of willing workers so long as he had favors to bestow. Loyalty and friendship also played an important role in keeping the organization intact. Organization politics, moreover, afforded social and political opportunities for immigrant and minority groups such as they could never find in "respectable" society. In fact, the machine was one of the few cohesive and unifying forces in the social chaos of metropolitan life.

The oil best calculated to lubricate the political machine was the loot that it received. On the lower levels, bribery—in the form of money paid to politicians and policemen by criminals, prostitutes, saloon keepers, and others —was extremely widespread, highly organized, and fabulously profitable. The Chicago Vice Commission reported in 1911, for example, that the annual profit from vice in that city was $15 million, and that one-fifth of this sum was paid to the police in the form of graft.

The most dangerous kind of bribery was the money paid by businessmen for protection, special privileges, and public rights. To begin with, the great economic interests in the cities turned "their dollars into votes and their property into political power" by buying control of the political machines. Corruption was inevitable so long as businessmen wanted exemption from equitable taxation. In addition, there were numerous opportunities in large and rapidly growing cities for bribery of another kind—purchase of franchises and contracts. New city railway lines had to be constructed; sewerage, gas, electrical, and water lines had to follow new areas of development. The boss usually had franchises and contracts at his disposal; even perpetual franchises could be bought. It was top-level bribery of this kind that was most dangerous to the public interest and most profitable to the machine.

This, therefore, was the "System," as Lincoln Steffens called it. This was the pattern of corruption that characterized American municipal politics at the turn of the century. Some cities, to be sure, outshone the others in refining the art of misgovernment. In St. Louis, for example, the Democratic boss systematically sold franchises, licenses, and exemptions to the respectable leaders of the business community. The boss of Minneapolis operated the most spectacular system of police graft in the country. In Pittsburgh two Republican leaders owned the city council and grew rich on contracts and utilities. Philadelphia presented the sorriest sight of all—a place where the citizens cheerfully acquiesced in the total subversion of representative government.

28. The Municipal Reform Movement

The general prevalence of municipal corruption and misrule stimulated the first important *political* development in the progressive movement—the crusade for municipal reform. It began in a sporadic way in the 1890s, with the emergence of Hazen S. Pingree, mayor of Detroit, as the first significant progressive municipal reformer. The widespread breakdown of city social services during the Panic of 1893 led to the formation of the National Municipal League, the temporary overthrow of Tammany Hall in New York in 1894, and the triumph of a reform coalition in Baltimore a year later.

The years 1896–1897, however, seem to mark a dividing line between spasmodic uprisings and widespread revolt. The first of these insurrections occurred in Chicago, where the city council was busily selling the public's most valuable rights to Charles T. Yerkes, a utilities magnate. As protests against the corrupt selling of franchises began to swell, some 232 civic leaders met in 1895, organized the Municipal Voter's League, and launched a nonpartisan campaign to clean up the city government. By pitilessly exposing the records of corrupt aldermen, the league won control of the city council in the aldermanic elections of 1896 and 1897. In the latter year, moreover, the league helped elect a progressive mayor, Carter Harrison, and Chicago was saved from the grafters, at least momentarily.

The reform movement in Chicago illustrated what could be accomplished by an aroused citizenry without an outstanding single leader. Elsewhere the municipal reform movement followed a similar pattern. Various nonpartisan good government leagues combined in New York City in 1913 to overthrow Tammany rule and elect a young reform mayor, John Purroy Mitchel. In Minneapolis an energetic citizens' committee and a fearless grand jury exposed the system of police graft operated by Mayor A. A. Ames and put Ames and his henchmen in prison.

The dominant pattern of municipal reform, however, was redemption through leadership of some dynamic and often colorful popular tribune. The most famous and influential member of this group was Tom L. Johnson of Cleveland. Elected mayor in 1901 on a platform demanding equal taxation and the three-cent fare on trolley lines, Johnson gathered some of the ablest young municipal administrators in the country and moved first against the inequalities of the tax lists. He next opened fire on railroads and utilities, which owned extensive property in Cleveland but paid hardly any taxes. The state legislature doubled railroad taxes in 1903–1904, while the utilities consented to a doubling of their assessments. All these battles were mere skirmishes compared to the great campaign that Johnson waged for the three-cent fare. The climax came when Johnson and his council established competing trolley routes and invited outside capitalists to bid for them. The local traction interests appealed to the state Republican ring for protection. The state ring, in turn, appealed to the supreme court of Ohio; it declared that all charters of Ohio cities were void because they had been created by special legislation. With all city governments of Ohio thus destroyed, the ring called the legislature into special session to adopt a uniform municipal code. It replaced the old system of concentrated power that had prevailed in Cleveland with government by divided authorities and independent boards.

Such tactics did not daunt Tom Johnson. He kept on appealing to the people and winning mayoralty campaigns. Eventually he concluded that public ownership of utilities and traction properties was the only way to eliminate the worst source of municipal corruption. Johnson was finally beaten in 1909, less than a year before his death. But his program was saved by the election of his chief lieutenant, Newton D. Baker, as mayor in 1911.

Such was the kind of men who led the progressive movement in the cities. All municipal reformers fought common enemies: entrenched and corrupt politicians allied with privileged business and criminal elements. They all sought the same goals: impartial government, fair taxation, regulation of public service companies, and expanded social services for the lower classes. These remained always the chief objectives. But progressives soon learned that it was not enough to throw the rascals out and inaugurate a program of economic and social reform. Politics remained; and reformers could never rest secure so long as bosses controlled the party structure. Thus, inevitably, progressives turned also to the task of changing the political mechanisms in the hope that greater popular participation and control would lay a secure basis for economic and social reforms that were already begun.

Progressives in the cities, therefore, joined hands with other reform groups in a frontal assault on bosses and machines by establishing the direct primary for nominating candidates and adopting the short ballot, initiative, referendum, and recall. As these campaigns were part of the progressive movement on the statewide level, we will discuss them later in this chapter.

Municipal reformers also fought hard to obtain home rule and an end to legislative interference in municipal administration. As Tom Johnson and other progressives soon discovered, city machines were invariably components of state rings. After smashing the local machine, it profited progressives little if the state ring, acting through the legislature, could nullify all their gains. This often happened because in most states city governments were creatures of the legislature and completely under its control. Municipal reformers were not notably successful in their struggle to be free from legislative interference, because rural and small-town legislators were loath to yield control over metropolitan revenues. Four states, Missouri, California, Washington, and Minnesota, had granted home rule to cities by the turn of the century. Eight other states granted this coveted privilege from 1900 to 1914, but only two of them, Michigan and Ohio, had any large cities of consequence.

The most far-reaching progressive proposal for institutional change struck at the heart of the problem of municipal government and seemed to offer the greatest hope of saving the cities. This was the plan to abolish the old mayor-council system entirely and to substitute government by a commission of nonpartisan administrators. The commission form, much discussed in the 1890s, was first put to use when a hurricane and tidal wave devastated Galveston, Texas, on September 8, 1900. With a corrupt city council utterly incapable of facing the tasks of reconstruction, leading property owners of Galveston appealed to the state legislature to assume the government of the city. The legislature responded by establishing a government by five commissioners, elected, after 1903, by the people.

The commission plan first won nationwide prominence when the Iowa legislature in 1907 adopted a more elaborate version of the Texas model. The Iowa statute allowed cities over 25,000 to adopt the commission form. More important, it incorporated the initiative, referendum, and recall as part of the machinery of city politics and provided for nomination of commissioners in nonpartisan elections. At once Des Moines adopted the commission form, and thereafter it was known as the "Des Moines Idea." More than one hundred cities had adopted commission government by 1910; by the eve of the First World War the number had exceeded four hundred—chiefly medium-sized cities in the Middle West, New England, and the Pacific states.

Experience soon demonstrated that the commission form had inherent weaknesses that were not evident at the outset. It failed really to concentrate responsibility for administration, since there was no guarantee that the commissioners would be expert managers. Progressives slowly evolved a refinement of the commission form. The final product was the city manager plan, first adopted in its complete form by Dayton, Ohio, in 1913, after a great flood had inundated the city and the mayor and council could not cope with the emergency. This innovation preserved the best features of the commission plan and eliminated most of its weaknesses. All authority was vested in a board of commissioners, elected on a nonpartisan basis, who made laws and policies for the city. The commissioners appointed a city manager, usually a trained expert, to administer the various departments of the government, and the city manager, in turn, was responsible in all matters to the commissioners.

The new form seemed such a logical way to achieve responsible and expert administration without sacrificing the principle of democratic control that it spread rapidly and soon displaced the commission form in many cities. More than three hundred cities had adopted the city manager plan by 1923.

Thus the progressive movement in the cities stimulated the rise of a host of new leaders and the development of political institutions calculated to facilitate popular rule and responsible government. To charge, as certain critics have done, that city reformers did not abolish all evils and bring the millennium is at best naive. For the most part they were tough-minded men, who well knew that venality and corruption would survive, regardless of the form of government, so long as men profited thereby. They must be judged on a basis of the obstacles that they faced and what they accomplished rather than condemned for failing to change human nature or reconstruct society. Surveying the American scene at the end of the progressive period, competent authorities concluded that the municipal reformers had in large measure succeeded. The era of flagrant corruption had by and large passed. Cities were governed more efficiently than they had been a decade before, and a new class of professional municipal administrators were in training throughout the country. In short, if the city was not yet the hope of American democracy, it was no longer its nemesis.

29. The Shame of the States

Corruption and special privilege held sway in many states around the turn of the century in the same manner and for the same purpose that they reigned in the cities. Just as the city machine was the medium through which corrupt businessmen obtained contracts, franchises, and immunities from the city government, so also was the state machine, or ring, the medium through which such favors were bought on the state level.

The boss system in the states varied greatly from state to state and from party to party. City organizations usually formed the basis for the state machine, although in rural states the county courthouse rings were the important components. In states with a tremendous concentration of population in one metropolis, the boss of the great city machine was often head of the state organization. In other states political power was more widely dispersed. In any event, party authority was concentrated in the state committee, headed by a state chairman who represented the dominant leader or leaders in the state. It was the state chairman who usually organized the legislature, controlled legislation, and made deals with railroad and corporation lobbyists.

Two states, Missouri and New Jersey, afford exaggerated but vivid illustrations of how the so-called system operated in most states of the Union at the turn of the century. In Missouri the bribery or "boodle" system worked at peak efficiency to govern the state in the interest of railroads and corporations. The corrupting agency was the lobby at the state capital, representing important railroad and business interests. The medium through which the lobby worked in this case was the party caucus in the legislature. Because the lobby bought control of the caucus, even honest legislators were caught in its net and forced to do its bidding. In Missouri, as in many other states, the lobby was the real, the living government that operated behind the façade of constitutional forms.

The control of state politics by a corporation-machine alliance reached its apogee in New Jersey. The leaders of the business and financial communities were in fact often the leaders of the dominant Republican party, and it was usually unnecessary for businessmen to corrupt legislators and state officials. The railroad lobby in 1903, for example, furnished the chief justice of the state, the attorney general, the state comptroller, the commissioner of banking and insurance, and one of the members of the state board of taxation. It was probably no coincidence that railroads at that time paid only one-third of their just share of the tax burden. Moreover, both United States senators from New Jersey were interested in public utilities, while the retiring attorney general was on the boards of three public service corporations. It was not surprising that public utilities in the state enjoyed immunity from equitable taxation and public regulation.

30. The Progressive Movement in the States

Like the municipal reform movement, the great revolt against the system in the states was a culmination rather than a beginning. In the South and West, agrarian radicalism was supplanted by progressivism from 1896 to 1900, as urban spokesmen assumed leadership in the struggle against railroad and corporation dominance. The Middle West, where the dominant GOP was firmly controlled by the vested interests at the turn of the century, was convulsed by a series of spectacular revolts from 1900 to 1908. Under insurgent leaders like Robert M. La Follette of Wisconsin, Albert B. Cummins of Iowa, and Albert J. Beveridge of Indiana, the midwestern states were transformed from bastions of conservative republicanism into strongholds of progressivism. In the East the progressive revolt had a more decidedly urban complexion, as it often grew out of earlier campaigns in the cities. But progressivism was no less spectacular in the East than in the Middle West. The following developments, among others, signified the power and strength of eastern progressivism: Charles Evans Hughes's election as governor of New York in 1906 and 1908 and his courageous battles for the direct primary and public regulation of utilities and railroads; the New Idea movement in New Jersey, which began in 1906 as a rebellion within the Republican party and culminated in the election of a Democrat, Woodrow Wilson, as governor in 1910; and the sweeping triumph of progressivism in Ohio, with the adoption of a new constitution and the election of a Democratic progressive, James M. Cox, as governor in 1912. The politics of the Pacific Coast states, too, was transformed by the trimuph of such reformers as Hiram W. Johnson of California and William S. U'Ren of Oregon.

What we are dealing with here was obviously no minor phenomenon but a political revolt of national proportions and momentous consequences for the future of American politics. So successful were progressive leaders in the several states by 1912 that all observers agreed that a thoroughgoing revolution had been accomplished since 1900. In most states the power of the bipartisan machines had been shattered or at least curtailed, and an older generation of conservative leaders had been supplanted by younger newcomers. State governments were more representative of the rank and file and more responsive to their economic and social needs.

"Give the government back to the people!"—the battle cry of progressivism in the states—not only reflected the conviction that state governments had ceased to be representative but also pointed up the major objective of the movement. But how could the system be destroyed? What were the processes and techniques of this counterrevolution against privilege?

The first, indeed the absolutely essential, ingredient was leadership. In every state in which progressivism triumphed there was some aggressive leader who carried the fight to the people and, after winning, provided responsible and effective government. Indeed, it is now evident that the progressives' most lasting contribution to American political practice was not the mechanical changes that they instituted, but rather the fact that they awakened the American people to the necessity for responsible leadership in a democracy.

Progressive leaders in the states, moreover, made a concerted campaign to overhaul the existing structure of political institutions. If representative government had broken down under the old forms, progressives argued, then new institutions had to be devised to facilitate popular control of parties and governments. Invariably, the first objective of reform leaders was the inauguration of the direct primary system of nominating candidates and party officials. This objective took priority because the old system of nomination by conventions seemed to afford the bosses an easy means of perpetuating their control. Practically all city and state elective officials before 1900 were nominated at party conventions on district, county, and statewide levels. Normally such conventions were easily bought or controlled; usually they were well-oiled cogs in the machine. Reform forces might capture the conventions and momentarily subdue the bosses, but it was an extraordinarily difficult undertaking.

The progressive remedy was simple and direct: make it easier for voters and more difficult for bosses to control the party by instituting a system of nominating candidates directly by the people. The direct primary apparently originated in Pennsylvania in the 1840s, but it was not used extensively on the local level until the 1890s, and then it was to be found mainly in the South. Mississippi in 1902 was the first state to adopt a compulsory, statewide primary law. Wisconsin enacted similar legislation the following year as the first major item in Governor La Follette's reform program. From this time on the system spread rapidly through all sections, so that by 1916 only Rhode Island, Connecticut, and New Mexico had failed to enact primary legislation of some kind.

State progressives usually campaigned next for a variety of institutional reforms: the short ballot, to reduce the number of elective officials and concentrate responsibility in government; corrupt practices legislation, to control and limit campaign contributions and expenditures; and the direct election of United States senators by the people instead of by the state legislatures. Progress in the field of short ballot reform was notable only in the area of municipal government with the rapid spread of the commission and city manager forms. Practically every state adopted stringent corrupt practices laws, while Congress in 1907 and 1909 prohibited corporations, insurance companies, banks, and railroads from contributing to campaign funds in federal election contests. For many years, however, reactionary forces in the Senate would not allow a constitutional amendment for direct election of senators to pass. Many states, therefore, turned to an indirect method of electing senators directly. This was accomplished by requiring senatorial candidates to be nominated in primary elections and candidates for the state legislature to swear that they would vote for the senatorial candidate thus nominated by the people. The United States Senate, after a scandal involving the election of William Lorimer, Republican boss of Illinois, to that body in 1909, approved the Seventeenth Amendment for direct election in 1912. It became a part of the Constitution on May 31, 1913.

Many skeptical progressives refused to agree that the foregoing reforms sufficed. Convinced that representative government might become subverted by the forces of privilege even under the new and more democratic forms, they proposed to give the people an alternative and a last resort—the initiative and referendum.[3] The initiative and referendum were used most widely in the West, where South Dakota first adopted them in 1898. During the next ten years only Utah, Oregon, Nevada, Montana, and Oklahoma joined the experiment in direct legislation. But fifteen other states, including several in the East and South, adopted the measures from 1908 to 1915. The movement came to a virtual standstill in 1915, however, as conservatives launched a vigorous counterattack, and experience soon proved that the mass of voters were not competent to deal with technical matters of legislation.

As a further safeguard of the popular interest, progressives championed the recall, a device that afforded the voters a handy means of removing unsatisfactory elective officials. First used in Los Angeles in 1903, the recall found widest acceptance in cities that adopted the commission and city manager forms. Oregon made the recall applicable to elective state and local officials in 1908, and nine other states, most of them in the West, followed suit from 1911 to 1915. This form of recall provoked strenuous opposition from conservatives, but defenders of the status quo saved their choicest invectives for the recall of judges. If the people could remove judges for making unpopular decisions, then what minority and property rights would be safe from the assaults of an irrational majority? Seven states—Oregon, California, Arizona, Nevada, Colorado, Kansas, and North Dakota—adopted the recall of judges. The violent controversies over the measure at the time now seem rather pointless; not a single judge of a superior or state supreme court has been removed since the recall of judges was first proposed. As an alternative means of protecting the right of the states to use police power for social and economic ends, Theodore Roosevelt in 1912 proposed the recall of decisions by state courts that nullified such legislation. Only Colorado, in 1913, adopted this measure, and the Colorado supreme court in 1921 declared the statute unconstitutional.

Critics have accused progressive leaders of naively believing that representative and truly democratic government could be restored by mere alterations in the mechanics of politics. The charge reveals a profound ignorance of the progressive era. There were undoubtedly fools among the leaders of the reform movement in the states. But the great majority were realistic politicians who well knew that the changes they proposed were merely instruments to facilitate the capture of political machinery. They used these instruments, therefore, to gain and hold power. And they must be judged for what they accomplished or failed to accomplish on the higher level of substantive reform.

Their achievements in the realm of social and economic legislation were

[3]The initiative is a device whereby the electorate may enact legislation against the will of the legislature. Upon petition of a stipulated percentage of the voters, the legislature must consider the measure that the petitioners propose. If the legislature refuses to approve the bill it must call a special election in which the voters may enact or reject the measure. The referendum, on the other hand, is a device by which voters may nullify a measure already approved by the legislature.

imposing indeed. We have already related the progress of the movement in the states for social justice legislation, so-called moral reform through prohibition, and the development of public education. In the realm of strictly economic legislation, progressive leaders in the states made substantial progress toward subjecting railroads and public service corporations to effective public control. Beginning with the Georgia Railroad Commission of 1879 and culminating in the adoption by the Wisconsin legislature of Governor La Follette's bill for a railroad commission in 1905, the movement for state regulation advanced steadily. Indeed, so effective had it become by 1914 that the railroad managers were then begging Congress to save them from harassment by state commissions. It was during the progressive era, too, that the movement for expert regulation by state commissions of rates and services of public service corporations and of insurance and investment companies began and reached its first culmination.

These were all important substantive reforms and together constitute an imposing record. But in assessing progressivism's achievement we should not dismiss lightly the political changes that it effected. By their emphasis on simplified forms of government, greater popular participation in, and control over, the electoral process, and responsible leadership, the progressive leaders transformed the theory and practice of politics in the United States. Looking back in 1913 upon his hard battles for the people as governor of Wisconsin, Robert M. La Follette penned a fitting epilogue, not only for the progressive movement in Wisconsin, but for progressivism in many other states as well: "This closes the account of my services in Wisconsin—a time full of struggle, and yet a time that I like to look back upon. It has been a fight supremely worth making, and I want it to be judged, as it will be ultimately, by results actually attained. If it can be shown that Wisconsin is a happier and better state to live in, that its institutions are more democratic, that the opportunities of all its people are more equal, that social justice more nearly prevails, that human life is safer and sweeter—then I shall rest content in the feeling that the Progressive movement has been successful."[4]

[4]*Autobiography of Robert M. La Follette* (Madison, Wis., 1913), pp. 368-369; see also Belle Case La Follette and Fola La Follette, *Robert M. La Follette,* 2 vols. (New York, 1953), I, p. 192.

Chapter 4

Politics and Problems of the Republican Era, 1901-1910

It was inevitable that the progressive revolt should soon spread from the cities and states into the larger arena of national politics. This was true because there is no real dividing line between state and federal politics in the American system. It was true even more because the spread of the railroad, financial, and industrial networks across state boundaries created important problems with which the federal government alone could constitutionally cope.

This and following chapters relate the impact of the progressive upheaval upon national politics and policies. At the beginning of the twentieth century the dominant Republican party was controlled by men who frankly urged a program of generous assistance to the business interests and who abhorred the very concept of public regulation. Under William Jennings Bryan, some of the minority Democrats were cautiously moving toward a more progressive position, but they had mounted no comprehensive and rational attack on the system of privilege. Within less than a decade, however, the progressive ferment had wrought mighty changes in the American political scene. Advanced progressives, who sought to make the federal government a positive, regenerative force, were a large element in the Republican party by 1910. Moreover, the Democrats were united and confident under new leadership.

In brief, the progressive movement, which had already brought important changes in federal policies, stood on the verge of culmination and fulfillment.

31. Theodore Roosevelt and the Progressive Movement[1]

No account of national progressivism would be complete without some note of its most extraordinary leader during its early period. Theodore Roosevelt, who came to the presidency by a tragic circumstance, presided over the nation's destinies during a time of agitation for, and development of, a national reform program. He opportunely adapted his policies to meet the changing configurations of political power. He was, however, no mere creature of circumstance, but rather a prime moving force in history.

Born on October 27, 1858, the scion of a well-to-do mercantile and banking family, he was reared in the genteel Knickerbocker traditions of New York City. Afflicted with a frail body and weak eyes, while still young he determined to make himself physically strong. He overcame his weakness by dint of exhausting labors and ever after gloried in the strenuous life and manly virtues. Whether as cowboy and gunfighter, Rough Rider during the Spanish-American War, or big game hunter in Africa, Roosevelt proved that physically he was as good as the best and that he did not know the meaning of fear.

From his social environment and especially from his father, Roosevelt acquired a compulsion to do good for people less fortunate than himself. While most persons of his class gave money to settlement houses or home missions, Roosevelt went into politics after graduating from Harvard in 1880. Part of his motivation must have been the strong moral sense he acquired from his Dutch Reformed religion and its Calvinistic emphasis upon righteousness. In any event, Roosevelt usually viewed political contests as struggles between the forces of good and evil and, like Wilson and Bryan, he became a preacher-at-large to the American people.

Background, training, temperament, and personal associations all combined in Roosevelt to produce a fundamentally cautious and conservative, rather than doctrinaire, approach to politics. Justice to all classes, and therefore legislation in the general interest, became his guiding principle. A patrician, he viewed with righteous anger the vulgarity and materialism of the newly rich captains of industry, financiers, and railroad speculators. Yet experience and a sense of justice prevented him from condemning whole

[1]Parts of the following section first appeared in Arthur S. Link, "Theodore Roosevelt in His Letters," *Yale Review,* 43 (Summer 1954), pp. 589–598; reproduced by permission of the editors of the *Yale Review.*

classes or accepting the socialist dictum that it was the economic system that was alone responsible for social wrongdoing. Roosevelt's conservatism, moreover, was manifested in his insistence upon continuity and his abhorrence of men who advocated unnatural change. Believing that progressive adaptation to new circumstances could not occur unless order and social stability first existed, he feared a mob as much as he feared the malefactors of great wealth.

It is proof of his complexity that Theodore Roosevelt must be reckoned a progressive in spite of his basically conservative approach to politics. On a bedrock of democratic idealism he built a structure of legislative policies the shape of which was usually determined by the pragmatic need of the hour. Experience, whether as governor of New York or president of the United States, led him to the conclusion that only organized political power, that is, government, could meet the manifold challenges that industrialism raised in city, state, and nation. For this reason he was primarily a progressive, even though he refused to be doctrinaire about his progressivism.

In the practice of politics Roosevelt was as hardheaded a realist as ever sat in the presidential chair. He was a realist because he recognized and respected power. Thus, while he was governor of New York, he worked with the Republican boss of that state as long as he could do so honorably. When he assumed the presidency in 1901 he found political power in the Republican party concentrated in the state organizations and exercised by their representatives in Congress. He did not attempt to destroy the party hierarchy; indeed, he worked with and through it. The important point is that Roosevelt not only accepted existing power structures as he found them in New York and Washington but that he also became a master politician, able to use his party for his own and the country's interests.

Indeed, in the way in which he conceded the smaller points in order to win the important objectives and mastered the political game without yielding his own integrity, Roosevelt symbolized the moral man confronted by the dilemmas of an immoral society. Doctrinaire reformers demanded the whole loaf of reform and denounced Roosevelt when he accepted half or two-thirds of the loaf. Roosevelt knew that he could not transform society and politics by one bugle blast. He knew that men are usually governed by selfish motives and that politics is fundamentally not a moral profession. Knowing these things, he tried to use selfishness to achieve a moral end—the advancement of human welfare. He also tried to strengthen altruistic tendencies whenever he found them.

These, then, were some of the features of Roosevelt's personality and philosophy. There was, however, another trait that to a varying degree dominated all the rest—his love of power, which mounted as the years passed and at times verged on megalomania. Love of his own opinions often obscured the truth in Roosevelt's mind and caused him to think that he was above the law and ordinary conventions. Yet his confidence was as much a source of strength as of danger, giving him the self-confidence essential to leadership.

Combined with intelligence and energy, it made him a superb administrator, precisely because he was bold enough to do unprecedented things.

Personal judgments of Roosevelt will vary, but no one should make the mistake of not taking him seriously. Because he was a leader of men it was given to him to make a large contribution to the progressive movement, to the art of government in the United States, and to the diplomacy of his country. In fact, since Lincoln, only two other presidents, Wilson and Franklin Roosevelt, have made comparable contributions.

Theodore Roosevelt's most lasting contribution to American political practice was his exercise of leadership and revitalization of the presidency. A long line of second-rate politicians had occupied the White House from 1865 to 1901. With the exception perhaps of Cleveland they were not even leaders of their own party, much less of the country. Because of the entrenched position of the Old Guard professionals in Congress, Roosevelt was never able to dominate the veterans on Capitol Hill. But he was able to bend a stubborn Congress to his will by making himself the one great popular spokesman in the country. By exploiting some of the powers inherent in the presidency, he proved that effective national leadership was possible in the American constitutional system.

Roosevelt's contributions to the science of administration alone would entitle him to distinction among the presidents. Perceiving that the only alternative to rule by private wealth was the development of a strong, efficient administrative state, democratically controlled but powerful enough to make important economic decisions, he advanced the science of administration as no president before him had done. He and his able associates strengthened the Civil Service, put the consular service on a professional basis, modernized the army's command structure, brought the navy to an unprecedented peak of efficiency, and carried forward a scientific program of conservation of natural resources. Moreover, he helped to broaden the powers of an old agency, the Interstate Commerce Commission, and created a new one, the Bureau of Corporations. In brief, during the Roosevelt era democracy learned to become efficient.

A third contribution is almost as important as Roosevelt's development of the presidential power. It was his vindication of the national, or public, interest over all private aggregations of economic power. The open contempt that bankers, monopolists, and railroad managers displayed toward the law and the highhanded manner in which they dealt with the people filled him with loathing and anger. He retaliated by asserting the supremacy of the people over private interests in three far-reaching ways. First, he withdrew more than 200 million acres of public lands to curb the plunder of a great national heritage. Second, he activated the Sherman Antitrust Act and began a movement that succeeded in curbing industrial monopoly in the United States. Third, he forced adoption of the Hepburn Act of 1906, which deprived the railroads of ultimate sovereignty in the rate-making process. In the anthracite coal strike of 1902, he was prepared to go the full limit in asserting the public interest—by seizing and operating the coal mines if the operators should refuse to mediate the controversy. Such actions marked the momentous beginnings of legislation and administration that culminated in the New Deal and the democratic welfare state.

32. Roosevelt and the Republican Party, 1900–1904

The leaders of the Republican party laid their plans carefully for the election of 1900. President William McKinley was of course the inevitable presidential choice of the GOP. The death in 1899 of Vice-President Garret A. Hobart left the second place on the ticket open and created an unusual opportunity for Thomas C. Platt, Republican boss of New York State. Platt had nominated Theodore Roosevelt, the hero of the Spanish-American War, for governor of New York in 1898 in order to win. Elected easily, Roosevelt attacked corruption with vigor, championed social legislation, and was consequently soon at odds with Platt. Hobart's death offered a dignified yet final method of getting Roosevelt out of New York. The Republican Old Guard could silence Roosevelt by elevating him to the vice-presidency, and Platt would be saved the embarrassment of having to nominate him again for governor in 1900.

McKinley and his adviser, Mark Hanna, responded coldly when Platt first presented his plan. "Don't any of you realize," Hanna is later alleged to have remarked, "that there's only one life between this madman and the White House?" But Platt was so persistent that Hanna finally gave in. Roosevelt, with his usual perception, at once saw through Platt's scheme. He had grave misgivings about accepting his consignment to oblivion. His friends, however, suggested that he would be the logical presidential candidate in 1904, and when the nomination was offered to him, he could think of no alternative but to accept.

The Democrats nominated Bryan for a second time, and the Nebraskan made his campaign chiefly on the issues of imperialism and trust control. Bryan soft-pedaled the silver issue and tried to make the election a solemn referendum on imperialism. As one diplomatic historian has shown, the election was more a repudiation of Bryanism and a thumping endorsement of prosperity than a popular expression on colonial policy. McKinley was elected by an even greater majority than in 1896.

Therefore, McKinley and Roosevelt were inaugurated on March 4, 1901. Platt said a pleasant good-by; Hanna stood at McKinley's right hand; and businessmen thanked God that all was right with the world. But the point of Platt's joke was lost in September 1901 when an assassin mortally wounded McKinley at Buffalo. "That damned cowboy," as Hanna called Roosevelt, was now president of the United States!

Those impatient reformers who expected Theodore Roosevelt to reorganize the Republican party and assume control of Congress at once understood neither the political situation nor the new president. The great industrial and financial interests since the Civil War had constructed an organization within the Republican party that could not be overthrown by direct assault. The preeminent leader of the party was Mark Hanna of Ohio, McKinley's adviser and a member of the Senate. Nearly equal in power was Senator Nelson W. Aldrich of Rhode Island, the avowed spokesman of Wall Street. Allied with Hanna and Aldrich in the upper house were John C. Spooner of Wisconsin, William B. Allison of Iowa, and Orville H. Platt of Connecticut. They and other Old Guardsmen controlled the Senate and protected the industrial, financial, and railroad interests. Furthermore, the Old Guard were firmly entrenched in the House of Representatives. The Speaker after 1902 was Joseph G. Cannon of Illinois, a thoroughgoing reactionary, who ruled the House with rural wit and an iron hand. Cannon not only appointed all committees but was also chairman of the rules committee that determined the priority of bills. It was not difficult for him to block "dangerous" legislation.

Advice came to Roosevelt from all sides in the autumn of 1901 to move slowly. It was unnecessary. Since he was in no position to challenge the Old Guard, Roosevelt determined to work with them for a time. He announced immediately after his accession that he would continue McKinley's policies and retain his Cabinet. Obviously, Roosevelt was feeling his way and assuring his nomination in 1904. Not yet ready to make war on the Old Guard, he came to terms with them. He went to Aldrich's home in Rhode Island in August 1902 and a short time later conferred at Oyster Bay, Long Island, with leading Republican senators. The upshot of these negotiations was Roosevelt's promise to leave the protective tariff system and monetary structure essentially undisturbed. The senators, in return, gave Roosevelt freedom of action in other matters.

The enormous agitation for railroad regulation and destruction of so-called trusts was beginning to have a significant impact on the Middle West, where a popular revolt against the policies of Hanna and Aldrich was getting under way. The first signs of this upheaval were the election of Robert M. La Follette as governor of Wisconsin in 1900, on a platform demanding the direct primary and effective railroad regulation, and the rise of Albert Baird Cummins as the dominant political leader in Iowa in 1901. Roosevelt realized far better than Aldrich and his friends the necessity of appeasing midwestern opinion. His first move was to instruct the attorney general in February 1902 to announce that he would soon institute proceedings to dissolve the Northern Securities Company, the gigantic railroad combination that J. P. Morgan had recently formed (See pp. 34–35).

The midwestern progressives could not be propitiated by this one act alone. They demanded drastic tariff reductions, federal regulation of railroad rates, and more vigorous action against the large corporations. Roosevelt made a tour through the Middle West in August 1902; the following year, in April, he returned to the region. The more he said the more it was clear that he understood and sympathized with the midwestern antagonism to Hanna and the Wall Street crowd.

This became dramatically clear in Roosevelt's first hard fight in Congress for reform legislation. It occurred in the early months of 1903 as a consequence of Roosevelt's demand for a provision, in a bill creating a Department of Commerce and Labor, for establishment of a Bureau of Corporations with full power to investigate business practices. Opposition from the big business interests was immense, but Roosevelt won his measure by stirring public opinion.

33. The Election of 1904 and the Emergence of a Progressive Leader

As the time for the national conventions of 1904 drew near, Roosevelt laid careful plans for winning his chief objective, the chance to be president in his own right. Quietly but surely he retired Hanna as chief dispenser of patronage and made his own alliances with dominant state organizations, especially in the South. Hanna was Roosevelt's only serious rival, but the Ohioan died on February 15, 1904, and no one stood in Roosevelt's way. He therefore received the nomination at the Republican convention on June 23, 1904, without even a show of opposition.

Having twice failed with Bryan, the Democrats decided to try a conservative to offset the impulsive Roosevelt. They nominated Judge Alton B. Parker of New York, an obscure and ineffectual third-rate politician. On the whole, the campaign was a drab affair. Near the end, however, Parker enlivened the contest by charging that Roosevelt was blackmailing Wall Street into supporting the Republican ticket. The charge was false, but somehow Roosevelt became badly frightened by rumors that certain Wall Street interests were pouring huge sums into the Democratic war chest. Rejecting the suggestion that he appeal directly to the people for small contributions, Roosevelt allowed his manager to raise money in the usual way.[2] The voters could not

[2]Edward H. Harriman, the railroad magnate, contributed $50,000 personally and collected $200,-000 more from other sources. J. P. Morgan gave $150,000, and the three life insurance companies that he controlled added another $148,000. Two Standard Oil partners, H. H. Rogers and John

have taken Parker's blackmail charge seriously, for they elected Roosevelt by the largest popular majority that had ever been given a presidential candidate. He received 7,628,500 votes to 5,084,000 for Parker and 421,000 for Eugene V. Debs, the Socialist candidate.

Events soon proved that Roosevelt had given no hostage to Wall Street by accepting its lavish contributions. On the contrary, he had won more real power with the people by 1904 than any president since Lincoln. The wine of victory exhilarated him and strengthened his determination to be the real leader of the country, the spokesman of the majority. His Annual Message of 1904 gave hints of an advanced position, but it was his address before the Union League Club of Philadelphia, delivered in January 1905, that blazoned his new progressivism. Great industries and wealth, he warned, must submit to public control; specifically, the public interest demanded effective regulation of railroad rates.

Pressure on Roosevelt from the Middle and Far West to support such causes as railroad regulation, the direct election of senators, and control of corporations mounted incessantly from this time forward. Moreover, Bryan and progressive Democrats were charging that the president talked loudly but was essentially a straddler. Roosevelt, however, did not merely give in to these pressures. Haunted by the fear that failure to appease popular demand would provoke revolution, he took personal control of the reform movement in the summer and fall of 1905. He launched an attack on the meat packers, beginning with a thorough investigation of the industry. And when Congress assembled in December 1905, he demanded a stringent railroad-regulation law, a pure food and drug law, publicity for campaign contributions, and additional conservation legislation.

The more vigorously Roosevelt asserted leadership, the more successes he won. He succeeded in pushing through a pure food and drug law; he forced the passage of a railroad-regulation bill in 1906; and he advanced the cause of conservation through executive action. Moreover, he attacked the so-called trust problem with renewed vigor, not only by many dissolution suits, but perhaps even more effectively through a number of searching exposures by federal agencies. He recognized the intensity of the midwestern demand for tariff reduction, but he never thought that the tariff was an important factor in preserving the system of privilege. He knew, also, that the country needed currency reform and more effective regulation of the banking system, but he never pressed these issues before Congress and the country.

Day in and day out during 1906 and most of 1907, however, Roosevelt gave eloquent voice to the demand for extension of public authority over great

---

D. Archbold, gave $100,000; and although Roosevelt demanded that this gift be returned, his managers quietly ignored his request. In all, corporations contributed nearly three-fourths of the $2,195,000 collected by the Republican National Committee.

aggregations of wealth. It is easy to condemn Roosevelt for not doing more than he did—for not fighting hard for tariff and banking reform, for example. It is also easy to forget that the national progressive movement was only yet in the making, that conservative Republicans controlled Congress (in fact, there were few if any progressives in the Senate until Roosevelt's second administration), and that his leadership of the reform cause was courageous and effective.

Roosevelt was forced to restrain his reform energies during the last months of 1907 in the wake of a severe panic in Wall Street. Bankers and railroad men blamed the administration for loss of public confidence, but the panic was brought on by a worldwide credit stringency and by the very speculative excesses that Roosevelt had condemned.

Depressed economic conditions only momentarily paralyzed Roosevelt's reform impulses. He knew that the popular desire for progressive change was as strong as ever and bound to grow. Thus, while congressional leaders awaited his abdication in pleasant anticipation, Roosevelt intensified his propaganda for reform. A special message to Congress on January 31, 1908, sounded the keynote of a campaign for advanced national legislation that would culminate in a political revolt in 1912 and other consequences. Roosevelt was outraged by the Supreme Court's nullification of the federal Employers' Liability Act of 1906 and demanded new legislation; he also urged the states to adopt accident compensation systems. Moreover, he condemned the courts for using injunctions merely to protect property in labor disputes and urged Congress to empower the Interstate Commerce Commission to make a physical valuation of railroad property and supervise the financial operations of the railroads. Finally, he suggested closer supervision of corporations, either through federal licensing "or in some other way equally efficacious"; and denounced speculators and dishonest businessmen. "The Nation," he warned, "will not tolerate an utter lack of control over very wealthy men of enormous power in the industrial, and therefore in the social, lives of all our people. . . . We strive to bring nearer the day when greed and trickery and cunning shall be trampled under feet by those who fight for the righteousness that exalteth a nation."

34. The Election of 1908

Roosevelt by the end of 1907 was the spokesman for the masses of Republican voters and the real leader of his party. Even the special interests who could delay or defeat his program in Congress could not have prevented his renomination in 1908. He enjoyed being president and delighted in the thought of another four years at the helm. But he had given a pledge after the election of 1904 that he would not run again, and an inner compulsion urged him to stand by his promise.

It was the most fateful decision of Roosevelt's career and perhaps the unwisest. By refusing to heed the popular call in 1908 he denied himself the opportunity to render his greatest service to the Republican party. A Roosevelt in the White House from 1909 to 1913 might well have averted the disastrous rupture that occurred in 1912. In any event, he had the power to name his successor and was determined to use it.

The ablest member of the constellation around the president was Elihu Root, who had served as secretary of war from 1899 to 1904 and as secretary of state since 1905. Roosevelt was sorely tempted to make this able corporation lawyer his successor, but he knew that the Middle West would never accept Root because of his Wall Street connections. Finally Roosevelt turned to William Howard Taft of Ohio, his secretary of war, who was one of his staunchest supporters in the Cabinet. Taft had a distinguished record as a federal judge, governor general of the Philippines, and secretary of war. He had good family connections, an eastern education, an excellent mind, and unquestioned integrity. Most important, he seemed eager to carry forward the Roosevelt policies.

Roosevelt, in January 1908, began to set all the machinery of the party organization in motion to assure Taft's nomination. Asserting publicly that the Republican convention should be free to choose its candidate, Roosevelt by the end of May was privately boasting that he had prevented his own renomination and could dictate the naming of Taft. At the Republican convention that met in Chicago in June, therefore, the Ohioan was nominated on the first ballot on a platform that promised, among other things, tariff revision and a federal system of postal savings banks.

The Democrats, meeting in Denver, turned again to Bryan in this year of Rooseveltian supremacy. Although he was by now something of a perennial candidate, the Nebraskan at least seemed able to save his party from another such disaster as it had suffered in 1904. Bryan had come a long way toward progressivism since 1896. He was not a great intellect, but he had a keen ear for the voice of the people and was free from any connection with special privilege. He made his campaign largely on the tariff and trust questions and, promising relief from indiscriminate injunctions, made a frank appeal for labor support. Taft, on the other hand, attacked Bryan as a demagogue, pledged himself to continue the Roosevelt policy of substantial justice to all classes, and promised tariff revision.

As all observers predicted, Taft won easily (he received 7,675,000 votes to 6,412,000 for Bryan); but it was significant that Bryan increased the Democratic vote by a million and a third over 1904 and carried the South, Oklahoma, Colorado, Nevada, and Nebraska. More significant for the future was the marked rise of Republican insurgency, or advanced progressivism, in the

Middle West. Heretofore the midwestern progressive Republican bloc in Congress had been a small minority. In the Sixty-first Congress, which would meet in 1909, they would be a powerful force in both houses.

35. Republican Troubles under Taft

Roosevelt left the United States soon after Taft's inaugural to hunt big game in Africa and then to go on an extended tour of Europe. His departure was applauded in financial circles, where many wished luck to the lions. Conservatives, generally, were sure that Taft would align himself with the Old Guard in Congress. Progressives, on the other hand, were certain that he would come to their support. As it turned out, neither group was entirely right—or wrong.

It would be unkind to say that Taft took the presidency under false pretenses. On the eve of his magistracy he thought that he was a progressive. He shared Roosevelt's belief in the supremacy of the public over the private interest. He believed in railroad regulation, was ruthlessly opposed to monopolies, and honestly wanted to continue Roosevelt's policy of preserving the nation's heritage of natural resources. In a normal period of political quietude he would have been a beloved president.

The years of Taft's reign, however, were highly abnormal. It was a time of agitation and revolt. Civil war within the Republican party impended, and open party warfare could have been averted only by bold presidential leadership. Unhappily, Taft was temperamentally unfit to play the role that history demanded. He could not lead in a time of trouble because leadership in such circumstances required wholehearted commitment and abandonment of the judicial quality that was dominant in his character. Taft was a philosophical progressive, but he could not get on with progressive leaders in Congress because they were too harsh in their denunciations, too impatient, too willing to experiment with untried measures.

The new president was forced to choose between the Old Guard leadership in Congress and the insurgent Republican bloc at the very outset—that is, at the beginning of the special session that convened in March 1909 to consider tariff revision. As the Republicans now had a majority of only forty-seven in the House of Representatives, insurgent leaders concluded that the time had come to combine with Democrats to unhorse the tyrannical Speaker, Joe Cannon. When it seemed that the insurgents were bound to succeed, the Speaker appealed to Taft for help, promising to support the president's legislative program in return. Taft was in a perplexing dilemma because he did not like Cannon and yet he needed his cooperation. He made his first mistake:

he endorsed Cannon and hinted that the insurgents should give up their campaign if they wanted a share in the patronage. In the end it was the defection of a group of southern and Tammany Democrats, not Taft's opposition, that frustrated the insurgents' coup d'état. Yet many progressives suspected that the president had betrayed them.

This incident only marked the beginning of the alienation of the progressives from the president. Effective White House leadership in the future could easily have repaired the damage done during the fight over the speakership. Instead of leading boldly, however, Taft soon blundered again, this time in a battle over tariff revision that split the Republican party in the spring of 1909. (For details of this epochal conflict, see pp. 94–95).

There is no doubt that Taft sincerely desired substantial tariff reductions. But he erred in the beginning by refusing to interfere in the fight in Congress and by failing to rally public opinion behind the cause of tariff reform. When he finally did intervene, moreover, he acted in such a manner as to cause midwestern insurgents, who were leading the fight for tariff reduction, to believe that he had deserted them and surrendered to special privilege. Although the president won a few noteworthy concessions, the bill that was signed—the Payne-Aldrich Act—represented a substantial victory for the eastern manufacturers. By this time—the late summer of 1909—the Middle West was seething with rebellion. Although few men realized the fact, the doom of the Taft administration had been sealed.

Taft embarked in September 1909 upon a 13,000-mile speaking tour from Boston to the West Coast to assuage popular discontent. Instead of calming the storm, he arrayed the insurgent masses decisively against himself by a series of indiscreet speeches. He publicly eulogized Nelson W. Aldrich of Rhode Island, leader of the Old Guard in the Senate. He rebuked midwestern senators who had voted against the tariff bill. And he climaxed his blunders by declaring at Winona, Minnesota, that the measure was the best tariff act that the Republican party had ever passed. After the Winona address, Midwesterners were certain that Taft had deserted to the Old Guard.

No sooner had public agitation over the Payne-Aldrich debacle quieted than a worse catastrophe completed the alienation of the progressives. This was the Ballinger affair, which grew out of a feud between the secretary of the interior, Richard A. Ballinger, and the chief of the Forestry Service in the Department of Agriculture, Gifford Pinchot. The root of the trouble was the fact that Pinchot was a conservationist and Ballinger was not. An investigator in the Interior Department, Louis R. Glavis, told Pinchot that Ballinger had connived with the Morgan-Guggenheim syndicate to validate certain withdrawals of Alaskan coal lands. Pinchot believed the accusation, urged Glavis to present his evidence to the president, and publicly denounced Ballinger as a traitor to conservation.

Glavis presented his indictment to the president, who accepted Ballinger's rebuttal and authorized the secretary to dismiss Glavis for insubordination. Pinchot, however, refused to halt his attack and virtually forced Taft to remove him from the Forestry Service in January 1910. Meanwhile, the controversy had developed into a national cause célèbre, with conservatives defending the administration and progressives charging treachery and fraud.

The climax came when Democrats and insurgent Republicans in Congress forced an investigation of the Interior Department. A packed committee voted Ballinger a clean bill of health. But the trenchant questions asked by Louis D. Brandeis, who represented Glavis, exposed Ballinger, not as a corrupt public official, but as an opponent of conservation and a champion of the far western demand for rapid distribution of the remaining public domain. Instead of dismissing Ballinger and appointing a genuine conservationist in his stead, Taft continued stubbornly to defend him and thus exacerbated popular discontent.

Progressive Republicans in the House of Representatives were ready in the early months of 1910 to try again to shear Speaker Cannon of his dictatorial control over legislation. Aware of the impending attack, the Speaker struck back by declaring that he would fight to the end. An insurgent Democratic coalition, led by George W. Norris of Nebraska, deposed the Speaker from the rules committee in March 1910 and deprived him of power to appoint members of standing committees. Certainly Taft secretly approved, for he well knew what a liability Cannon was. Yet because he did nothing by word or deed to encourage the insurgents, the country concluded that Taft was on Cannon's side.

The misunderstanding about Taft's position in the fight against Cannon caused a final and complete break between the administration and the insurgents. They quarreled with Taft over the terms of a bill to strengthen the powers of the Interstate Commerce Commission. They accused him of conspiring with Wall Street when he proposed establishment of a postal savings system. Convinced that the insurgents were maneuvering in every possible way to destroy him politically and goaded by incessant and often unfair attacks, Taft turned fiercely against the progressives and joined the Old Guard in a powerful campaign to destroy insurgency. Taft, Aldrich, and Cannon conferred in March 1910 and formulated a plan of attack. It involved using money and patronage, first to build up strong conservative organizations in the Middle West and then to defeat insurgents for renomination in the impending spring primary elections. The plan was quickly carried out. Patronage in the midwestern states was given to supporters of the president, while Old Guard spokesmen invaded the region and exhorted voters to support administration candidates.

In fighting bitterly for their political lives, the insurgents virtually declared their independence of the party dominated by Taft, Aldrich, and Cannon. It was a momentous battle, for its outcome would determine the fate of the

GOP, not only in the Middle West but in the nation as well. The railroad, industrial, and financial interests of the Midwest supported the administration almost solidly, but the people in every state supported their rebel leaders. Nothing was more indicative of the inevitable doom of the Taft administration than the failure of its anti-insurgent campaign. The flames of midwestern progressivism had grown into a raging prairie fire of insurgency. Already insurgents were talking about organizing a new party if Taft were renominated; already midwestern eyes were turning to Theodore Roosevelt for leadership in the impending battle. Before we discuss these events, however, let us turn back and see how political leadership confronted issues that agitated the American people during the Republican era.

36. Struggles for Tariff and Tax Reform, 1894–1913

No public questions were more potentially explosive and at the same time more perpetually discussed after the Civil War than tariff and tax policies. By the turn of the century the elaborate system of tariff protection and the virtually complete immunity from taxation that wealth enjoyed had become to progressives the very symbol of control of the federal government by allied industrial and banking interests.

The Democrats had made a fumbling effort at tariff and tax reform during the second Cleveland administration. The outcome, the Wilson-Gorman Tariff Act of 1894, represented at best a feeble effort at downward revision and left the protective structure essentially unimpaired. But a coalition of western and southern representatives forced into the tariff bill an amendment levying a 2 percent tax on all net incomes of individuals and corporations over $4,000.

By a strained and obviously class-conscious opinion, a bare majority of the Supreme Court ruled the income tax unconstitutional in 1895. It would be many years before progressives were strong enough to overcome the Old Guard's opposition to an income tax amendment. Meanwhile, Republicans would have spared themselves much future trouble if they had left well enough alone in tariff legislation. However, McKinley was eager to propitiate the agrarian Middle West after his close victory over Bryan in 1896, and so he called a special session of Congress in March 1897 to consider tariff revision. The president desired only a moderate revision of the Wilson-Gorman rates. But senators from western states held the balance of power and forced a substantial increase in duties on agricultural raw materials like wool and hides. Eastern senators, in turn, obtained increased duties on woolens, silks, and other manufactured products. The upshot of this log-rolling was the Dingley tariff, the highest tariff in American history to that time.[3]

Manufacturing interests and western agricultural producers were able to forestall any attempt at general revision for twelve years after the adoption of the Dingley Act. At the same time conservatives kept an equally firm hand on tax policy. Congress imposed a moderate estate tax during the Spanish-American War. But this impost was repealed in 1902, and the federal government reverted to its usual practice of obtaining revenue almost entirely from consumption taxes—customs duties and excise taxes on tobacco and alcoholic beverages—that fell most heavily on the lower and middle classes.

Nevertheless, strong forces were at work during the first years of the twentieth century to culminate eventually in an irresistible movement for tariff and tax reform. First, the passage of the Dingley Act at the beginning of the period of frantic industrial combination lent apparent proof to the charge, often pressed by Bryan and other Democrats, that the high protective system stimulated the growth of monopolies and supercorporations at home. Second, the cost of living increased nearly one-fourth between 1897 and 1907, and the average consumer saw a close relation between high tariffs and high prices, although there was often no connection between the two. Third, widespread discussion of the increasing concentration of incomes and wealth alarmed the middle class and stimulated the conviction that only income and inheritance taxes could reverse a process that seemed to threaten the future of American democracy.

The most significant factor in the beginning of a powerful movement for tariff and tax reform was the awakening of the Middle West. After an epochal struggle in 1901, Iowa Republicans nominated the progressive Albert B. Cummins for governor and wrote into their platform his proposal to remove all duties on articles manufactured by so-called trusts. Thereafter the "Iowa Idea," as Cummins's suggestion was called, became a stock feature of most midwestern state Republican platforms. Although the movement for downward revision soon became nationwide and included many small businessmen, the midwestern insurgents remained the most consistent advocates of tariff reform in the GOP.

Roosevelt recognized the potential danger of popular discontent and was often tempted to take leadership of the movement for tariff revision. He failed to act for three reasons. First, he agreed with his Old Guard friends that such

---

[3]The Dingley Act, however, authorized the president to negotiate reciprocal agreements on certain enumerated articles, principally in the French and Latin American trade. Such agreements were later made with France, Italy, Brazil, and other nations. Section 4 of the Dingley Act, moreover, authorized the president to negotiate commercial treaties under which the American tariff might be reduced up to 20 percent in return for reciprocal benefits. These treaties had to be approved by both houses of Congress and could not run for more than five years. The State Department subsequently negotiated eleven such treaties, none of which Congress approved.

a move would disrupt the GOP. Second, he shrewdly struck a bargain with Speaker Cannon in late 1904 by which he agreed to jettison tariff revision in return for Cannon's promise to clear the road for a railroad regulation bill in the House of Representatives. Third, and most important, Roosevelt thought that the tariff was a question of expediency, not of principle. In this belief he revealed progressivism's divided mind on the issue. On the other hand, both Roosevelt and Taft agreed in 1908 that the tariff question could no longer be evaded. At their insistence, a plank declaring "unequivocally for the revision of the tariff" was written in the Republican platform. Moreover, by 1908 both Roosevelt and Taft had come out squarely for graduated federal estate, gift, and income taxes.

Thus it seemed that the movement for genuine tariff and tax reform had reached a point of culmination when President Taft called Congress into special session in March 1909 to consider tariff revision. The administration's bill, sponsored by Sereno E. Payne of New York, chairman of the House ways and means committee, put a number of important raw materials on the free list and substantially reduced rates on iron and steel products, agricultural implements, sugar, and lumber. The measure included a federal inheritance tax ranging from 1 to 5 percent. Although the Democrats made an unsuccessful effort to add an income tax amendment and then voted against the Payne bill for party reasons, they, like midwestern insurgents, were pleasantly surprised when the House approved the bill.

It was an altogether different story in the Senate. There Senator Aldrich and his finance committee took the Payne bill in hand and reported it on April 12, 1909, without the provision for an inheritance tax and with 847 amendments, the majority of which effected increases. Instead of lowering the Dingley rates, as the Rhode Island senator claimed, the Aldrich bill actually increased the ad valorem duties from 40.21 to 41.77 percent. In all fairness, it should be added that Aldrich and his committee were under almost unbearable pressure for rate increases and that the Rhode Islander usually acted under this goad and not on his own initiative.

A wave of indignation swept over the country, and especially the Middle West, as the implications of Aldrich's surrender to the special interests became clear. In the Senate a group of insurgent Republicans waged an open fight against the finance committee's amendments. They also joined Democrats to include an income tax as a substitute for the discarded inheritance tax. So effective was their campaign that Aldrich headed it off only by accepting Taft's proposal for a 2 percent tax on the net incomes of corporations and by agreeing to the passage of an income tax amendment to the Constitution.

With strong administration support in the violent intraparty battle in the Senate, Aldrich put his bill across on July 8, 1909. It included the corporation income tax, restored the duties on hides, iron ore, and lumber, and greatly increased the Payne rates on a number of manufactured products. The final struggle came when the conference committee met shortly afterward. At last bestirring himself in behalf of lower rates, Taft persuaded the committee to accept free hides and reductions in prevailing duties on shoes, lumber, coal, and iron ore. Nonetheless, the bill that the committee approved and Taft signed was a victory for the manufacturing East and an affront to the insurgent Middle West.[4]

The Payne-Aldrich debacle had profound and almost immediate repercussions. For one thing, it widened to an even greater extent the gulf between insurgents and the Taft administration. For another, it enabled the Democrats to capture the House of Representatives in the congressional elections of November 1910. Following hard on the heels of this disaster for the GOP, Taft proceeded further to alienate midwestern opinion by driving for reciprocity with Canada.

Confronted with an impending trade war between the United States and her northern neighbor, the State Department concluded a reciprocal trade agreement with the Canadian government in January 1911 that promised to draw the two nations into an economic union. The agreement placed all important agricultural products, industrial raw materials, and raw lumber and wood pulp on the free list. Moreover, it substantially reduced prevailing rates on many manufactured products. The president presented the agreement to Congress on January 26, 1911, for approval by joint resolution; and when the Senate refused to act before the regular session ended, Taft called Congress into special session for the first week in April.

In the subsequent battle over reciprocity that raged from April nearly to August, the recently formed alignment of progressive Republicans was totally destroyed. The Democrats joined Taft's friends in Congress in supporting the agreement because it represented a tremendous victory for free trade. For the same reason the Old Guard fought the measure. The midwestern insurgents, on the other hand, accused the administration of sacrificing midwestern farm interests in order to widen the foreign market for eastern manufactured products. They fought the treaty, therefore, even more bitterly than did the Old Guard. For once Taft exerted himself strenuously and won the fight in Congress with the nearly solid support of the Democrats. The House approved the agreement on April 21, the Senate on July 22, 1911. But it seemed that Taft could not succeed, even when he did the statesmanlike thing. Aroused by talk in the United States of annexation, Canadian voters on September 21, 1911, repudiated the Liberal government that had negotiated the reciprocity agreement.

The antireciprocity coalition of insurgents and the Old Guard was short-

---

[4]As the matter of tariff rates is infinitely complicated, it is almost impossible to specify the average rates of the Payne-Aldrich bill. The figure usually given by authorities is 37 percent. The measure also established a tariff board to make scientific studies of various phases of the tariff question and to advise Congress and the president.

lived. In fact, insurgents combined with Democrats even while the battle over reciprocity was raging to pass three tariff bills—a farmers' free list bill, which removed duties from about one hundred articles that the farmer bought; a wool and woolens bill; and a bill reducing duties on iron and steel products, cotton goods, and chemicals. Taft vetoed these measures on the ground that they were not "scientific." Moreover, progressive Democrats and Republicans joined hands throughout the country during 1911 and 1912 to obtain ratification of the Sixteenth, or income tax, Amendment, which Congress had submitted to the states in 1909. The first chapter in the history of twentieth-century tax reform was completed on February 25, 1913, when the amendment became a part of the Constitution.

37. The Railroad Problem

Agitation for effective public control of railroad rates and services antedated the progressive revolt by several decades. First came efforts by midwestern and southern legislatures during the 1870s and 1880s to institute regulation, either by statute or commission. Some of these attempts succeeded partially; others failed completely. In any event, during the 1880s the conviction grew that only Congress could deal effectively with rebating, stock watering, pools that destroyed competition, and exorbitant rates for goods and passengers in interstate commerce. Experience, and the Supreme Court's decision in the Wabash case of 1886, forbidding the states to regulate *interstate* rates, demonstrated that the really important railroad evils were beyond the jurisdiction of the states.

As a result the American people by 1886 had firmly determined to institute federal regulation and end the reign of unbridled freedom in the field of transportation. The legislative response to this overwhelming demand, the Interstate Commerce Act of 1887, was avowedly tentative in character. It specifically forbade pooling, discrimination, rebating, and higher charges for a short haul than a long one. As for rates, it declared that all charges should be reasonable and just and required railroads to publish rate schedules. Finally, the measure established the Interstate Commerce Commission, the first federal regulatory agency, to administer the law. Adoption of the Interstate Commerce Act, unenforceable though it turned out to be, marked a turning point in the exercise of federal power in the United States. For the first time the federal authority had been extended into an important area of private economic activity.

Railroad managers seemed eager to abide by the law for a brief time after the adoption of the act of 1887. But the ICC ran head on into the refusal of railroad managers to testify when it tried to stamp out rebating, and it required years of adjudication to establish the commission's authority to compel testimony. However, it was the Supreme Court's narrow interpretation of the commerce act that deprived the ICC of any real power. In the maximum freight rate cases of 1896 and 1897, the court ruled that the commission did not have the power to fix rates. Moreover, in the *Alabama Midlands* case of 1897 the Supreme Court practically emasculated the prohibition against discrimination in charges for long and short hauls. Indeed, after these decisions the ICC became nothing more than a fact-finding·body and openly confessed its inability to cope seriously with the problem of regulation.

Thus by 1900 the whole problem of federal railroad regulation had to be fought out all over again in Congress and the country. The first amendment to the Interstate Commerce Act, the Elkins Act of 1903, was adopted, ironically enough, in response to the pleas of the railroad managers themselves. The rebating evil, they warned, had grown to such monstrous proportions that it threatened to bankrupt the railroads. Congress responded at once with the Elkins Act, which outlawed any deviation from published rates.

The "railroad senators" who framed the Elkins Act carefully avoided giving the ICC any authority over the rate-making process. Yet it was obvious on all sides that this was what the great majority of farmers and businessmen wanted most. At this high point of public agitation, Theodore Roosevelt took leadership of public opinion. In his Annual Message of December 1904 he recommended that the ICC be empowered, upon complaint of shippers, to fix maximum rates, subject to review by the courts. The House of Representatives in response passed the Esch-Townshend bill, implementing the president's suggestion, by the impressive majority of 326 to 17. Seeking to delay or postpone further action, Republican leaders in the upper house instructed the commerce committee to investigate the railroad problem during the spring and summer of 1905. As it turned out, the committee's investigation was no whitewash but rather uncovered a far-flung propaganda campaign by the railroads against federal regulation.

Armed with this new evidence of railroad misdoing, Roosevelt pressed his campaign for legislation all during the summer and fall of 1905. So enthusiastic was the popular response that even the railroad senators began to tremble. The House of Representatives quickly passed the administration's measure, the Hepburn bill, in February 1906. Although it fell short of what advanced progressives wanted, the bill went straight to the core of the railroad problem by empowering the ICC, upon complaint by shippers, to lower rates already established.

The Hepburn bill was referred in the Senate to the commerce committee, the chairman of which was the multimillionaire Stephen B. Elkins of West Virginia, who, along with Aldrich, led the railroad senators. Realizing that he could not control the administration majority on the committee, Aldrich allowed it to report the Hepburn bill unamended. In order to outflank the committee, Aldrich arranged to have the fiery Democrat, Ben Tillman of South Carolina, report the bill and defend it on the Senate floor. At this stage, the astute Rhode Islander proposed amendments to cripple the bill. The most important of these endowed the courts with sweeping authority to review and nullify the ICC's rate decisions.

Debate raged for two months in the Senate over Aldrich's amendment. Roosevelt contended that judicial review should be limited solely to determining whether the ICC had exercised due process in fixing rates. He fought with unusual resourcefulness for a time. Then, when it seemed that a coalition of Democrats and administration Republicans could put the measure across without Aldrich's consent, several Democrats deserted the coalition. At this point—that is, early May 1906—Roosevelt executed a brilliant maneuver. Instead of going down to defeat with progressives who still demanded narrow court review, Roosevelt maneuvered Aldrich into accepting a compromise amendment. Framed by Aldrich, sponsored by William B. Allison of Iowa, and approved by the president, it was accepted; and the Hepburn bill became law on June 29, 1906.

Some progressives charged that Roosevelt had betrayed the cause of railroad regulation, but the verdict in this historic dispute must go to Roosevelt. The Allison amendment authorized district courts to issue interlocutory, or suspensive, injunctions against the ICC's decisions, it is true; but it also provided for speedy appeals to the circuit courts and the Supreme Court. Moreover, only these courts could reverse the commission's rulings, and they were instructed to pass upon such rulings with the same seriousness that they would have in passing upon acts of Congress, with the presumption always in favor of the ICC. Thus so-called broad court review was hedged about with such effective limitations that judicial nullification of the Hepburn Act was well-nigh impossible.

Furthermore, an examination of the general provisions of the Hepburn Act emphasizes the dimensions of Roosevelt's victory. To begin with, the ICC was empowered, upon complaint, to investigate and lower rates. In other words, ultimate control over rates was taken from private hands and given to an agency of the people. The commission, in addition, gained jurisdiction over express and sleeping car companies, switches and spurs, and pipe lines. Finally, the act required a uniform system of cost accounting by the railroads, eliminated the old free-pass evil, and required railroads to divest themselves of outside properties after 1908. The latter provision was aimed chiefly at the anthracite coal monopoly controlled by nine eastern railroads.

The effect of the broadening of the ICC's power was at once apparent. Shippers made more than 9,000 appeals to the commission within two years, while railroad managers seemed almost in a chastened mood. Then railroad managers began suddenly to challenge the ICC in 1908, and their action in turn caused a crowding of the dockets of the circuit courts. In addition, the railroads made general rate increases in 1909, and the masses of people realized for the first time that the commission could deal only with specific increases, upon complaint, and lacked power to suspend or revoke general rate advances.

The railroads' resistance to regulation and the general rate increases of 1909 at once stimulated increased agitation for a further strengthening of the ICC's power. In response, President Taft, in the summer of 1909, requested Attorney General George W. Wickersham to prepare a new railroad bill. The measure that Wickersham drafted greatly enlarged the commission's rate-making power and established a commerce court, which should have original jurisdiction in appeals from the rulings of the ICC. The midwestern insurgent senators were disappointed because the Wickersham draft made no provision for valuation of railroad property by the commission, and they strongly disapproved the proposal for a commerce court, with power of broad review. Even so, the insurgents' opposition to the president's bill might have been less violent had it not seemed that Taft was willing to change the measure to satisfy the demands of railroad spokesmen. Taft conferred with six railroad presidents early in January 1910, even before the measure was introduced in the House, and he changed the bill to allow railroads to acquire competing lines. To progressives, this looked suspiciously like collusion. And when Senator Aldrich announced that he would support the bill, they were certain that some evil scheme was being plotted.

The president's measure, introduced in the House of Representatives in January 1910 as the Mann bill, at once fell into the hands of a progressive Republican–Democratic coalition. It struck out the provision permitting mergers of competing lines, added amendments for physical valuation and equality in charges for long and short hauls, and brought telephone and telegraph companies under the jurisdiction of the Interstate Commerce Commission. Meanwhile, insurgents in the Senate had launched a violent attack on the president's bill, which the commerce committee reported without amendments. Taft made the measure a test of party loyalty, and insurgents joined Democrats and threatened to rewrite the bill altogether. After the progressive coalition struck out the provisions contrary to the Sherman Antitrust Act, Aldrich turned to the Democrats. If they would support the administration's railroad bill, Aldrich said, the administration would agree to approve statehood acts for New Mexico and Arizona. As the Democrats were eager for the admission of the two territories, they sealed the bargain. Thus the progressive Republican–Democratic coalition changed into a Democratic–Regular Republican majority, and the administration's railroad bill passed the Senate essentially intact.

Nonetheless, the bill that emerged from the conference committee, which Taft approved as the Mann-Elkins Act, represented more a victory for the progressives than for the administration. The new legislation empowered the ICC to suspend general rate increases and revise rates on its own initiative. It also established a commerce court to hear appeals directly from the commission. These provisions had been originally parts of the president's bill. On the other hand, all important progressive amendments, except the provision for physical valuation, were retained by the conference committee. Railroads were not allowed to acquire competing lines. Telephone, telegraph, cable, and wireless companies were defined as common carriers. The prohibition in the act of 1887 against discriminations in charges for long and short hauls was strengthened. As a result of the hard fight that progressives made in support of these amendments, the Mann-Elkins Act of 1910 had become legislation comprehensive in character, not merely supplementary.

Progressives in Congress now redoubled their efforts to obtain physical valuation as the basis for rate making by the ICC. Valuation of railroad property would enable the commission to fix rates on a basis of the true value of railroad property, rather than on a basis of watered capitalization. This was the chief reason why progressives supported and railroad spokesmen opposed the proposal. To conservatives, moreover, physical valuation seemed to be the first step in eventual nationalization. Nonetheless, the insurgent-Democratic congressional coalition won this last objective in the closing months of the Taft regime. The Physical Valuation Act of 1913 required the Interstate Commerce Commission to report the value of all property owned by every common carrier subject to its jurisdiction, including the original cost, the cost of reproduction new, and the cost of reproduction less depreciation. When completed, the act declared, such valuations were to be accepted as prima facie evidence of the worth of the property in all actions by the commission.

38. The Federal Antitrust Policy, 1890–1913

Almost simultaneous with the beginning of the agitation for railroad regulation was a widespread movement to destroy the infant industrial combinations of that day, the trusts. (For a discussion of the origins and progress of the trust movement in the United States, see pp. 31–33). At least fourteen states and territories had written antitrust provisions into their constitutions by 1890, while thirteen others had adopted antitrust laws. Almost without exception, these were western and southern states—a reflection of the impact of the agrarian crusade against railroads and monopolies. The state antitrust crusade gained new momentum from 1890 to 1900. By the latter date forty-two states and territories attempted to outlaw monopolies, either by constitutional provision or by statute.[5]

It became increasingly obvious that sporadic and uncoordinated action by the states could neither destroy monopoly nor restore competition, especially when New Jersey in 1888 permitted the legal incorporation of trusts as

[5]Practically all these states and territories prohibited restraint of trade that was contrary to the public interest. Some twenty-nine states prohibited suppression of competition through pools, agreements to limit quantity or divide sales territories, price-fixing agreements, and so on. A number of states, moreover, attempted to outlaw cutthroat practices, such as price cutting to destroy competition, so-called tying contracts, and discriminations in prices made for the purpose of destroying competition.

holding companies. By this date the popular agitation had reached such a high pitch that both major parties incorporated antitrust planks in their platforms. And when President Benjamin Harrison endorsed the demand for a federal antitrust law in his Annual Message of December 1889, Congress did not dare refuse to act.

Its response, the Sherman Antitrust Act of 1890, was brief and to the point. The core was embodied in Section 1. It prohibited "every contract, combination in the form of trust or otherwise, or conspiracy, in restraint' of trade or commerce among the several States, or with foreign nations," and provided punishment for such misdoing. Section 7, moreover, stipulated that any person injured by illegal combinations or conspiracies might sue and recover threefold damages and the cost of the suit.

No statute ever enacted by Congress reflected more accurately an overwhelming popular demand. Yet the Sherman law, after several prosecutions by the Harrison administration, fell into neglect and general contempt until 1902. Effective enforcement of the law depended largely upon the Justice Department. But attorneys general during the Cleveland and McKinley administrations did little to carry out the popular mandate to destroy the trusts because neither Cleveland nor McKinley had any sympathy for the objectives of the Sherman Act—except insofar as the provisions of the law might be applied against labor unions.

A case in point was *E. C. Knight* v. *United States,* 1895, in which the government challenged the monopoly recently acquired by the American Sugar Refining Company of Philadelphia. Instead of vindicating the Sherman law, Cleveland's attorney general, Richard Olney, presented the government's case in such a manner that the Supreme Court thought that it had to declare that the Sherman Antitrust Act did not apply to combinations in manufacturing. The consequences of Olney's calculated subversion were far-reaching, but we should not fall into the common error of thinking that the Supreme Court entirely emasculated the antitrust law. As we shall see later, on every opportunity afforded by the government, that tribunal evidenced its willingness to carry out the mandate embodied in the statute.

It was obvious as the new century opened that only a president's determination to give teeth to the measure was needed to make the Sherman law a really effective measure. Theodore Roosevelt understood the dimensions of the popular fear of trusts, abhorred monopoly, and personally resented the power that uncontrolled wealth exercised over the nation's destiny. He therefore resolved to vindicate national sovereignty by bringing great combinations to book. His chief weapons were publicity and the Sherman law. He made investigations and publicity of mergers and so-called trusts possible on a systematic scale by his victory in the fight in 1903 for establishment of the Bureau of Corporations in the Department of Commerce and Labor.

In the form of direct attack, the Justice Department under Roosevelt instituted eighteen proceedings in equity, obtained twenty-five indictments, and participated in one forfeiture proceeding. Beginning with his first prosecution, the suit to dissolve the Northern Securities Company in 1902, Roosevelt pressed relentlessly forward against combinations. The president, later in 1902, ordered prosecution of the Swift, Armour, and Nelson Morris companies—the so-called Beef Trust—for organizing the National Packing Company to acquire control of independent packing firms in the Middle West. The Supreme Court rendered a unanimous verdict for the government in 1905. But the packers continued to defy the government, and it was not until 1920 and 1921 that competition was effectively restored to the meat industry. The climax of Roosevelt's campaign came with sweeping indictments by the Justice Department of the Standard Oil Company in 1907 and of the American Tobacco Company in 1908. These two cases, the most important in the history of the antitrust movement before 1945, did not reach final settlement until 1911.

Roosevelt's contribution to the antitrust cause has been derided by most historians in spite of this effort and achievement. Their failure to understand his contribution stems, among other things, from a faulty appreciation of his objectives. Unlike some progressives, who would have limited the size of corporations, Roosevelt never feared bigness in industry—unless bigness was accompanied by monopolistic control and a disposition on the part of management to defy the public interest. Thus, he never moved against two prominent combinations, United States Steel and International Harvester, because he never had good evidence to prove they were monopolies or were illegally suppressing competition. The Taft administration later instituted dissolution proceedings against these two corporations, but the Supreme Court confirmed Roosevelt's judgment in both cases.

Roosevelt's aggressive program of publicity and prosecution was carried forward at an even more intensive pace by President Taft and his attorney general, George W. Wickersham. When Congress refused to enact Taft's proposal for federal incorporation, a corporation commission, and legislation against stock watering, the Taft administration moved in a wholesale way against combinations. All told, Taft instituted forty-six proceedings for dissolution, brought forty-three indictments, and instituted one contempt proceeding. His two most important cases, those against United States Steel and International Harvester, ended in failure. His two most important victories, over Standard Oil and American Tobacco, were scored in proceedings that Roosevelt had instituted. The government, after five years of legal warfare, won complete victory in 1911 with the Supreme Court's order for dissolution of the gigantic oil and tobacco monopolies. The Court implicitly repudiated the *Knight* decision and made it plain that the holding-company form could not be used to evade the Sherman law. The primary objectives of the antitrust movement had been fairly accomplished by the end of the Taft administration. There was no longer any constitutional doubt that the federal government possessed ample power to prevent monopoly and suppress unfair trade practices in the day-to-day operations of businessmen. Because of Roosevelt's and Taft's vigorous prosecutions, moreover, the age of monopoly was over. Great corporations remained and dominated certain industries, but these oligopolies existed by the sufferance of public opinion and a government that jealously guarded their smaller competitors.

39. The Supreme Court and Economic Policy before the First World War

In the American constitutional system Congress proposes and the Supreme Court disposes. The phrase is of course a hyperbole, but it points up a problem that continually perplexed progressives who were struggling to extend the boundaries of governmental power. Unlike their counterparts in other countries, American reformers in state and nation were never free to develop at will a system of administrative regulation. For one thing, they were bound by a written constitution capable of being construed as the bulwark of a laissez-faire policy. For another, they were restrained by the fear that a conservative Supreme Court, which insisted upon having the final word, would not tolerate the extension of governmental power that they sought to accomplish.

To begin with, the Supreme Court by 1900 had established the right to review all state attempts to regulate railroads and corporations. This power the court had assumed as a result of one of the most important revolutions in judicial theory in American history. It began when Roscoe Conkling, while arguing the case of *San Mateo County* v. *Southern Pacific Railroad* before the Supreme Court in 1882, asserted that the congressional committee that framed the Fourteenth Amendment had intended to confer federal citizenship upon corporations. As Conkling had been a member of the committee and produced its secret journal, the court listened carefully to his argument, although it did not take judicial cognizance of it. In *Santa Clara County* v. *Southern Pacific Railroad,* 1886, and in the *Minnesota Rate* case, 1889, however, the court accepted Conkling's reasoning and declared that corporations were federal citizens, entitled to protection by the Fourteenth Amendment against action of the states that would deprive them of property, or income, without due process of law. Finally, in *Smyth* v. *Ames,* 1898, the Supreme Court reached the last stage in its judicial revolution. Nebraska had established maximum charges on freight carried entirely within the state. Overturning the Nebraska statute, the court reaffirmed the federal citizenship of corporations, declared that rates must be high enough to guarantee a fair return to railroads, and warned state legislatures that the courts existed, among other reasons, for the purpose of protecting property against unreasonable legislation.

In none of these cases did the Supreme Court deny the right of the states to regulate railroads and other corporations. It only insisted that state regulation be reasonable and fair and not invade the jurisdiction of Congress. Until a body of doctrine defining due process regarding state regulation had been built, however, the effect of the court's new departure was to create a twilight zone of authority. Judges of the numerous federal district courts could prevent the states from acting; and the states had no recourse but to await the verdict of the high tribunal.

Progressives, therefore, charged that the Supreme Court had usurped the administrative function of the states and imposed its own notion of due process and reasonableness on state commissions. They resented even more bitterly the systematic manner in which the court narrowed the authority of the ICC under the act of 1887 and even reduced that great statute to an unenforceable platitude. In view of the absence of any specific delegation of the rate-making authority to the commission by the Interstate Commerce Act, the court could probably not have ruled otherwise. Impatient progressives, however, found the court a more vulnerable scapegoat than Congress.

Progressives were on more solid ground when they denounced the Supreme Court's nullification of the income tax provision of the Wilson-Gorman Tariff Act of 1894. By a five-to-four decision in *Pollock* v. *Farmers' Loan and Trust Company,* 1895, the court reversed precedent by declaring that the income tax was in part indirectly a tax on land and would therefore have to be apportioned among the states according to population. It was easily the most unpopular judicial ruling since the *Dred Scott* decision of 1857. For one thing, the income tax decision effectively blocked the movement for a more democratic tax policy until a constitutional amendment could be adopted. For another, the court's majority had obviously made a political rather than a judicial judgment. Coming as it did in the same year in which the court upheld the conviction of Debs and other officials of the American Railway Union for violating the Sherman law, the income tax decision only deepened the popular conviction that the highest tribunal in the land had become the tool of railroads, corporations, and millionaires.

Popular distrust was further intensified in 1895 when the Supreme Court, in the case of *E. C. Knight* v. *United States,* seemingly emasculated the Sherman Antitrust Act's prohibition against industrial monopoly. That the court was actually willing to interpret the Sherman law liberally was demonstrated, however, in a series of important antitrust cases from 1897 to 1899. In the *Trans-Missouri Freight Association* case of 1897, the justices affirmed that the Sherman law applied to railroads and outlawed a pool operating south and west of the Missouri River. The court reaffirmed this judgment in the *Joint Traffic Association* case of the following year. And in the *Addyston Pipe Company* case, 1899, the justices made it clear that the Sherman law applied also to manufacturers who combined in pools to eliminate price competition.

Thus by the turn of the century the Supreme Court had firmly established the rule that combinations formed directly to suppress competition in the transportation and distribution of products were illegal. Promoters of industrial combinations and their lawyers, however, continued to assume on account of the *Knight* decision, discussed earlier, that manufacturing consolidations did not fall under the prohibitions of the antitrust act. This illusion the court finally and completely shattered in its decisions in the *Standard Oil* and *American Tobacco* cases rendered in 1911.

The *Standard Oil* and *American Tobacco* decisions represented, therefore, a complete accommodation of legal doctrine to prevailing antitrust sentiment. But even more important was the fact that they marked the end of a long struggle within the court itself over the basic meaning of the Sherman Antitrust Act. Did that statute forbid all restraints of trade, or did it prohibit only unreasonable, that is, direct and calculated, restraints? The Supreme Court's majority had consistently ruled before 1911 that the Sherman law proscribed all restraints, reasonable and unreasonable.[6] However, Justice Edward Douglas White had vigorously dissented in the *Trans-Missouri Freight Association* case of 1897, declaring that the framers of the antitrust law had intended to outlaw only unreasonable restraints. He reiterated his position over the years and won converts to it. He finally won a majority to his side in the *Standard Oil* and *American Tobacco* cases and, as chief justice, he wrote the "rule of reason" into American legal doctrine. The Sherman law, he declared, prohibited only unreasonable restraints of trade. Actually, the rule of reason was the only standard by which the antitrust law could be enforced, as the court had tacitly admitted years before. Hence the promulgation of the rule of reason represented the greatest victory thus far accomplished in the long fight to destroy monopoly in the United States.

[6] In common law doctrine a reasonable restraint of trade is any restraint that is ancillary to an otherwise legal contract. Almost any form of contract involves such reasonable restraint of trade. By agreeing to sell his product to one person, for example, a manufacturer restrains trade to the extent that he cannot sell the same goods to another person. An unreasonable restraint of trade, on the other hand, occurs when businessmen enter into agreements, the objectives of which are to restrain trade. Thus conspiracies to control prices, restrict production, divide markets, and so on are unreasonable restraints of trade.

Chapter 5

Woodrow Wilson and the Flowering of the Progressive Movement, 1910-1916

The years from 1910 to 1916 were a time of fulfillment for American progressivism. We have seen how various reform movements in the cities and states came to fruition during this period. In addition, a virtual revolution took place in the more important area of national politics. The Republican party was convulsed by internal schisms and suffered a violent rupture from 1910 to 1912; and Theodore Roosevelt attempted in the latter year to rally progressives of all parties under the banner of a third party. As the Democrats now had a reform leader of their own in Woodrow Wilson, Roosevelt failed to build either a solid progressive phalanx or a permanent party. Instead, he split the Republican majority and enabled the Democrats to capture control of the presidency and of Congress.

But Roosevelt did more than make possible a Democratic victory in 1912. By championing an advanced program of federal economic and social regulation, he also pointed up the major dilemma confronting American progressives. Could national regeneration be achieved, as most Democratic progressives thought, merely by destroying special privilege and applying the rule of equity to all classes? Or could the promise of American life be fulfilled only through a program of federal intervention and participation in economic and social affairs, as Roosevelt and Herbert Croly contended?

Advocates of these two concepts of progressivism battled all during the first

Wilson administration to shape the form and character of federal legislation. As the new president exercised an extraordinary control over Congress, the outcome of the conflict—in fact, the future destiny of the progressive movement—was largely in his hands. Let us now see how progressivism came to flood tide, how Wilson guided it from one channel into another, and how the basis for a later and bolder program of federal action was laid by the time the United States entered the First World War.

40. The Disruption of the Republican Party and the Reorganization of the Democratic Party

There were numerous warnings in all parts of the country during the spring and summer of 1910 that a violent storm impended in the Republican party. The most portentous was the near hurricane velocity of the insurgent revolt in the Middle West. President William Howard Taft hastily sought to make peace with his enemies and save his party from disaster after the failure of his concerted attempts to purge midwestern progressives in the primary campaigns of 1910. The insurgents, now determined to seize control of the GOP. and prevent Taft's renomination in 1912, rebuffed the president's overtures and began a search for a leader of their own.

A second signal of Republican distress was the estrangement between Roosevelt and Taft, which was fully evident by the time the former president returned from Europe in June 1910. The coolness that Roosevelt felt toward his former friend was the outgrowth partly of incidents like the Ballinger affair, but above all it was the result of Roosevelt's growing conviction that Taft had allowed the Old Guard to maneuver him into a position that made the revolt of the insurgents inevitable. Roosevelt was firmly committed to the progressive cause, but he tried hard to bring the warring factions together. Feeling rebuffed by the administration when he endeavored to mediate between conservatives and progressives in New York State, the former president set out upon a speaking tour in the summer of 1910 to kindle the flames of progressivism. So enthusiastic was the popular response that he was catapulted into leadership of the rebellion against Taft and the Old Guard.

Democrats harvested the fruits of Republican dissension and popular protest against the Payne-Aldrich tariff and the Ballinger affair in the congressional and gubernatorial elections of November 1910. The House of Representatives went Democratic for the first time since 1892, and Democratic governors were elected in many normally Republican states in the East and Middle West. There could be no doubt that progressive agitation was rising to flood tide or that a Republican party dominated by Taft, Aldrich, and Cannon faced almost certain defeat in 1912.

The Republican insurgents, on the other hand, were determined to win in

1912, but to win with their own ticket and platform. Many signs in 1910 and early 1911 pointed to Senator Robert M. La Follette of Wisconsin as the leader of the rebels, especially after prominent insurgents formed the National Progressive Republican League in January 1911 to fight for the Senator's nomination. La Follette had the support of a small and dedicated band of idealists, but the great mass of Republican progressives wanted Roosevelt. Convinced that his party faced certain defeat if Taft was renominated and persuaded that La Follette could never be nominated, Roosevelt at last gave in to the pleas of his friends and announced his candidacy for the Republican nomination on February 24, 1912.

The battle for control of the GOP that occurred from March through May 1912 was bitter and violent. In the thirteen states that held presidential primaries, Roosevelt won 278 delegates, as compared to 48 for Taft and 36 for La Follette. On the other hand, Taft controlled the southern states, had the support of Old Guard strongholds like New York, and dominated the Republican National Committee. Consequently the Taft forces organized the national convention that met in Chicago on June 18, awarded themselves 235 of the crucial 254 contested seats, and proceeded ruthlessly to renominate the president on the first ballot on June 21.

Meanwhile, over three hundred Roosevelt delegates had stormed out of the convention and, in consultation with Roosevelt, had decided to return to Chicago and form a new party dedicated to advancing the cause of progressivism. The outgrowth of the insurgents' anger and dedication was the Progressive party, organized in Chicago on August 5 and 6, 1912. Roosevelt, saying that he felt like a bull moose, came in person on August 6 and delivered his acceptance speech, "A Confession of Faith."

The high excitement of these events at Chicago should not be allowed to obscure their significance or the importance of the platform, the "Contract with the People," that the convention of the new Progressive party adopted. It erected mileposts that the American progressive movement would follow for the next fifty years. It was, in fact, the most important American political document between the Populist platform of 1892 and the Democratic platform of 1936. The Progressive party platform of 1912 approved all objectives of the social justice reformers—minimum wages for women, child labor legislation, workmen's compensation, and social insurance. It endorsed neodemocratic demands for the initiative, referendum, and recall, the recall of state judicial decisions, nomination of presidential candidates by preferential primaries, and woman's suffrage. Finally, it demanded establishment of powerful new agencies—a federal trade commission and a federal tariff commission—to regulate business and industry. In brief, it proposed to transform state and federal governments into positive, dynamic agencies of social and economic regeneration.

A crucial struggle had also been occurring in the meantime for control of the Democratic party. Bryan remained titular head, but he announced soon after the elections of November 1910 that he would not be a candidate for a fourth nomination, and a host of new leaders rose to claim his mantle. Woodrow Wilson, who had made a brilliant and successful campaign for the governorship of New Jersey, quickly emerged as the most formidable Democratic claimant. In a spectacular display of leadership, Wilson forced through an unwilling legislature a series of measures that implemented the program for which New Jersey progressives had been fighting for almost a decade. As a consequence of these triumphs, many progressive Democrats throughout the country by the summer of 1911 were thanking God that they had a new leader and spokesman. For his part, Wilson threw himself into the movement for his nomination for the presidency with such vigor that it seemed at the beginning of 1912 that he would easily win leadership of the Democrats.

Wilson's apparent success made the meteoric rise of his chief rival, Champ Clark of Missouri, Speaker of the House of Representatives, all the more surprising. In contrast to the New Jersey governor, who represented the newcomer and the nonprofessional in politics, Clark was an old-line politician who had served without distinction in the House since the 1890s. Temperamentally and intellectually unfit to be president, Clark nonetheless inherited most of Bryan's following in the West, made alliances with a number of eastern and southern state organizations, and won the support of William Randolph Hearst and his chain of newspapers.

Thus, while Wilson campaigned fervently and won not quite one-fourth the delegates to the Democratic National Convention, Clark negotiated shrewdly and harvested a crop nearly twice as large. To make matters worse for Wilson, Oscar W. Underwood of Alabama, chairman of the House ways and means committee, had entered the contest and won over one hundred southern delegates who probably would have otherwise gone to Wilson.

It was a critical moment in the life of the Democratic party and, indeed, in the history of the country, when the delegates assembled for the national convention in Baltimore on June 25, 1912. As nothing less than control of the federal government was at stake, the convention was a bitter affair from the beginning. The outcome of preliminary contests over organization, in which Bryan and the Wilson forces were defeated by the conservative leaders with the help of the Clark delegates, seemed to forecast Clark's impending victory. Clark took a commanding lead in the early balloting. Then the ninety Tammany-controlled New York delegates went to the Speaker on the tenth ballot, giving him a majority—but not the then necessary two-thirds. Yet the expected and seemingly inevitable Clark landslide did not materialize; in fact, Clark lost votes on the next few ballots. A long and grueling battle followed in which the Wilson managers gradually undermined Clark's strength and finally won a two-thirds majority for the New Jersey governor on the forty-sixth ballot.

It has long been mistakenly assumed that Bryan's action in changing his vote from Clark to Wilson on the fourteenth ballot was the decisive factor in this miraculous conclusion. Actually, a number of other circumstances were more responsible for Wilson's victory. However, Bryan did at least dominate the writing of the historic Democratic platform of 1912. It denounced the Payne-Aldrich tariff, promised honest downward revision, and demanded legislation to destroy so-called trusts and establish a decentralized banking system free from Wall Street control. It held out hope for early independence to the Filipinos. Finally, it approved the amendments for the income tax and direct election of senators and favored exempting labor unions from prosecution under the Sherman law. Although it was neither as advanced nor as nationalistic as the Progressive party's "Contract with the People," the Democratic platform did promise at least the destruction of the system of special privileges for business that Republicans had carefully erected since 1861.

41. The Campaign and Election of 1912

A meaningful division in American politics occurred for the first time since 1896 during the presidential campaign of 1912. The four parties and tickets in the field offered programs that well reflected the existing divisions of political sentiment. Although the Republican platform contained concessions to the dominant progressive sentiment, voters understood that Taft's reelection would mean a continuation of Old Guard leadership and policies. In extreme contrast stood Eugene V. Debs, the Socialist candidate, and his party. Offering a program envisaging the gradual nationalization of resources and major industries, Debs campaigned as if he thought he had a chance to win.

The campaign, however, soon turned into a verbal duel between Roosevelt and Wilson. Both men were progressives, yet they reflected in their respective programs and philosophies a significant ideological divergence in national progressivism. Roosevelt's program, the New Nationalism, represented the consummation of a philosophy that had been maturing in his mind at least since 1908, if not since 1905. Like Herbert Croly, Roosevelt urged progressives to examine their basic political assumptions and to see that the historic American democratic creed, which was intensely individualistic, was no longer adequate for an urbanized and industrialized society. Practically, Roosevelt declared, this meant that progressives must abandon laissez faire for democratic collectivism and be willing to use the federal government as a regulator and protector of business, industry, and workers. It meant, in brief, that progressives must surrender their hostility to strong government and espouse instead a New Nationalism that would achieve democratic ends through Hamiltonian, or nationalistic, means.

In expounding this philosophy in the campaign of 1912, Roosevelt advocated a policy toward big business that was entirely at variance with the individualistic tradition. Let us recognize, he said, that concentration and bigness in industry are inevitable in many fields. At the same time, let us subject the large corporations to comprehensive public control through a powerful federal trade commission. Let us also recognize that the great mass of American workers, especially women and children, are powerless to protect themselves, and hence let us use the state and federal governments to improve their lot—among other things by minimum wages for women, workmen's compensation, federal prohibition of child labor, and expanded public health services.

Wilson, a recent convert to progressivism, had no such well-constructed program in mind. Still imbued with a strong residue of laissez-faire concepts, he believed that the federal authority should be used only to destroy artificial barriers to the full development of individual energies, not to rearrange social and economic relationships or to give protection to special classes. He was also a States' rights Democrat, fundamentally suspicious of bold use of federal power. Acting like a traditional Democrat, Wilson began his campaign by promising to destroy the Republican system of tariff protection as the first step in restoring competition. When this issue failed to catch fire, he followed the suggestion of Louis D. Brandeis and moved to what he made the fundamental issue of his campaign—emancipation of business and labor from monopolistic control. Lashing out at Roosevelt's proposals for social legislation and control of corporations, he warned that the New Nationalism could end only with big businessmen controlling the federal government and enslaving workers. In contrast, he promised to destroy monopoly and unleash the potential energies of businessmen by restoring conditions under which competition could flourish. This he would do, specifically, by instituting tariff reform, freeing credit from Wall Street control, and strengthening the Sherman Antitrust Act so as to outlaw unfair trade practices and break up interlocking directorates. This program Wilson called the New Freedom. In brief, it envisaged the destruction of special privileges, restoration of the reign of competition, and reliance for future progress on individual enterprise. On social and economic justice, Wilson was somewhat ambiguous. Since his own ideas were in flux, it is difficult to know precisely where he stood. In any event, he offered no definite program like Roosevelt's.

The most striking fact of the campaign was Roosevelt's failure to split the Democratic ranks and create a solid progressive coalition. The results, therefore, were obvious long before election day. Wilson polled 6,286,214 popular votes; Roosevelt, 4,126,020; Taft, 3,483,922; and Debs, 897,011. Although Wilson received slightly less than 42 percent of the popular votes, his victory in the electoral college was overwhelming because of the multiple division of popular votes. The disruption of the GOP, moreover, gave the Democrats a large majority in the House and a small but workable majority in the Senate.

The election of 1912 seems to have demonstrated that the American people

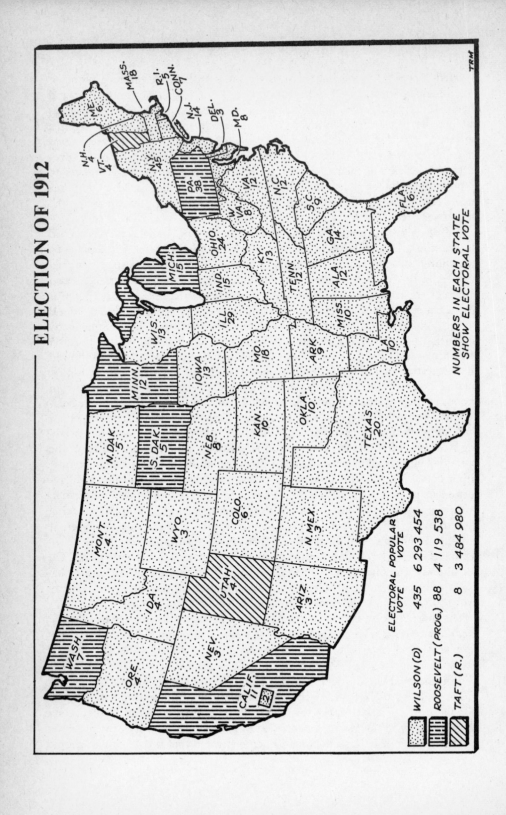

ELECTION OF 1912

NUMBERS IN EACH STATE
SHOW ELECTORAL VOTE

	ELECTORAL VOTE	POPULAR VOTE
WILSON (D)	435	6 293 454
ROOSEVELT (PROG.)	88	4 119 538
TAFT (R.)	8	3 484 980

TRM

were in an overwhelmingly progressive, if not rebellious, mood. Had progressive Republicans and progressive Democrats been able to unite behind a single ticket and platform, progressivism's triumph would have been even more spectacular. As it was, the Democrats would control the federal government chiefly because of the disunion among their opponents. The future of the progressive movement in the United States would depend upon Wilson's ability to bring the reform program to fulfillment and unite the two divergent wings.

42. Woodrow Wilson and the Progressive Movement

No man in American history before 1910 had such a meteoric rise to political preeminence as Woodrow Wilson. Born in a Presbyterian manse in Staunton, Virginia, on December 29, 1856, he grew to boyhood in a South convulsed by Civil War and Reconstruction. After graduating from Princeton University in 1879, Wilson studied law at the University of Virginia and tried unsuccessfully, in 1882 and 1883, to practice law in Atlanta. Disillusioned by the sharp practices of lawyers in Atlanta at that time, he entered the new Johns Hopkins University in Baltimore and won a doctor's degree in political science and history in 1886. He taught successively at Bryn Mawr College, Wesleyan University, and Princeton University from 1885 to 1902. He found an outlet for his political energies in lecturing and writing, and above all in analyzing the weaknesses inherent in the structure of the national government. The basic cause of the failure of leadership in the American political system, he asserted in his most famous work, *Congressional Government,* (1885), lay in the separation of executive from legislative responsibility and leadership.

Wilson's election as president of Princeton University in 1902 gave him his first opportunity to practice the principles of leadership that had been maturing in his mind. Visualizing himself as a prime minister, he put into operation a reorganized curriculum and a new method of undergraduate instruction, the preceptorial system of discussion in small groups. As he emerged as an educational leader of national prominence, he also became increasingly articulate as a spokesman of Democratic conservatism.

Wilson probably would not have allowed his suppressed political ambitions to revive had events continued to go well for him at Princeton. He attempted in 1906 and 1907 to reorganize the social life of undergraduates by abolishing their eating clubs and substituting quadrangles, or residential colleges, in their stead. Students and alumni were so bitterly opposed that the trustees felt compelled to withdraw their approval of the quadrangle plan. This first reversal was so humiliating that Princeton's prime minister nearly resigned.

But the really crushing blow, the event that made Wilson willing to embark upon an uncertain political career when the opportunity arose in 1910, was his defeat in a personal controversy in 1909 and 1910 with the trustees and dean of the graduate school over the establishment and control of a graduate college.

While the graduate college controversy was at its height in the spring of 1910, George Harvey, editor of *Harper's Weekly*, persuaded the leading Democratic boss of New Jersey, James Smith, Jr., to nominate Wilson for the governorship. Wilson accepted the nomination chiefly because the situation at Princeton had become personally intolerable to him. Once in politics, however, he refused to play the role that Harvey and Smith had cut out for him. Sensing that the progressive movement in his state was at flood tide, he came out squarely behind the progressive program and, with the support of insurgent Republicans, won a startling victory in November 1910. As we have mentioned, he boldly seized control of the Democratic party in New Jersey, pushed a comprehensive reform program through an assembly heretofore dominated by bosses and lobbyists, and then undertook a nationwide campaign that carried him into leadership of the Democratic party in 1912 and the White House in 1913.

For the next four years Wilson occupied the same position with regard to national progressivism that Theodore Roosevelt had occupied from 1905 to 1909. However, changed circumstances and differences in personality made Wilson's role in the development of the movement considerably different from Roosevelt's. Unlike Roosevelt, Wilson had not participated in any early progressive movement. In Trenton and later in Washington he was given leadership of state and national movements ripe for fulfillment. The chief thing required of him was to act as the catalytic agent of his time—to rally and strengthen his forces, to synthesize ideas and proposals, and then to use his incomparable powers of articulation and leadership to translate these ideas into statutory realities.

Roosevelt had never really mastered the powerful and entrenched Old Guard machine in Congress. By appealing to the country he had forced Congress to act, but he never actually led the legislative branch of the government. In contrast, Wilson found a congressional situation in 1913 that afforded a unique opportunity for a strong executive. For one thing, there was no Democratic machine in Congress. For another, Democratic leaders, after wandering in the wilderness for twenty years, were determined to make good and cooperate for the success of their program and party. Wilson was thus privileged to be the best and most effective kind of leader in the American system—the parliamentary leader of a cooperative congressional majority. A strong believer in party government and responsibility, Wilson prepared a legislative program, personally guided congressmen in drafting measures, and mediated between various factions when disputes inevitably arose over principles and details.

Wilson's first and most important contribution to the national progressive movement, therefore, was his strengthening and extension of the power of the presidency. By his own example he demonstrated that the president has it in his power not only to represent the majority opinion, as Roosevelt had done, but also to destroy the wall between the executive and legislative branches. His second great contribution was a more immediate one—the manner in which he used this leadership to bring the national progressive movement to legislative consummation.

Men followed Wilson because he was determined to fulfill party pledges and to act for the good of the country, and above all because he nobly articulated their own highest ideals and aspirations. Among friends and associates Wilson was usually warm and intimate. He was in most circumstances an excellent administrator who gave the greatest possible rein to subordinates. But he commanded loyalty by superior intelligence and by appealing to principles and moral purposes more than to personal friendship. Wilson's leadership succeeded so long as his massive intelligence and moving eloquence survived the hazards of an increasingly demanding presidential career. Even so, his leadership was impaired by certain defects even during the heyday of his powers. The most striking of these was a tendency to value his own intuitive and moralistic judgments over conclusions deduced from an analysis of sometimes unpleasant facts. Moreover, he too often assumed that others were as high-minded as he; consequently, he was sometimes a poor judge of men. Finally, his strong activism and urge to achieve his own solutions sometimes, although not always, prevented him from making necessary compromises.

Most historians agree that these were usually minor flaws. Wilson brought to the presidency new life and vigor informed by an almost intuitive ability to probe and understand public opinion. Perhaps better than any other president he was adept at the alchemy of transforming broad principles and traditions into statutory realities. He gave leadership in nobility of character and eloquence of language unrivaled since Lincoln, indeed, unexcelled by any president in our history.

43. The New Freedom

The first item on Wilson's legislative schedule was tariff revision, for Democratic promises would be hollow so long as the Payne-Aldrich Act—that symbol of business privilege—remained in force. On the day of his inauguration, March 4, 1913, therefore, Wilson called a special session of Congress; and he went in person before the two houses on April 8. By breaking the precedent established by Jefferson, Wilson asserted his personal leadership in legislation and focused the attention of the country on Congress. Even more, he conferred frequently with Chairman Oscar W. Underwood while the House ways and means committee prepared the new tariff bill.

The measure that Underwood presented to the House on April 22, 1913, honestly fulfilled Democratic promises of tariff reform. It was not a free trade bill, but rather it was an attempt to place American industries in a genuinely competitive position with regard to European producers. All products manufactured by so-called trusts, such as iron and steel products and agricultural machinery, were placed on the free list, while most raw materials, clothing, food, shoes, and other such items were either put on the free list or given only incidental protection. The general average of the Underwood duties was about 29 percent, as contrasted with the 37 to 40 percent level of the Payne-Aldrich Act. Finally, to compensate for the anticipated loss of revenue, the ways and means committee added a provision levying a graduated but slight tax on incomes.[1]

The Underwood bill passed the House by a thumping majority on May 8, but the battle for tariff reform had only just begun. By insisting on free sugar and free wool, Wilson had antagonized Democratic senators from Louisiana, Montana, and Colorado, the states that produced these raw materials, and a change of three Democratic votes in the upper house could change a Democratic majority into a minority. It was a dangerous situation, but the president took unprecedented steps. First he applied heavy personal and political pressure on wavering Democrats. Then on May 26 he issued a statement to the country denouncing the swarms of lobbyists who infested Washington and were hard at work to defeat tariff reform.

This bold strategy succeeded far beyond the president's expectations. In response to Wilson's indictment of the lobbyists, La Follette and other progressives in the Senate instituted a searching inquiry into lobbying and compelled senators to reveal personal property holdings that might be affected by tariff legislation. Under such penetrating publicity the opposition of Democratic senators, except for the two Louisiana senators, vanished, and the road ahead was clear for honest reform. In fact, by putting food and other farm products on the free list, the Senate finance committee, headed by Furnifold Simmons of North Carolina, actually reduced the Underwood rates by 4 percent. Moreover, a threatened rebellion of progressive senators of both parties forced the finance committee to increase the levy on incomes from a maximum of 4 percent to a maximum of 7 percent.[2] The Senate approved the tariff bill on September 9, 1913; the House conferees accepted the Senate

[1]It levied a flat tax of 1 percent on all personal and corporate incomes over $4,000 and an additional surtax of 1 percent on incomes from $20,000 to $50,000, 2 percent on incomes from $50,000 to $100,000, and 3 percent on incomes over $100,000.
[2]The Senate bill, to which the House agreed, levied an income tax of 1 percent on income over $4,000 and an additional surtax ranging to 6 percent.

amendments; and Wilson signed the revised and strengthened Underwood-Simmons bill on October 3.

It was fortunate for Wilson that he emerged from this first and crucial test stronger than before, for at the moment he signed the Underwood-Simmons Act a controversy provoked by his attempt to reorganize the national banking and currency systems was brewing furiously. Practically every authority recognized the imperative need for speedy reform, lest the entire awkward banking structure collapse in another depression.[3]   The trouble was that different interests and groups demanded different kinds of legislation. The banking community and conservative Republicans almost unanimously supported the plan proposed by the Aldrich Commission, appointed in 1908 to study banking reform, to establish a great central bank, with branches, controlled by the dominant banking interests. The Democrats had condemned the Aldrich plan in their platform of 1912, but they were well-nigh fatally divided. The progressive faction demanded a reserve system and currency supply owned and controlled by the government. They pointed to the revelations of the Pujo Committee, which investigated the so-called Money Trust in early 1913, to prove that only decisive public control could destroy the existing concentration of credit resources in Wall Street. On the other hand, conservative Democrats, still fearful of Bryan's monetary heresies, proposed a decentralized reserve system, free from Wall Street domination, but owned and controlled by private interests.

It was amid such confusing and divided counsels that Wilson tried to steer a middle course and evolve a policy that would be acceptable to all factions. He commissioned Carter Glass of Virginia, chairman of the House banking committee, to prepare a preliminary bill. As Glass was a leader of the conservative Democratic faction, he drafted a measure that would have established a system consisting of as many as twenty reserve banks, under private control and without central direction. At Wilson's insistence, Glass added a provision for a central governing board on which bankers would have minority representation to coordinate the far-flung reserve system.

The publication of the original Glass bill set off a controversy in administration circles that threatened for a time to disrupt the Democratic party. Bryan, Secretary of the Treasury William G. McAdoo, and Robert L. Owen, chairman of the Senate banking committee, led progressive Democrats in demanding a reserve and currency system owned and controlled entirely by the government. In addition, agrarian spokesmen in the House denounced the

[3]The banking and currency systems established by the Civil War legislation were totally unfit for the needs of a great industrial and commercial nation. For one thing, the currency was based upon the bonded indebtedness of the United States and was therefore inflexible; worse still, the national banking structure was without any effective central control or workable machinery for mobilizing banking reserves. The Panic of 1907 had prompted Congress to enact the Aldrich-Vreeland Act of 1908, which allowed banks to issue emergency currency against securities and bonds, but this measure was never meant to be a long-run solution and was devised only to meet emergencies.

Glass bill because it made no provision for destroying the Money Trust or furnishing credit to farmers. Confronted by a seemingly impossible situation, Wilson moved serenely but decisively. Upon the advice of Louis D. Brandeis, the president decided that the bankers should be denied representation on the proposed Federal Reserve Board and that Federal Reserve currency should be the obligation of the United States. At Bryan's urging, he allowed the agrarian faction to amend the Glass bill to provide short-term credit facilities for farmers in the new system. On the other hand, private banking interests would own and largely control the Federal Reserve banks and have a voice in an advisory commission that would counsel the Federal Reserve Board. Thus Wilson's mediating leadership in this first great crisis in banking reform enabled the progressive, agrarian, and conservative Democratic factions to find an acceptable compromise.

No sooner had the controversy within the administration been settled than another more violent storm burst over the country. Bankers and their spokesmen were up in arms, denouncing the revised Glass bill as harebrained, socialistic, and confiscatory. Organized banking groups and banking journals raged all during the late summer and autumn of 1913, but gradually preponderant general opinion turned in the administration's favor. The Glass bill passed the House in September by a large majority; considerably revised, it passed the Senate on December 19, and the president signed it four days later.

The Federal Reserve Act established twelve Federal Reserve banks owned by member banks[4] and controlled by boards of directors, the majority of whom were chosen by member banks. As the central banks of their various districts, reserve banks held a portion of member banks' reserves and performed other central banking functions. The Glass measure also created a new currency, Federal Reserve notes, issued by the reserve banks to member banks on the basis of collateral consisting of commercial and agricultural paper and a 40 percent gold reserve. This Federal Reserve currency was flexible, that is, it would expand or contract in volume in direct relation to the needs of the business community. Uniting and controlling in a limited fashion the entire system was a Federal Reserve Board of seven members, appointed for long terms by the president with the consent of the Senate.

It was the great merit of the Federal Reserve Act that it provided means to mobilize the major part of the banking reserves of a region, indeed of the entire country; created a new and flexible, yet absolutely sound, currency; effectively destroyed the concentration of credit resources in a few financial centers; and reinforced private control on the local level, tempered by a degree of public supervision and national coordination. Doctrinaire progressives like La Follette denounced the Federal Reserve Act because it did not provide for comprehensive federal control or ownership and operation of the

[4]All national banks were required to join the Federal Reserve system. State banks were free to join the system but were not compelled to do so.

national banking system. Yet the framers of the measure never intended to implement such far-reaching policy. In the spirit of Wilson's New Freedom they conceived a banking and currency system in which the private interest would predominate and the public interest would enjoy only a supervisory function.

44. The Turning Point in Wilsonian Progressivism

The Federal Reserve Act marked the high tide of the New Freedom doctrines. Wilson gave numerous evidences throughout 1913 and the early months of 1914 of his determination to adhere strictly to his limited reform program and his resolution not to surrender to the movements then on foot to commit the federal government to advanced social and economic legislation. The root of the disagreement between the president and the agrarian, labor, and social justice reformers stemmed from divergent conceptions of the proper role that the federal government should play. Like Theodore Roosevelt, advanced progressives championed measures aimed at using federal authority to benefit special, if underprivileged, classes. Thus controversy inevitably arose when Wilson invoked New Freedom concepts to thwart the demands of these powerful pressure groups.

So resolutely did the president stand in defense of the New Freedom, in fact, that for a time he obstructed or refused to encourage the fulfillment of a large part of the progressive program. We have already seen how he blocked the AF of L's campaign to obtain immunity for labor unions from application of the antitrust law to their illegal strike activities (see pp. 48–49). In the same manner, Wilson in the spring of 1914 prevented passage of a bill that would have established a system of long-term rural credits financed and operated by the federal government. Or, again, when the National Child Labor Committee's child labor bill passed the House in 1914, Wilson refused to fight for its approval by the Senate because he thought it unconstitutional. He also refused to support a woman's suffrage amendment because he thought that suffrage qualifications should be determined by the states.

Three other incidents revealed the extent to which the president opposed or refused to encourage advanced progressive legislation. The first was his momentary obstruction of the movement to reduce the number of immigrants coming to American shores. Restriction, or outright exclusion, of immigration had long been an objective of the AF of L, many sociologists, and many social workers. The instrument proposed by these groups, the literacy test, was embodied in the Burnett immigration bill that passed Congress on January 2, 1915. Wilson vetoed this measure, and his veto held. Two years later, in January 1917, Congress overrode his veto of a similar bill.

The second incident was Wilson's near veto of the La Follette seamen's bill in March 1915. Initiated by Andrew Furuseth, president of the International Seamen's Union, this measure imposed rigorous safety requirements on all vessels in the American maritime trade. More important, it freed American and foreign sailors on vessels coming to American ports of their bondage to labor contracts. Wilson at first supported the seamen's bill, as it conferred no special privileges and did no more than place maritime workers on an equal footing with other workers. The State Department, however, strongly opposed the measure because it unilaterally abrogated some thirty treaties with the maritime powers. After much soul-searching and after Senator La Follette, the measure's chief sponsor, agreed to give the State Department ample time to renegotiate the treaties, Wilson approved the seamen's bill on March 4, 1915. Obviously, it was not an administration measure.

The third incident was perhaps the most revealing. It came early in the New Freedom dispensation, when Wilson permitted his secretary of the treasury and postmaster general to segregate certain Negro and white workers in their departments. This provoked such a storm of protest from Negroes and from white progressives in the North that the administration reversed what was in fact a very limited segregation policy late in 1914. The incident, nonetheless, revealed the absence in administration circles of any strong concern for social justice, at least for Negroes.

The first important turning point or movement toward more advanced progressivism occurred in the early months of 1914 as Wilson and congressional leaders set about to prepare antitrust legislation. Advanced progressives demanded establishment of an independent trade commission armed with a kind of freewheeling authority to oversee business activities and suppress unfair trade practices. At the outset of these discussions Wilson insisted upon a solution more in accord with the New Freedom doctrine of limited intervention. His original antitrust program was embodied in two measures, the Clayton bill and the Covington interstate trade commission bill. The former enumerated and prohibited a series of unfair trade practices, outlawed interlocking directorates, and gave private parties benefit of decisions in antitrust suits originated by the government. The Covington bill created an interstate trade commission to supplant the Bureau of Corporations. The new commission would have no independent regulatory authority but, like the Bureau of Corporations, would act merely as a fact-finding agency for the executive and legislative branches.

The publication of the administration's bills provoked such an outbreak of confusing dissent that it seemed for a time that there might be no legislation at all. Because the Clayton bill failed to provide immunity from antitrust prosecution for labor unions, spokesmen of the AF of L were up in arms. Because the measure attempted to enumerate every conceivable restraint of trade, advanced progressives in both parties denounced it as futile. Because it did not attempt to destroy outright the oligarchical financial and industrial structure, agrarian radicals from the South and West claimed that the Clayton bill was a betrayal of Democratic pledges. Wilson was visibly shaken by these attacks, but in the confusion of voices he did not know where to turn.

When the president seemed most uncertain, his informal adviser, Louis D. Brandeis, came forward in April 1914 with an alternative that involved virtually abandoning the effort to prohibit unfair trade practices by the statutory method. Instead Brandeis proposed outlawing unfair trade practices in general terms and then establishing a federal trade commission endowed with ample authority to suppress restraints of trade whenever they occurred. Brandeis's solution had been embodied in a trade commission bill, introduced earlier by Representative Raymond B. Stevens of New Hampshire.

Although Brandeis's proposal envisaged at least something like the kind of regulation of business that Roosevelt had advocated and Wilson had at least implicitly condemned in 1912, it seemed to be the only practical answer to an otherwise insoluble problem. Thus Wilson at once made the Stevens bill the cornerstone of his new antitrust policy, and administration leaders in Congress sidetracked the Covington bill and pressed the Stevens measure instead. Wilson also lost all interest in the Clayton bill, except to maintain his inflexible opposition to granting labor unions the privilege of using illegal strike weapons. In consequence, the Clayton bill was cut adrift in the Senate, where most of its strong provisions were seriously weakened. The measure that Wilson signed on October 15, 1914, was, Senator James A. Reed of Missouri complained, "a sort of legislative apology to the trusts, delivered hat in hand, and accompanied by assurances that no discourtesy is intended."[5]

Meanwhile, the president had bent all his energies toward obtaining congressional approval of the Stevens trade commission bill. After a hard battle he won a decisive victory because the Federal Trade Commission Act that he approved on September 26 committed the federal government to a policy of vigorous regulation of all business activities. In sweeping terms it outlawed, but did not attempt to define, unfair trade practices. Moreover, it established a Federal Trade Commission to supersede the Bureau of Corporations, armed with authority to move swiftly and directly against corporations accused of suppressing competition—first by issuing cease and desist orders and then, if that recourse failed, by bringing the accused corporations to trial.

Wilson's acceptance of what might very roughly be called a Rooseveltian legislative solution was matched to a considerable degree on the level of direct antitrust activity. Rejecting agrarian radical demands for a relentless cam-

[5]The Clayton Act forbade contracts requiring purchasers to buy from only one producer or seller; forbade corporations to purchase the stock of other corporations when the result would be to lessen competition substantially; outlawed interlocking directorates, when their existence operated substantially to lessen competition; and made court decisions in antitrust suits initiated by the government prima facie evidence in private damage suits.

paign against bigness, per se, Wilson and his attorneys general instead continued the Roosevelt-Taft policy of moving only against combinations that seemed obviously to have been in restraint of trade. For example, they continued Taft's case against United States Steel, in spite of that corporation's offer to settle out of court. What was new in the antitrust story under Wilson was the eagerness of officials of several important combinations to accept government-dictated reorganizations in order to avoid prosecution. The American Telephone & Telegraph Company, the New Haven Railroad, and the Southern Pacific Railroad, among others, accepted consent decrees proposed by the Justice Department in 1913 and 1914. The Federal Trade Commission never seemed able to fulfill the hopes of its founders during the balance of the Wilson era. It was hobbled first by incompetence and internal dissension. It had little to do during the period of American belligerence, 1917–1918, as antitrust prosecutions were then generally suspended. It finally came to life in 1919–1920 in a victorious campaign to destroy the old Beef Trust.

Wilson's acceptance of the Federal Trade Commission bill during the congressional discussions of 1914 was also an important turning point in the history of the national progressive movement. It was the first important sign that the president might be willing to abandon his doctrinaire New Freedom concepts and surrender to the rising progressive demands for bold social and economic legislation in other fields. Any such surrender, however, would have to come in the future, for adoption of the Clayton and Federal Trade Commission acts in the autumn of 1914 seemed to signal the completion of the president's reform program. In a public letter to Secretary of the Treasury McAdoo on November 17, Wilson asserted that the legislation of the past eighteen months had destroyed the Republican system of special privilege and ended the antagonism between business and the public. The future, he added, would be a time in which businessmen would adapt themselves to changed conditions and the nation would enter a new era "of cooperation, of new understanding, of common purpose." In brief, the reconstructive phase of the national progressive movement was over; reform would now give way to readjustment.

45. The Triumph of the New Nationalism

As it turned out, Wilson's forecast of future political developments was somewhat naive. By the time that the president wrote his letter to McAdoo a profound upheaval in American politics—the virtual disappearance of the Progressive party—had occurred during the congressional elections of November 3, 1914. The outbreak of war in Europe a few months before had diverted American attention from the campaign and evoked a general disposition to stand by the president. Even so, the Democratic majority in the House of Representatives was reduced from seventy-three to twenty-five, and Republicans swept back into power in key states like New York, Pennsylvania, Illinois, and New Jersey. So powerful was the tide that it seemed that a general Republican victory in 1916 was probable.

The months passed, and the nation was convulsed by alarms of war with Germany and a great debate over preparedness. It was obvious by January 1916 that Theodore Roosevelt would abandon his third party and join with his erstwhile enemies to drive the Democrats from power. Democratic defeat in the impending presidential campaign was virtually inevitable if he succeeded in leading most Progressives back into the Republican camp. The urgent necessity facing Wilson and his party at the beginning of 1916, therefore, was to find some means of luring at least a large minority of the former Progressives into the Democratic ranks. This strategy offered the only possible hope of converting a normal Democratic minority into a majority in November 1916. To execute the strategy, however, Wilson and the Democratic party had to cast off the shackles of States' rights and laissez faire doctrines and convince still suspicious Progressives that they offered the best hope of positive economic and social reform.

Although adopting advanced progressive concepts and legislation required abandoning some of the ideological foundations upon which the New Freedom rested, Wilson did not shrink from the necessity. Moreover, it is probably accurate to say that changed convictions, growing out of his own experience during the past two years, were as much responsible for Wilson's change of course as was political expediency. Beginning in January 1916, he embarked upon a new course of action; and because his new departure seemed to offer the only hope of staying in power, most Democrats in Congress followed him willingly.

The first sign of this metamorphosis was Wilson's appointment of Louis D. Brandeis to the Supreme Court on January 28, 1916. Progressives of both parties were delighted, for Brandeis was one of the leading exponents of social and economic reform in the country. The president called the sponsors of the much controverted rural credits bill to the White House shortly afterward and told them that he would support their measure. He was as good as his word, and the Federal Farm Loan Act passed Congress in May.[6] A few months later, after the presidential campaign had begun, spokesmen of the social justice forces informed Wilson that they regarded the pending child labor and federal workmen's compensation bills as the acid tests of his progressivism. Wilson had said not a word to this point in advocacy of these

---

[6]This measure established twelve Federal Farm Loan banks capitalized at $750,000 each, which should extend long-term credit to farmers on a basis of land and improvements. It also created a Federal Farm Loan Board to supervise the new system.

measures. Now he immediately applied heavy pressure on Democratic leaders in the Senate and obtained their passage in August.[7]

The extent of Wilson's commitment to advanced progressivism can best be understood when we perceive the long-run significance of the Child Labor Act of 1916. By this measure, Congress for the first time used its power over interstate commerce in an important way to control conditions under which employers might operate their industries. Did this signify the beginning of a new and enlarged federal regulation under the commerce clause, as the spokesman of the NAM declared, "of any commodity produced in whole or in part by the labor of men or women who work more than eight hours, receive less than a minimum wage, or have not certain educational qualifications"? Progressives hoped and conservatives feared that it did. In any event, it seemed that a constitutional way had been found to extend federal control over all phases of the manufacturing process.

Nor did the foregoing measures alone represent the full extent of Wilson's espousal of the program embodied in the Progressive platform of 1912. Echoing a proposal Roosevelt had made in 1912, Wilson in 1916 sponsored and obtained passage of a bill to establish an independent tariff commission, allegedly to remove the tariff issue from politics. Moreover, in language that Roosevelt might have used, Wilson publicly reversed historic Democratic policy and approved the principle of rational protection for certain infant industries. He supported and won passage of a series of measures launching the federal government upon a new program of aid to the states for education and highway construction.[8] Finally, he sponsored but did not obtain adoption until January 1918 of the Webb-Pomerene bill to permit American manufacturers to combine for the purpose of carrying on export trade.

Thus it was that political necessity and changed political convictions compelled a president and party who had taken office in 1913 for the purpose of effectuating a limited reform program to sponsor and enact the most far-reaching and significant economic and social legislation in American history before 1933. Looking back in 1916 upon the development of the progressive movement since 1912, observers might well have been puzzled by the revolution that had occurred. On the one hand, Wilson and his party had tacitly

[7]Drafted by the American Association for Labor Legislation, the Kern-McGillicuddy Compensation Act established a model workmen's compensation system for federal employees. The Keating-Owen child labor bill, sponsored by the National Child Labor Committee, which became the Child Labor Act of 1916, forbade the shipment in interstate commerce of goods manufactured in whole or in part by children under fourteen, and of any products manufactured by children under sixteen employed more than eight hours a day.

[8]These were the Bankhead Good Roads Act of 1916, which provided federal funds to match state appropriations for interstate highways and the Smith-Hughes Act of 1917, providing federal funds on a matching basis for vocational education in public high schools. An earlier measure, the Smith-Lever Act of 1914, provided federal money on a matching basis for agricultural extension work.

abandoned the New Freedom, and the president could justly claim that Democrats were also Progressives and boast that his party had enacted practically all the Progressive platform of 1912. On the other hand, Theodore Roosevelt, the great expounder of the New Nationalism in 1912, had by 1916 abandoned his platform to the Democrats and was striving mightily to defeat the party that had carried out his proposals.

Chapter 6

The Growth of the United States as a World Power, 1898 - 1917

Between the end of the Napoleonic Wars in 1815 and the outbreak of the Spanish-American War in 1898, the American people enjoyed such freedom from foreign vexations as they had never known before 1815 and would not experience in the twentieth century. The United States was not normally active in world politics before 1898, for the American people did not want to sit in the councils of the mighty, nor engage in the scramble for colonies and concessions, nor play the game of power politics. They only desired to be let alone. They were determined to defend the Monroe Doctrine, that cornerstone of their foreign policy. But defense of the Western Hemisphere was defense of America's splendid isolation.

Yet a nation is not isolated merely by wishing to be. In fact, forces were at work during the high tide of American insularity, 1865–98, to make continued isolation soon impossible. First, the United States during this period was emerging as the dominant industrial power in the world. American financiers and manufacturers were beginning to export capital and goods and to acquire markets and interests abroad that their government could not ignore. Moreover, because of their strategic economic position, the American people would find it difficult to avoid involvement in a future European war.

Thus, although few Americans realized the fact in 1900, the United States had a vital stake in the peace of Europe. Second, swift technological advances during the half-century before the First World War were drawing the world closely together and diminishing the strategic value of America's oceanic defensive barriers. Finally, the rise of Germany as the dominant military power in Europe and Japan as an aspiring power in Asia during the last quarter of the nineteenth century upset the old balance of power upon which American security had in some measure depended.

46. The Acquisition and Administration of the American Colonial Empire, 1898–1917

The American people entered blithely upon the war with Spain only for the purpose of freeing Cuba from Spanish tyranny. Even so, a few thoughtful leaders of the war movement like Theodore Roosevelt and Henry Cabot Lodge of Massachusetts welcomed the war for the opportunity it offered to acquire bases in the Caribbean and Pacific. Looking toward the day when the United States would construct an isthmian canal and need naval bases to guard its approaches, they urged annexation of Puerto Rico, Spain's other Caribbean possession, and retention of naval bases in Cuba. As for the Pacific, they urged and won annexation of Hawaii a few months after the war with Spain began. As assistant secretary of the navy, Roosevelt, on February 25, 1898, had instructed Commodore George Dewey, commanding the Asiatic squadron then at Hong Kong, to prepare to attack the Spanish fleet in Manila Bay in the event that war occurred. But neither Roosevelt nor any other responsible spokesman of the administration contemplated taking the Philippine Islands.

Yet the American commissioners at the peace conference that met in Paris from October 1 through December 10, 1898, demanded and won not only Cuba's freedom and the transfer of Puerto Rico to the United States, but also the cession of Guam and the entire Philippine archipelago. The United States by this act extended its frontiers far out into the Pacific and assumed the burden of pacifying the Philippines and then defending them against future aggression.

The immediate issue of imperialism was settled for a time after the ratification of the Treaty of Paris by the Senate in 1899 and McKinley's second victory over Bryan in 1900. The United States would continue to hold and administer the Philippines, at least until the Filipinos were ready for self-government. But the American people soon discovered that it is far easier to acquire a colonial empire than to govern it. On the outbreak of the war with Spain, Commodore Dewey and the American consul at Singapore had helped

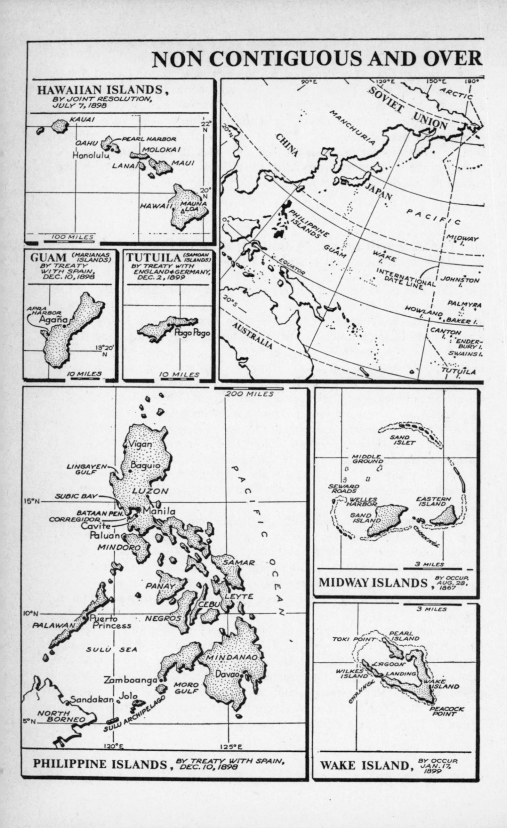

NON CONTIGUOUS AND OVER

HAWAIIAN ISLANDS, *BY JOINT RESOLUTION, JULY 7, 1898*

KAUAI · OAHU · PEARL HARBOR · Honolulu · MOLOKAI · LANAI · MAUI · HAWAII · MAUNA LOA · 22°N · 20°N · 100 MILES

GUAM (MARIANAS ISLANDS) *BY TREATY WITH SPAIN, DEC. 10, 1898*

APRA HARBOR · Agaña · 13°20'N · 10 MILES

TUTUILA (SAMOAN ISLANDS) *BY TREATY WITH ENGLAND & GERMANY, DEC. 2, 1899*

Pago Pago · 10 MILES

90°E · 120°E · 150°E · 180° · ARCTIC · SOVIET UNION · MANCHURIA · CHINA · JAPAN · PACIFIC · MIDWAY I. · PHILIPPINE ISLANDS · GUAM · WAKE · INTERNATIONAL DATE LINE · JOHNSTON I. · EQUATOR · PALMYRA I. · HOWLAND I. · BAKER I. · CANTON I. · ENDERBURY I. · SWAINS I. · TUTUILA I. · AUSTRALIA · 20°S

PHILIPPINE ISLANDS, *BY TREATY WITH SPAIN, DEC. 10, 1898*

200 MILES · Vigan · Baguio · LINGAYEN GULF · LUZON · SUBIC BAY · BATAAN PEN. · Manila · CORREGIDOR · Cavite · Paluan · MINDORO · SAMAR · PANAY · LEYTE · CEBU · PALAWAN · Puerto Princess · NEGROS · SULU SEA · MINDANAO · Davao · Zamboanga · MORO GULF · Sandakan · Jolo · NORTH BORNEO · SULU ARCHIPELAGO · PACIFIC OCEAN · 15°N · 10°N · 5°N · 120°E · 125°E

MIDWAY ISLANDS, *BY OCCUP. AUG. 28, 1867*

SAND ISLET · MIDDLE GROUND · SEWARD ROADS · WELLES HARBOR · EASTERN ISLAND · SAND ISLAND · 3 MILES

WAKE ISLAND, *BY OCCUP. JAN. 17, 1899*

3 MILES · TOKI POINT · PEARL ISLAND · WILKES ISLAND · LAGOON · WAKE ISLAND · LANDING · PEACOCK POINT

SEAS EXPANSION, 1867-1914

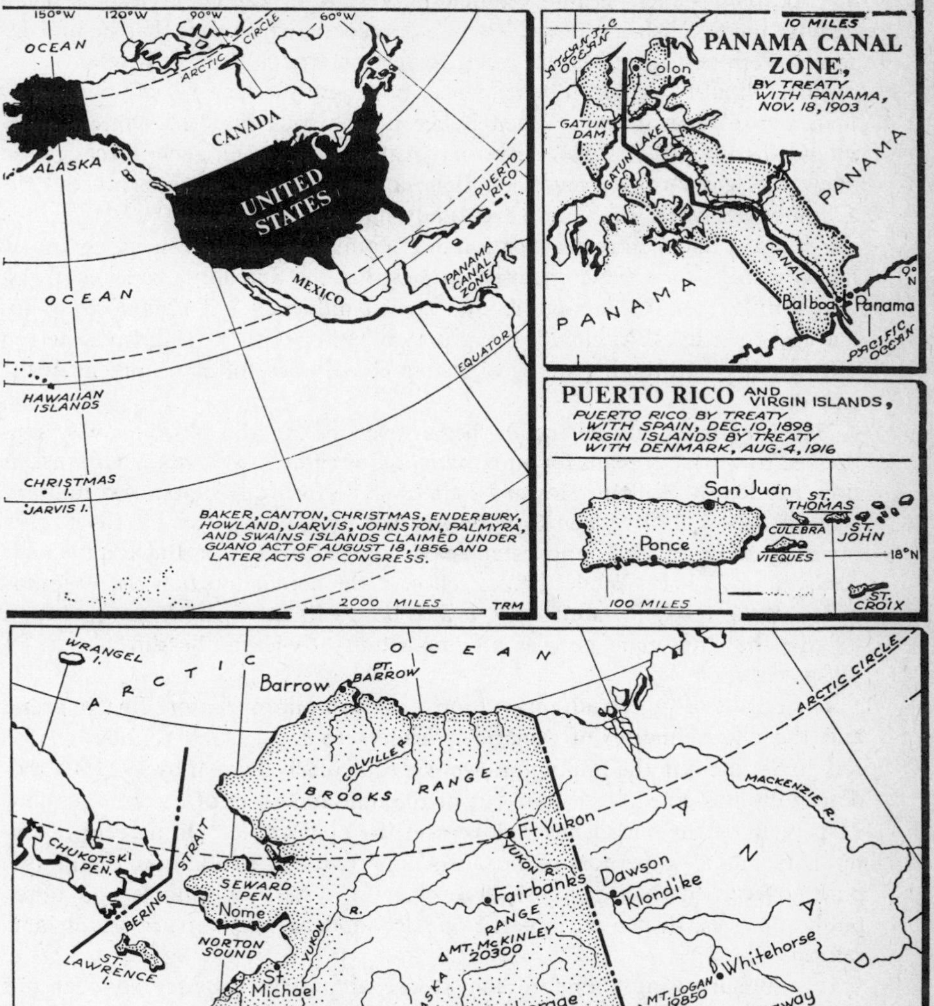

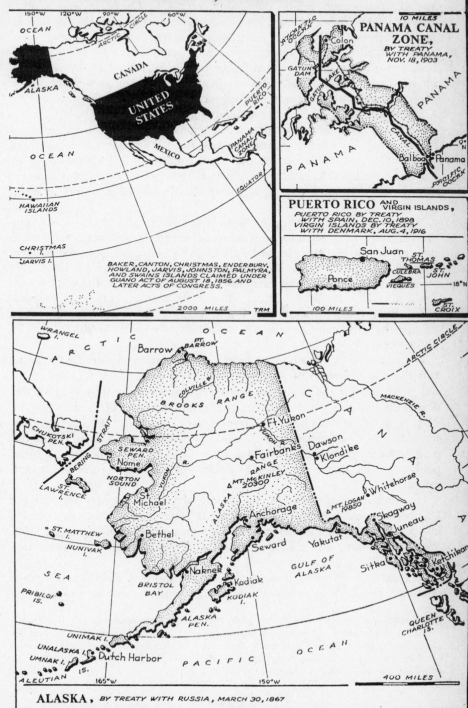

150°W
120°W
90°W
60°W
OCEAN
ARCTIC CIRCLE
CANADA
ALASKA
UNITED STATES
PUERTO RICO
MEXICO
PANAMA CANAL ZONE
OCEAN
EQUATOR
HAWAIIAN ISLANDS
CHRISTMAS I.
JARVIS I.
BAKER, CANTON, CHRISTMAS, ENDERBURY, HOWLAND, JARVIS, JOHNSTON, PALMYRA, AND SWAINS ISLANDS CLAIMED UNDER GUANO ACT OF AUGUST 18, 1856 AND LATER ACTS OF CONGRESS.
2000 MILES
TRM
10 MILES
PANAMA CANAL ZONE,
BY TREATY WITH PANAMA, NOV. 18, 1903
ATLANTIC OCEAN
Colon
GATUN DAM
GATUN LAKE
PANAMA
CANAL
PANAMA
Balboa
Panama
9°N
PACIFIC OCEAN
PUERTO RICO AND VIRGIN ISLANDS,
PUERTO RICO BY TREATY WITH SPAIN, DEC. 10, 1898
VIRGIN ISLANDS BY TREATY WITH DENMARK, AUG. 4, 1916
San Juan
ST. THOMAS
CULEBRA
ST. JOHN
Ponce
VIEQUES
18°N
100 MILES
ST. CROIX
WRANGEL I.
ARCTIC OCEAN
PT. BARROW
Barrow
ARCTIC CIRCLE
COLVILLE R.
BROOKS RANGE
CANADA
MACKENZIE R.
CHUKOTSKI PEN.
BERING STRAIT
Ft. Yukon
YUKON R.
SEWARD PEN.
Nome
Dawson
Fairbanks
Klondike
NORTON SOUND
YUKON R.
ALASKA RANGE
MT. McKINLEY 20300
ST. LAWRENCE I.
St Michael
Whitehorse
MT. LOGAN 19850
Skagway
Anchorage
Juneau
ST. MATTHEW I.
Bethel
Seward
Yakutat
NUNIVAK I.
GULF OF ALASKA
Sitka
Ketchikan
SEA
Naknek
Kodiak
BRISTOL BAY
KODIAK I.
PRIBILOF IS.
ALASKA PEN.
QUEEN CHARLOTTE IS.
UNIMAK I.
OCEAN
UNALASKA I.
Dutch Harbor
UMNAK I.
PACIFIC
ALEUTIAN IS.
165°W
150°W
400 MILES

ALASKA, BY TREATY WITH RUSSIA, MARCH 30, 1867

a Philippine leader, Emilio Aguinaldo, return to Luzon to lead a revolt against the Spanish authority. Aguinaldo succeeded so well that he and his forces were besieging Manila when American troops occupied the city.

The Filipinos wanted independence, not merely a transfer of sovereignty to a new foreign master. When it became obvious that the United States intended to impose its own authority, Aguinaldo and his rebel forces raised anew the standards of revolt on February 4, 1899. So stubbornly did the Filipinos fight that McKinley eventually had to send some 70,000 troops to the islands; and before pacification was completed American commanders had resorted to the same primitive tactics that the Spaniards had unsuccessfully employed in Cuba; and about 10,000 Americans and 100,000 Filipinos had lost their lives. Aguinaldo's capture on March 23, 1901, signaled the end of resistance and the beginning of a long era of peaceful development of the islands.

The McKinley administration began even before the rebellion was suppressed to work out plans for a permanent government. A civilian administration, headed by William Howard Taft as civil governor, supplanted military rule on July 4, 1901. Then Congress passed an Organic Act for the Philippines on July 2, 1902, and established a government for the islands that survived until 1916. While the act reflected the conviction that the Filipinos were not yet ready for autonomy, it also bore witness to American intention to give the Philippine peoples an opportunity to learn the difficult art of self-government.[1]

The results of superb administration, generous appropriations by Congress, and the determination of American leaders to lay a solid foundation for self-government in the Philippines were spectacularly evident by 1913. By this date, Filipinos constituted four out of the nine members of the commission, 71 percent of the classified employees in the civil service, 92 percent of the teachers, and all governors of the Christian provinces. In addition, the Philippine government had established a splendid system of schools and other public services, dispensed impartial justice, and carried out important land reforms.

It is not surprising, therefore, that Roosevelt and Taft shuddered when the Democrats came to power in 1913, for the Democrats had advocated early independence for the Filipinos during every presidential campaign since 1899. Woodrow Wilson was elected in 1912 on a platform that reiterated this position, and the new Organic Act for the Philippines that Congress passed on August 29, 1916, the Jones Act, fell little short of giving the Filipinos dominion status. This measure created an elective senate to supplant the

---

[1]The Organic Act made Filipinos citizens of the Philippine Islands; created an executive branch consisting of the governor-general and a commission, to be appointed by the president with the consent of the United States Senate; established an Anglo-American system of courts; and provided for establishment of a two-house legislature, the lower house to be elected by the Christian tribes and the upper house to consist of the commission.

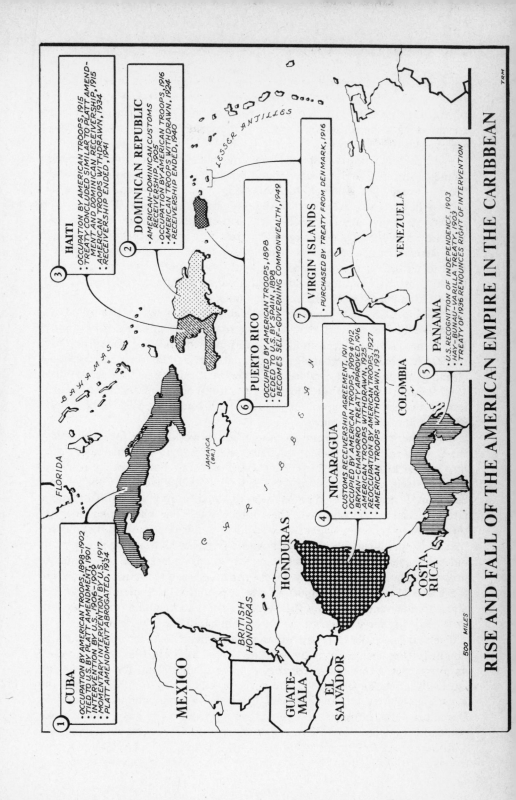

RISE AND FALL OF THE AMERICAN EMPIRE IN THE CARIBBEAN

① CUBA
- OCCUPATION BY AMERICAN TROOPS, 1898-1902
- TIED TO U.S. BY PLATT AMENDMENT, 1901
- INTERVENTION BY U.S. 1906-1909
- MOMENTARY INTERVENTION BY U.S., 1917
- PLATT AMENDMENT ABROGATED, 1934

③ HAITI
- OCCUPATION BY AMERICAN TROOPS, 1915
- TREATY CONCLUDED SIMILAR TO PLATT AMEND-MENT AND DOMINICAN RECEIVERSHIP, 1915
- AMERICAN TROOPS WITHDRAWN, 1934
- RECEIVERSHIP ENDED, 1941

② DOMINICAN REPUBLIC
- AMERICAN-DOMINICAN CUSTOMS RECEIVERSHIP, 1905
- OCCUPATION BY AMERICAN TROOPS, 1916
- AMERICAN TROOPS WITHDRAWN, 1924
- RECEIVERSHIP ENDED, 1940

⑥ PUERTO RICO
- OCCUPIED BY AMERICAN TROOPS, 1898
- CEDED TO U.S. BY SPAIN, 1898
- BECOMES SELF-GOVERNING COMMONWEALTH, 1949

⑦ VIRGIN ISLANDS
- PURCHASED BY TREATY FROM DENMARK, 1916

④ NICARAGUA
- CUSTOMS RECEIVERSHIP AGREEMENT, 1911
- OCCUPIED BY AMERICAN TROOPS, 1909 & 1912
- BRYAN-CHAMORRO TREATY APPROVED, 1916
- AMERICAN TROOPS WITHDRAWN, 1925
- REOCCUPATION BY AMERICAN TROOPS, 1927
- AMERICAN TROOPS WITHDRAWN, 1933

⑤ PANAMA
- U.S. RECOGNITION OF INDEPENDENCE, 1903
- HAY-BUNAU-VARILLA TREATY, 1903
- TREATY OF 1936 RENOUNCES RIGHT OF INTERVENTION

LESSER ANTILLES

BAHAMAS

FLORIDA

JAMAICA (BR.)

C A R I B B E A N

MEXICO

BRITISH HONDURAS

GUATE-MALA

EL SALVADOR

HONDURAS

COSTA RICA

COLOMBIA

VENEZUELA

500 MILES

TRM

commission as the upper house of the Philippine legislature, lowered suffrage requirements, and provided that the governor-general should appoint heads of executive departments, except the head of the Department of Public Instruction, with the consent of the Philippine senate. The Jones Act, however, reserved ultimate sovereignty to the United States.

With a view toward hastening independence, Wilson's governor-general, Francis Burton Harrison, cooperated with the native Nationalist leaders, Sergio Osmeña and Manuel Quezon, in transferring power to native departmental heads and to leaders of the assembly and senate. Filipinos were running their own affairs so well by the end of the Wilson era that Governor Harrison and the president urged Congress to grant independence at once. The Republicans, who now controlled Congress, refused and attempted in 1921 to restore a larger measure of American control. Even so, it was evident by this date that the logic and application of American policy since 1901 could culminate in only one solution—independence.

Pacifying Cuba and establishing a stable government in the island was considerably less difficult than the task that Americans confronted in the Philippines. An American military government did heroic work from 1898 to 1902 in repairing the damage of the civil war, building roads and schools, cleaning up cities, and establishing order in rural districts. Meanwhile, in 1900 the military governor, General Leonard Wood, had arranged the election of a constituent convention, which in 1902 adopted a frame of government for the new republic.

The American government was now ready to withdraw its forces and leave the Cubans to manage their own affairs. But President McKinley and Secretary of War Elihu Root agreed that the United States bore a special responsibility to itself, to the world, and to the Cubans themselves for Cuba's future behavior. Therefore, the administration resolved to draw the Cuban republic into a special relationship with the United States. The Platt Amendment to the army appropriations bill of 1901 spelled out this relationship. It stipulated that Cuba should make no treaties with other powers that might impair its independence, assume no debts it could not pay, carry on the sanitation program begun by the military government, and lease certain naval bases to the United States. Most important was a provision authorizing the United States to intervene in Cuba, if that were necessary to maintain orderly government and discharge Cuba's international obligations.

The Cubans under duress wrote the Platt Amendment into their constitution in 1902 and signed a treaty with the United States in 1903 that embodied its provisions. Peace and prosperity reigned in the island for a brief time, especially after the Cuban-American reciprocity treaty of 1903 opened the American market to Cuban sugar. After the second national elections in December 1905, however, widespread rioting against the government broke out, and President Tomás Estrada Palma appealed for American intervention.

Roosevelt was reluctant to undertake the thankless task. He finally sent troops into the island in 1906 and established a provisional government under

Charles E. Magoon, governor of the Canal Zone. There was some talk in administration circles at this time of making Cuba a permanent protectorate, but Roosevelt repudiated it angrily. New Cuban elections were held; a government was formed; and the Americans withdrew in January 1909. The State Department afterward intervened frequently on a diplomatic level, but American troops were sent into the republic to preserve order only in 1911 and 1917. On each occasion their stay was brief.

Governing America's other major island dependencies[2] proved a relatively simple task. Hawaii, annexed by joint resolution of Congress on July 7, 1898, was made an incorporated territory on April 30, 1900, and thereafter enjoyed all territorial rights of self-government. Puerto Rico, occupied by the American army in July 1898, was given civil government by the Foraker Act in 1900 and a large measure of self-government by the Jones Act of 1917, which also granted American citizenship to inhabitants of Puerto Rico.

The chief diplomatic objective of the American government after 1900 became, as we shall see more fully in the next and later sections, the building of an isthmian canal and the establishment of its own naval supremacy in the Caribbean. As the British withdrew the larger units of their West Indian squadron in 1904–1905, the United States was in fact the dominant power in the Caribbean after this date. But there was always the danger, often more illusory than real, that Germany would attempt to establish naval bases in the area, possibly by acquiring the Danish West Indies. Secretary of State John Hay negotiated a treaty with Denmark in 1902 for purchase of the Danish West Indies, or Virgin Islands; but the Danish Parliament, acting, Americans suspected, under pressure from Germany, refused to ratify the treaty. When the Danish government in 1916 offered to sell the islands at the inflated price of $25 million, the American government concluded the deal without haggling. The islands were transferred to American sovereignty on March 31, 1917, and were governed by the Navy Department until 1931.

47. The Panama Incident and Two Hemispheric Disputes

The dramatic voyage of the battleship *Oregon* from Puget Sound around Cape Horn to Cuban waters in 1898 to participate in the war with Spain underscored the absolute strategic necessity of a canal linking the Atlantic and Pacific oceans, while the development of the West Coast and anticipation

[2]It should be noted that the United States by 1900 had also acquired a string of coaling stations in the Pacific beyond Hawaii: Midway Island, acquired in 1867; the Samoan Islands, occupied jointly with Germany and Great Britain from 1889 to 1899 and divided between Germany and the United States in the latter year; Guam, ceded by Spain in the Treaty of Paris of 1898; and Wake, acquired formally in 1899. All these islands were governed by naval officers under orders from the Navy Department.

of a great American trade with the Far East highlighted the economic need. A diplomatic obstacle, however, stood athwart the achievement of what was by 1900 a great national objective. That obstacle was the Clayton-Bulwer Treaty of 1850, in which the United States and Great Britain had each agreed not to construct a canal without the other's participation. The British government was now eager to win American friendship and gave up its right to participate in building the canal in the first Hay-Pauncefote Treaty, negotiated at Washington in 1900. This treaty, however, forbade the United States to fortify the canal. The Senate refused to ratify the treaty without amendments providing for fortification. The British then went all the way, and the second Hay-Pauncefote Treaty, concluded on November 18, 1901, acknowledged the right of the United States exclusively to build and fortify the canal.

Discussion in Washington now centered on the proper route. President Roosevelt and a large majority of Congress favored the Nicaraguan route, and the Isthmian Canal Commission, which McKinley had appointed, officially concurred in November 1901. The House of Representatives approved the commission's recommendation on January 9, 1902. In the meantime, however, Philippe Bunau-Varilla and William Nelson Cromwell, agents of the French New Panama Canal Company, had been working assiduously to sell their company's rights to the route across the Isthmus of Panama.[3] Faced with the possibility of losing everything, the directors of the French company hastily cut their price from $109 million to $40 million. Their bargain offer, the advantages of the Panamanian route, and the providential eruption of a volcano in Nicaragua caused Roosevelt, the commission, and Congress to change their minds. The Spooner Act, approved by Roosevelt in June 1902, stipulated that the Panamanian route should be used, provided that a satisfactory treaty could be concluded with Colombia, which owned the Isthmus, within a reasonable time. Otherwise, the act declared, the Nicaraguan route should be chosen.

The State Department during the following months applied extraordinary pressure on the Colombian government to sign a treaty authorizing the construction of a Panamanian canal. The Colombian minister left for home in disgust. Secretary Hay then concluded a treaty with the Colombian chargé, Tomás Herrán, on January 22, 1903. It authorized the United States to build a canal across the Isthmus of Panama in return for payment of $10 million and an annual rental of $250,000. The American Senate approved the Hay-Herrán Treaty on March 17, 1903. The Colombian government, however,

---

[3]The builder of the Suez Canal, Ferdinand de Lesseps, organized a French company in 1879 for the construction of a Panamanian canal. Over $250 million had been wasted by 1889 in a vain attempt to conquer tropical diseases and the jungle, and the French company went into bankruptcy. The New Panama Canal Company was organized in 1894 to take over the assets of the bankrupt corporation. Bunau-Varilla, formerly chief engineer of the old company, was a large stockholder in the new concern. Cromwell was a prominent New York attorney with considerable influence in Republican circles.

balked. Public opinion in Colombia opposed the treaty because it impaired the nation's sovereignty in the proposed Canal Zone, but Colombia's leaders had an additional reason for refusing to ratify the treaty. The French company's concession would expire in 1904; all its rights and property would then revert to Colombia. By delaying action for only one year, the Colombian government would be in position to demand the $40 million that would otherwise be paid to the French company.

The fact that the Colombian government was acting well within its rights did not seem significant to President Roosevelt. It was, he said, as if "a road agent had tried to hold up a man," and Colombians were "entitled to precisely the amount of sympathy we extend to other inefficient bandits." He made plans, therefore, to seize the Isthmus and to justify such action by the Treaty of 1846 between the United States and New Granada (Colombia), under which the former guaranteed the neutrality and free transit of the Isthmus.

Meanwhile, Bunau-Varilla was setting plans on foot that would obviate the need for violent American action. Working through his agents in Panama, this astute Frenchman organized a Panamanian "revolution" against Colombia. The State Department took no part in these intrigues, but Bunau-Varilla informed the president and secretary of state of the plot, and he could deduce from what they said that Colombia would not be allowed to suppress a revolution. Roosevelt, moreover, dispatched U.S.S. *Nashville* to Colón, on the Atlantic side of the Isthmus. *Nashville* arrived at Colón on November 2, 1903; on the following day the army of patriots rebelled at Panama City, on the Pacific side. Thereupon the commander of *Nashville* landed troops at Colón and forbade Colombian troops in the city to cross the Isthmus and suppress the rebellion. In fact, the Colombian commander agreed to take his troops back to Colombia in return for a generous gift from Bunau-Varilla's agent.

At 11:35 in the morning of November 6 the American consul at Panama City informed the State Department that the revolution had succeeded. At 12:51 P.M. Secretary Hay instructed the consul to extend de facto recognition to the new government of Panama. Fearing that the Panamanians would now demand a share of the $40 million, Bunau-Varilla persuaded Roosevelt to receive him as the minister from Panama. He signed a treaty with Secretary Hay on November 18 that conveyed to the United States, in perpetuity, a zone ten miles wide across the Isthmus. In return the United States agreed to pay $10 million in cash and an annual rental of $250,000. The leaders of the new republic had no choice but to ratify this treaty.

The American government took possession of the Canal Zone on May 4, 1904, and set about preparing to excavate the great ditch. Before work could proceed, Colonel William C. Gorgas, one of the conquerors of yellow fever, had to clean up the region and subdue the fever-carrying mosquitoes. Congress approved a plan for a lock canal in 1906; Roosevelt gave responsibility to the army engineers in the following year. The first ship passed through the canal on January 7, 1914. Seven months later, on August 15, 1914, the canal was opened to the commerce of the world.

Many thoughtful Americans regretted the means that Roosevelt had employed to accomplish the objective even while they agreed that construction of the Panama Canal was a great boon to mankind. Criticism of Roosevelt's Big Stick diplomacy in Panama was bitter in 1903 and 1904, and the American public began to suffer from acute pangs of conscience as more details were revealed, especially by a congressional committee in 1912. On the other hand, never once did Roosevelt admit that he had perhaps acted unwisely or wrongly. Every action of his administration in the Panamanian affair, he once wrote, had been "in accordance with the highest, finest, and nicest standards of public and governmental ethics." Roosevelt grew bolder in his own defense as the years passed, until in 1911 he finally spoke the truth: "I am interested in the Panama Canal because I started it. . . . I took the Canal Zone and let Congress debate; and while the debate goes on the Canal does also."

Two other diplomatic incidents, the Venezuelan blockade and Canadian-American boundary disputes, revealed the arrogance, strident nationalism, and growing concern for American supremacy in the Western Hemisphere that characterized Roosevelt's diplomacy during the first years of his presidency. The Venezuelan trouble began when the dictator of that republic, Cipriano Castro, refused even to acknowledge his country's indebtedness to European creditors. Great Britain and Germany, later joined by Italy, instituted a blockade of Venezuela in December 1902 after obtaining the State Department's approval. American public opinion viewed the intervention suspiciously from the beginning of the affair. It became greatly agitated when the Germans bombarded Fort San Carlos and destroyed a Venezuelan town in January 1903. Meanwhile, Castro had signified his readiness to submit the debt question to the Hague Court.

The German bombardment also caused Roosevelt to suspect German intentions. For a moment it seemed that the Berlin government would refuse Castro's offer of mediation. Roosevelt, in February 1903, at once called in the German ambassador and told him that he had put Admiral George Dewey in charge of the Atlantic fleet for its annual maneuvers in West Indian waters. Public opinion was so aroused, Roosevelt went on, that he would regretfully be obliged to use force if the Germans took any steps toward acquiring territory in Venezuela or elsewhere in the Caribbean. Roosevelt's warning was probably unnecessary, for the Germans certainly had no desire to risk a serious incident with the United States. They and the British gladly accepted arbitration to escape from a potentially dangerous situation.

The boundary dispute with Canada involved the long finger of Alaska that runs from Alaska proper down the Pacific Coast to the latitude 54° 40'. It first became acute when gold was discovered in the Canadian Klondike region in 1896. Because it seemed clear that the United States had an airtight case, the State Department refused for several years to arbitrate the conflicting claims.[4] Roosevelt was at first inclined to let the matter rest; then he studied the case and concluded that the Canadians had completely fabricated their claim. Secretary of State John Hay, therefore, negotiated a convention with the British government in 1903 providing that six "impartial jurists of repute" —three appointed by the president of the United States and three by the king of England—meet in London and settle the question by majority vote.[5] The tribunal convened in London in September 1903. It soon became evident that the Americans would vote as a bloc, that the two Canadian members would support their country's claims, and that the decision would rest with the British commissioner, Lord Chief Justice Alverstone. Meanwhile, Roosevelt had already decided to ask Congress for authority to run the boundary line himself if the tribunal did not endorse the American claims. After the tribunal convened, Roosevelt carefully repeated this threat in conversation and letters for the benefit of the British foreign office. Whether Lord Alverstone was more influenced by the president's threat than by the merits of the American case, we do not know. In either event, to the disgust of the Canadians he voted consistently with the American commissioners and thus helped to cement Anglo-American friendship.

48. The Roosevelt Corollary to the Monroe Doctrine

On the day before the Senate ratified the Hay–Bunau-Varilla Treaty the Hague Court rendered a verdict that held significant implications for the United States. That tribunal ruled that Germany, Great Britain, and Italy, the very powers that used force against Venezuela, were entitled to first claim on payments by Venezuela to European creditors. In brief, the Hague Court's decision put a premium on intervention at a time when American security interests in the Caribbean were being multiplied by the decision to construct the Panama Canal.

Roosevelt knew after the Venezuelan blockade affair that the United States could not thereafter tolerate European armed intervention on a major scale in the Caribbean. On the other hand, he knew also that he could not command sufficient naval power to stand off Europe by announcing a policy of nonintervention by outside powers in the Western Hemisphere. Some other

[4]The Canadians claimed that the line should run thirty miles inland in a straight line from the sea and should not be adjusted to the heads of the bays and inlets. The Americans argued that the boundary should run along a line thirty miles inland from the heads of these bays and inlets.
[5]The American representatives were Secretary of War Elihu Root, Senator Henry Cabot Lodge of Massachusetts, and former Senator George Turner of Wisconsin, none of whom was either impartial or a jurist of any great repute.

way of reconciling American security needs with European economic interests in the Caribbean had to be found. The British prime minister, Arthur Balfour, had suggested one solution in 1902: Britain would support the Monroe Doctrine and abstain from intervention in the New World if the United States would take responsibility for seeing that the necessity for such intervention did not arise.

A situation developed only two years later in the Dominican Republic that compelled Roosevelt to work out some kind of policy. That Caribbean republic defaulted on its foreign debt of $32 million after prolonged civil war. As there was a strong probability that European powers would intervene if he did not, Roosevelt sent Admiral Dewey and the assistant secretary of state to the troubled republic to investigate. The latter recommended establishment of an American receivership to collect and disburse the Dominican customs. This course was soon agreed upon, and American representatives in Santo Domingo signed a protocol with Dominican officials on January 20, 1905. It stipulated that the United States should collect the Dominican customs, turn over 45 percent of the receipts to the local government, and apply the balance for liquidation of the Dominican Republic's foreign debt.

Roosevelt and Root put the new arrangement into operation so smoothly that neither Dominican pride nor Latin American sensitivity was offended. The American receiver general persuaded the Dominican Republic's creditors to scale down their claims from $32 million to $17 million, and the new debt was refunded at a lower rate of interest. More important was the fact that the little republic enjoyed peace and prosperity as it had never known before, since customs houses were no longer prizes to be won by successful revolutionists.

The Dominican incident was most important in the long run because Roosevelt seized the opportunity it afforded to announce a new Latin American policy—the Roosevelt Corollary to the Monroe Doctrine. Roosevelt forecast his corollary in a public letter to Secretary Root on May 20, 1904, and articulated it more fully in his Annual Message in the following December. Chronic wrongdoing by an American republic might require intervention by some civilized nation, he said on the latter occasion, and "the adherence of the United States to the Monroe Doctrine may force the United States, however reluctantly, in flagrant cases of such wrongdoing or impotence, to the exercise of an international police power." In other words, the president declared that the United States owed it to the European powers to guarantee that no cause for intervention should arise since the Monroe Doctrine prohibited European use of force in the Western Hemisphere.

The Roosevelt Corollary was based upon false assumptions and bad history, for no American statesman, not even Roosevelt, had ever before interpreted the Monroe Doctrine as forbidding temporary European interventions to compel Latin American states to pay debts or discharge international obligations. Roosevelt was simply invoking the sanction of a historic doctrine to justify a major change in American foreign policy: hereafter the United States would tolerate no further European interventions in the Caribbean region.

49. Theodore Roosevelt and the New Diplomacy in Europe and Asia

The years from 1901 to 1909 saw a perilous growth of international tension in Europe and the Far East. Germany's simultaneous determination to dominate the Continent and challenge Britain's naval supremacy brought about a diplomatic revolution in Europe by forcing Britain to seek rapprochement, first with France and then, in 1907, with Russia as well. In the Far East the old balance of power was upset by the rise of Japan and Russia's determination to control Korea and Manchuria. Theodore Roosevelt boldly grasped the nettle danger to help maintain the balance of power in the Far East and to avert a general European war into which the United States might be drawn. That attainment of these objectives required abandonment of the traditional posture did not deter Roosevelt. He played the game of power politics as if he were a divine-right monarch, but he played it well and for the peace of the world.

Roosevelt's chief objective in European affairs was to be an impartial friend in order to help to relieve the growing tension between the Entente powers and Germany. Friction between France and Germany centered during the early years of the twentieth century on Morocco, where France was closing the doors to German and other foreign merchants. France's ally, Russia, became embroiled in war with Japan in 1904, and the kaiser and his foreign office saw an opportunity to call France's hand and perhaps also to break the newly formed Anglo-French entente. The kaiser in 1905 thereupon demanded an international conference to define the status of Morocco. The French refused, and the kaiser appealed to Roosevelt for support. Although he was extremely reluctant to intervene, Roosevelt knew that war might break out unless the French gave in. Therefore, he brought such pressure to bear on England and France that they consented to attend a conference.

The kaiser had won the first round. But the Germans faced a solid Anglo-French bloc, which usually had the support of the American delegates, when the conference met at Algeciras in southern Spain in early 1906. The General Act of Algeciras, signed on April 7, 1906, represented superficially a victory for commercial freedom in Morocco. However, it gave the French such control over the sultanate that they were able quietly to close the door to non-French trade. But that was in the future. At the moment, when a general war seemed probable, Roosevelt had intervened decisively and helped Europeans to find a peaceful alternative.

Working out a viable Far Eastern policy posed an even greater challenge to Roosevelt's skill. The basic American objectives in the Far East had been defined by Secretary of State John Hay in the Open Door notes of 1899 and 1900—to preserve the commercial Open Door to, and the territorial integrity of, China, and to protect the vulnerable Philippines from Japanese attack. Moreover, the American emotional investment in China by 1905 was considerable as a result of a tremendous growth of American missionary, medical, and educational work. Indeed, most Americans now regarded their government as China's sole defender against allegedly rapacious European and Japanese imperialism.

The chief threat to the peace of the Far East in the late 1890s and early 1900s was Russian expansion into Manchuria and Korea. In order to halt Russian expansion, the British concluded an alliance with Japan in 1902. And, when war broke out between Japan and Russia in 1904, American sympathy went to the Nipponese. Convinced that Japan was playing America's game by curbing and offsetting a growing Russian preponderance of power in the Far East, Roosevelt supported the Japanese, even to the extent of warning Germany and France that he would not countenance their going to the support of Russia.

The Japanese had won a series of spectacular victories on land and sea by the spring of 1905, but the empire was so exhausted that it could not maintain a major effort much longer. The Japanese Cabinet, therefore, appealed secretly to President Roosevelt on April 18 to offer mediatory services. The American president was reluctant to undertake what was bound to be a thankless task, yet he believed that a Japanese victory was essential to maintenance of the existing power balance. Thus he invited the belligerents on June 8 to come to a peace conference to end the "terrible and lamentable conflict."

The conference opened at the Portsmouth, New Hampshire, Navy Yard on August 9, 1905. The Japanese commissioners, not satisfied with winning control of southern Manchuria, Korea, and the southern half of Sakhalin from Russia, also demanded a huge monetary indemnity. The latter demand caused American opinion to turn sharply against Japan, and the Japanese leaders, realizing that they had gone too far, yielded this point rather than risk resumption of hostilities.

The Treaty of Portsmouth of 1905 in effect preserved the balance of power that Russian expansion had threatened to destroy. Russia remained an important Pacific power, but Japan now stood as an effective counterpoise. Whether this configuration would protect American interests in the Far East depended upon many factors, the most important of which was the Japanese government's future conduct. Roosevelt could not control Japanese policy; he could only try to channel it in a direction advantageous to the United States. Even before the Portsmouth Conference opened, he sent Secretary of War Taft, then in Manila, to Tokyo to come to an immediate understanding with the Japanese Cabinet. Taft concluded an executive agreement with the prime minister, Taro Katsura, on July 25, 1905. By its terms the United States recognized Japan's suzerainty over Korea, and Japan disavowed any designs on the Philippines.

The Japanese welcomed Roosevelt's recognition of their new status in the Far East, but events were developing in the United States that threatened to impair good relations between the two countries. The most dangerous trouble was brewing in California on account of Japanese immigration into that state.[6] It seemed following the Russo-Japanese War that the relatively small stream of Japanese immigrants would become a rushing tide. With Congress indifferent to the problem, Californians organized to take matters into their own hands. As the first step in an anti-Japanese campaign, the San Francisco board of education adopted an order on October 11, 1906, requiring the segregation of all Oriental school children.

The Japanese people, still flushed with their victory over the largest power in Europe, were in no mood to let this insult pass. The Japanese ambassador lodged a formal protest with the secretary of state on October 25, 1906, while irresponsible newspapers in both countries tried to stir war passions. It was a dangerous situation, but Roosevelt acted with superb caution and good sense. He did not ignore the fact that war was a possibility, but he was certain that the segregation order violated the Japanese-American Treaty of 1894, which guaranteed most favored treatment to Japanese subjects in the United States. He was determined if necessary to use the army to protect the rights of the Japanese in California; at the same time he understood that Japanese immigration was the root of the trouble and resolved to bring it to an end.

Roosevelt solved the difficulty by a judicious mixture of courtesy and sternness. At his invitation the mayor and board of education of San Francisco came to the White House in February 1907. Roosevelt promised to use diplomacy to stop Japanese immigration; in return, the school board revoked the segregation order. Then the president negotiated, in 1907 and 1908, the so-called Gentlemen's Agreement with the Japanese. In this document the imperial government promised to issue no more passports to peasants or workers coming directly to the continental United States.

In order to disabuse the Japanese of any notion that he had acted out of fear of them, Roosevelt decided in the summer of 1907 to send an American fleet of sixteen battleships on a cruise around the world—by way of the Pacific. While the fleet was on its epochal voyage the Japanese foreign minister instructed his emperor's ambassador in Washington, Baron Takahira, to open negotiations for a comprehensive understanding with the American government on all phases of the Far Eastern question. The outcome was the Root-Takahira Agreement of November 30, 1908, by which Japan and the

[6]There were 12,000 Japanese in California in 1900. In that year the Japanese government announced that it would cease issuing passports to laborers who wished to go to the continental United States. Japanese kept coming to California, however, at the rate of 500 to 1,000 a year until 1905.

United States agreed to help maintain the status quo in the Pacific, to respect each other's territorial possessions, and to support jointly the Open Door in China and the independence and territorial integrity of that country. Here indeed was a program of cooperation which, if faithfully adhered to, might provide a modus vivendi for Japanese-American peace for all time to come.

The United States was a world power in fact as well as in name when Roosevelt left the White House in 1909. By blunt and sometimes questionable diplomacy Roosevelt had established undisputed American supremacy in the Caribbean area. By abandoning old traditions against interference in non-American affairs, he had helped to preserve the peace of Europe. And by a policy of realism, he had supported the rise of Japan and come to friendly understanding with that power. This was no mean record for a man who has often been described as an amateur diplomatist.

50. Taft and "Dollar Diplomacy" in the Caribbean and the Far East

William Howard Taft, who was unfit and unwilling to be a strong leader in world affairs, deliberately abandoned Roosevelt's policy of participation in European politics and blundered into partial reversal of Roosevelt's policy of maintaining Japanese good will. But the new president and his secretary of state, Philander C. Knox, could not reverse Roosevelt's policy of protecting American supremacy in the Caribbean area without endangering national security. In fact, they went far beyond the limited kind of intervention that Roosevelt and Root had practiced and devised a new policy, "dollar diplomacy," to strengthen American power in the approaches to the canal. It involved using private American banking resources to displace European concessionaires and creditors, and hence to strengthen American influence in the Caribbean region, where, as Knox said, "the malady of revolutions and financial collapse is most acute precisely . . . where it is most dangerous to us."

Soon after taking office in 1909, Knox tried to persuade American bankers to take over the debt owed British investors by Honduras. The secretary signed a treaty with the Honduran minister in 1911 for refunding of that country's foreign debt by American bankers and establishment of an American customs receivership. The government of Honduras, however, refused to ratify the convention. Again, in 1910, Knox persuaded four New York banking firms to invest in the National Bank of the Republic of Haiti in order to help the black republic to stabilize its currency.

These activities were merely a prelude to Knox's most important action in the Caribbean area, his intervention in Nicaragua. That country at the beginning of the Taft administration was ruled by a dictator, José Zelaya, who was nursing an old grudge against the United States. He vented his spleen on the United States–Nicaragua Concession, a mining company owned by Pittsburgh capitalists, and even went so far as to make plans to offer an option on the Nicaraguan canal route to the Japanese government. Officials of the United States–Nicaragua Concession helped to engineer a revolution against Zelaya in 1909, and the State Department sent marines to the Nicaraguan city of Bluefields to protect foreign nationals and property. As a consequence of Knox's interference, Zelaya was overthrown and Adolfo Díaz, former secretary of the United States–Nicaragua Concession, was installed as president in 1911 with the State Department's blessing.

Knox now moved swiftly to bring Nicaragua completely under American control. He signed a treaty with the Nicaraguan minister on June 6, 1911, for refunding of the Nicaraguan foreign debt by two New York banking firms and establishment of an American customs receivership. Democrats in the Senate blocked ratification of this, the Knox-Castrillo Treaty. At the request of the State Department, however, the New York bankers advanced $1,-500,000 to Nicaragua and received in return majority control of the state railways and the National Bank of Nicaragua. An American receiver-general of Nicaraguan customs was appointed by the banking houses and approved by the two governments later in the same year.

As it turned out, the new Díaz government did not have the support of a majority of Nicaraguans. In defiance of the State Department they continued to look to Zelaya and his Liberal party for leadership. The Liberals raised the standards of revolt in 1912, and Díaz would have fallen had not Taft rushed 2,700 marines to Nicaragua to suppress the uprising. So bitter was anti-Díaz and anti-American sentiment that the marines continued to occupy the country for many years.

The American intervention and occupation did not solve Nicaragua's most pressing requirement—her need for financial assistance in refunding her foreign debt and paying claims arising from the revolutions of 1909 and 1912. Chiefly to satisfy the national treasury's need for ready cash, Secretary Knox signed a treaty in 1913 with the Nicaraguan minister for payment by the United States to Nicaragua of $3 million. In return, Nicaragua granted to the United States an exclusive option on its canal route, the privilege of establishing a naval base on the Gulf of Fonseca, on the Pacific side, and a ninety-nine-year lease on the Great Corn and Little Corn islands in the Caribbean. The treaty was negotiated too late to be ratified before the Sixty-second Congress expired on March 4, 1913, and the Wilson administration inherited the unpleasant task of persuading the Senate to ratify the convention.

The objectives of dollar diplomacy in the Far East were nearly as ambitious as in the Caribbean. Toward the end of the Roosevelt administration a clique in the State Department headed by a young career diplomat, Willard Straight, began to lay plans to sponsor American investment in Manchuria in order to offset Japanese influence in that province. Restrained by Secretary Root's firm hand, Straight and his colleagues came into control of Far Eastern policy when Knox took the helm at the State Department. Their opportunity to press for a more aggressive policy came in 1909, when a consortium of British, French, and German bankers signed a contract with the Chinese government to build a network of railways in central and southern China.

Straight and his friends in the Far Eastern division of the State Department easily won Knox to their side by arguing that American participation in the consortium was necessary to enable the United States to defend the Open Door and the territorial integrity of China. Accordingly, the State Department in 1909 demanded that American bankers be permitted to participate in the loan. An American banking syndicate formed by J. P. Morgan & Company was admitted to the consortium, along with Japanese and Russian bankers, in May 1911. But for various reasons the project never prospered, and President Wilson, in March 1913, announced the withdrawal of the American group.

Meanwhile, Secretary Knox pressed forward in a more reckless move—that is, with his ill-fated proposal, made in late 1909, for internationalization of Manchurian railways in order to offset growing Japanese and Russian influence in the province. The British were at this very time encouraging Japanese expansion in Manchuria in order to keep the Japanese at safe distance from the British sphere of influence; they promptly rebuffed Knox's suggestion. The Japanese, on the other hand, regarded the proposal as an attempt to undermine their influence in an area that Roosevelt had tacitly recognized as being within the Japanese orbit. In short, Knox's proposal was ill conceived and naively made. It angered the British, drove the Japanese and Russians into an anti-American bloc, and even alienated the American banking group.

The historian must conclude that, on the whole, Taft's record in foreign affairs was even more barren than in domestic politics. The most important outcome of dollar diplomacy in Latin America was an armed intervention in Nicaragua that lacked strategic necessity, failed to bring peace to Nicaragua, and intensified anti-American feeling in Latin America. The result of dollar diplomacy in the Far East was an embittering of Japanese-American relations without any benefit to the United States. For the failure of his foreign policy Taft had only himself and his secretary of state to blame. Where Roosevelt had been wise and farsighted, Taft was indolently ineffectual; where Root had been suave, Knox was often offensive. The contrast goes far toward explaining the unsatisfactory state of American foreign relations when Woodrow Wilson took office on March 4, 1913.

51. The New Freedom Abroad

Humanitarians hailed Wilson's inauguration in 1913 as beginning a more idealistic era in American foreign relations. Most Democrats since 1901 had consistently condemned Roosevelt's and Taft's policies of military intervention, quasi-protectorates, and dollar diplomacy. They stood for early independence for the Filipinos and fought for a moderate naval building program designed only to implement a diplomacy of defense. The character and convictions of the new makers of American foreign policy also seemed to promise a new era in diplomacy. No public leader of his generation was more eloquent in articulating the liberal, idealistic international program than Woodrow Wilson. Long before he became the prime exponent of international organization and collective security, Wilson had championed a diplomacy that sought the good of mankind above the selfish interests of the United States. Moreover, Wilson's secretary of state, William Jennings Bryan, was easily the leading opponent of imperialism and navalism and a pioneer in the movement to advance peace through arbitration and conciliation.

The first sign of a New Freedom in foreign policy was Bryan's ambitious peace plan, launched only a few months after Wilson's inauguration. In its practical aspects, Bryan's plan was based soundly upon the experience of his predecessors in trying to steer arbitration treaties through the Senate. Secretary of State John Hay had negotiated a series of arbitration treaties that excluded all disputes involving vital interest and national honor. But the Senate in 1905 amended these treaties to make its consent to each arbitration necessary, and Roosevelt withdrew them. Secretary Root three years later persuaded Roosevelt to yield to the Senate's demand; he then negotiated twenty-five limited arbitration agreements in 1908 and 1909. However, the Senate rebelled again when President Taft and Secretary Knox signed new treaties with Britain and France in 1911 providing for arbitration of all "justiciable" questions, including disputes affecting national interest and honor. The upper house consented to ratification of these treaties in 1912 but exempted all important questions from possible arbitration. Taft in disgust refused to promulgate the mutilated treaties.

Bryan found a solution that he thought would achieve unlimited arbitration without arousing the Senate's suspicions. Bryan's treaties provided, not for arbitration, but for submission of all disputes to permanent commissions for investigation for a period of one year. Neither party would resort to war or increase its armaments during this interval of "cooling off." After the investigation was completed, the parties might accept or reject the commission's findings. Both countries would then be free to go to war, but Bryan was confident that hostilities could not occur in such circumstances. Bryan signed the first conciliation treaty with El Salvador on August 7, 1913, and negotiated twenty-nine other such agreements during the following year with Great Britain, France, Italy, and lesser powers.

Further evidence of New Freedom idealism was the administration's withdrawal of the American banking group from the six-power consortium that had been formed in 1911 to finance construction of the Hukuang Railway in China. The United States, Wilson said on March 18, 1913, could not approve the loan agreement because it would lead to intolerable interference in Chinese affairs. A few weeks later, as if to emphasize his determination to cut loose from all such imperialistic conspiracies, Wilson recognized the new Republic of China without first consulting other powers.

A third example of idealistic diplomacy was Wilson's settlement of the Anglo-American dispute provoked when Congress, in August 1912, exempted American ships engaged in coastwise trade from payment of Panama Canal tolls. The British foreign office objected soon afterward that the exemption violated the Hay-Pauncefote Treaty's promise of equal rates for ships of all nations. Wilson could not run the risk of splitting his party so long as the tariff and banking bills hung in the fire; but after these measures were safely passed, he met the Senate foreign relations committee, on January 28, 1914, reviewed the critical state of American foreign relations, and urged repeal of the exemption provision in order to restore fully cordial relations with the British government. The president reiterated his plea before a joint session of Congress on March 5, 1914. The Hearst press roared, and some Democrats in Congress threatened rebellion. But the House of Representatives approved a repeal bill on March 31, which the Senate then passed on June 11, 1914.

Wilson's and Bryan's determination to do the moral if unpleasant thing in foreign affairs was evidenced, finally, in the treaty of reparation that they negotiated with Colombia to make amends for Rooseveltian sins. In a treaty signed at Bogotá on April 6, 1914, the United States expressed "sincere regret" for anything that had occurred to impair good relations between the two countries, agreed to pay $25 million to Colombia for the loss of Panama, gave the government of Colombia free use of the canal, and assured Colombian citizens equality of treatment with Americans in the Canal Zone. Roosevelt's friends in the Senate blocked ratification in 1914 and again in 1917, but the Wilson administration's intentions had been clearly demonstrated. The sight of the great government of the United States apologizing to a helpless neighbor stirred a wave of warm and cordial feeling toward the United States throughout Latin America.[7]

52. New Troubles with Japan, 1913–1917

The record of the Wilson administration's relations with Japan from 1913 to 1917 demonstrates that good intentions alone do not always suffice to settle delicate international disputes. The possibility of new difficulties was raised during the campaign of 1912, when Democrats and Progressives launched a campaign in California for a law prohibiting Japanese ownership of land. Instead of perceiving the dangers, Wilson conferred with California leaders

[7]The Harding administration negotiated a new treaty in 1921 that awarded the Colombian government $25 million but omitted the specific apology.

and even volunteered a method to exclude Japanese from land ownership without violating a Japanese-American commercial treaty of 1911. Acting upon the president's suggestion, the California Assembly, on April 15, 1913, passed an alien bill prohibiting, in an indirect manner, Japanese ownership of land.

A crisis suddenly developed when news of the California Assembly's action was published in Japan. Then the California Senate exacerbated the tension on April 21 by adopting an alien land bill that was openly anti-Japanese. A rising war fever in Japan brought Wilson to his senses and compelled him to act. He first addressed a public appeal to the Californians, urging them not to make their alien land bill openly discriminatory. Next he sent Bryan to Sacramento to plead for caution. Wilson's and Bryan's supplications did not budge the California leaders from their determination to humiliate the Japanese people. The legislature on May 9, 1913, approved a bill excluding from land ownership persons "ineligible to citizenship"—words hateful to the Japanese. Governor Hiram W. Johnson signed the measure in spite of last-minute appeals from Wilson and Bryan.

For a brief moment it now seemed possible that Japan and the United States might be heading for war. The Japanese ambassador lodged a strong protest with the State Department on May 9; Japanese public opinion was at a dangerous point of anger. So explosive was the situation that the joint board of the army and navy warned Wilson on May 13 and 14 that war with Japan was "not only possible, but even probable." The joint board, besides, urged the president to transfer American warships in Chinese waters to the Philippines to help avert a surprise Japanese attack.

It was a dangerous situation, but Wilson and Bryan kept their heads. Correctly assuming that the Japanese government did not want war, they rejected the joint board's advice and relied exclusively on diplomacy. Many notes passed between Tokyo and Washington during the remainder of 1913 and the first months of 1914. The Japanese government proposed a treaty guaranteeing the mutual right of land ownership. In reply, Wilson and Bryan promised to negotiate such a treaty when it was politically possible to obtain ratification. But that time did not come soon enough, and the new Japanese foreign minister, Baron Kato, abruptly terminated the negotiations in June 1914. Thus relations between the two governments were gravely unsettled when the war in Europe spread to the Far East and raised new difficulties for the United States.

As Wilson and Bryan perceived, there was now the grave danger that Japan would take advantage of Europe's adversity to extend her influence in China. When Japan entered the war on the side of the Allies and seized the German naval base and concession in Shantung Province of China, the American leaders were disturbed but helpless to prevent such action. When the Japanese government proceeded in the early weeks of 1915 to attempt to impose a treaty embodying twenty-one demands on China, adherence to which would

have made China virtually a satellite of Japan, Wilson and Bryan entered the
ensuing controversy as defenders of China, voicing their opposition to the
more extreme Japanese demands in a series of statements to the press and in
notes to the Japanese and Chinese governments during April and May 1915.
The most important of these was a caveat that Robert Lansing, counselor of
the State Department, had drafted and that Bryan sent to Tokyo and Peking
on May 11. It declared that the United States would not recognize any
Sino-Japanese agreement violating the political and territorial integrity of
China and the Open Door policy. The British foreign office had meanwhile
become aroused and applied heavy pressure on the Tokyo Cabinet in favor
of a policy of moderation. The upshot of these Anglo-American protests was
the Japanese government's abandonment for the time being of its plan to
bring China under its control.

Following this crisis the Japanese pressed forward to enhance their economic position in China by offering capital that European bankers could no
longer supply. Wilson responded by reversing his position on an international
bankers' loan to China. Through the State Department he announced on
November 9, 1917, that the American government was contemplating creation of a new four-power consortium of American, British, French, and
Japanese bankers to supply desperately needed capital to China. Actually, the
American determination to offset Japanese economic expansion in China had
been evident months before the announcement of November 9 and had
prompted the Japanese government to ask the Washington leaders for a frank
avowal of their policy. When correspondence failed to yield satisfactory
understanding, the Tokyo foreign office sent a special envoy, Viscount
Kikujiro Ishii, to Washington. Intense if intermittent discussions between
Ishii and the secretary of state, Robert Lansing, ensued between September
6 and November 2, 1917. The extent of their divergence became clear when
Ishii insisted that the United States recognize Japan's paramount interest in
China, in the same way that Japan had recognized the paramount American
interest in Mexico. Lansing replied that Japan should reaffirm her allegiance
to the Open Door and help maintain Chinese independence.

The two men were unable to come to clear and firm agreement and, as
diplomats often do, used ambiguous language to make a show of accord. In
an agreement signed on November 2, 1917, the United States recognized that
Japan had special interests in China, especially in provinces contiguous to
Japanese possessions—presumably Manchuria and Shantung Province. In
return, Japan reaffirmed her support of the Open Door and the territorial and
administrative independence of China. Moreover, Japan promised in a secret
protocol not to take advantage of the war situation to seek special rights in
China that would abridge the interests of citizens of friendly powers. Ambiguous though it was, the Lansing-Ishii Agreement served to stabilize Japanese-
American relations until a more comprehensive understanding could be
achieved after the war ended.

53. Further Penetration of Central America and the Caribbean

In contrast to Wilson's and Bryan's promises of a new policy of nonintervention toward Latin America stands a record of wholesale diplomatic and military interference in the affairs of neighboring states unparalleled at any time in the annals of American diplomacy. How can this contradiction between promise and performance be explained?

To begin with, the Wilson administration inherited a foreign policy aimed primarily at protecting the future Panamanian life line. This policy could not be reversed without abandoning what seemed to be the cornerstone of the American security system. Actually, the Democratic leaders believed implicitly in the necessity of preserving American supremacy in the Caribbean and Central American areas, and they were willing to undertake even bolder programs than their Republican predecessors had envisaged.

In the second place, although Bryan and the Democratic party had solemnly condemned so-called dollar diplomacy as insidious financial imperialism, circumstances compelled the new secretary of state to use the very instrument that he had denounced. In the beginning, however, Bryan had other plans. To free Latin America from the snares of foreign concessionaires and bankers, he proposed a farsighted plan. It envisaged the assumption and refunding by the United States government of the external debts of the small Latin American states. But Wilson rejected this proposal as being too "radical," and Bryan concluded that he had no alternative but to continue to use private capital to consolidate American influence in a vital area.

These two points help to explain why there was no essential change in the Latin American policies of the United States in 1913. But the motives behind Wilson's and Bryan's extension of the Roosevelt-Taft policy lay deeper than simply a desire to protect American security interests. Wilson and Bryan were missionaries of democracy and freedom. They sincerely wanted to help less fortunate neighboring peoples to find peace and develop democratic institutions. Thus they intervened, not to subjugate and enslave, but to enlighten, instruct, and liberate.

The formulation of their program in Nicaragua shows how all these factors combined to shape and control policy. Bryan could not withdraw American troops from Nicaragua without inviting civil war and the inauguration of a bitterly anti-American regime in an area close to the canal. He continued, therefore, to support the Knox-sponsored Díaz government, which the Nicaraguan people would almost certainly have overthrown had they been free to do so.

Having concluded that it was necessary to control the government of Nicaragua, Bryan was also willing to go the whole way and regularize Nicaragua's special relation to the United States in treaty form. Counsel for the Nicaraguan government in June 1913 presented to the State Department the draft of a document that was later known as the Bryan-Chamorro Treaty. Like the agreement that Secretary Knox had negotiated and the Senate had refused to ratify a few months before, the Bryan-Chamorro Treaty provided for an American option on the Nicaraguan canal route for $3 million and also for other privileges. Unlike Knox's instrument, the Bryan-Chamorro Treaty also permitted the United States to intervene in Nicaragua to preserve order, protect property, and maintain Nicaraguan independence. The Senate approved the treaty on February 18, 1916, but only after the provision authorizing American intervention in Nicaragua's internal affairs had been removed. Actually, the deletion made no difference in State Department policy, which continued to be one of active interference in all phases of Nicaraguan politics.

The conclusion of this treaty marked only the beginning of a further penetration of the Caribbean area that culminated in the occupation of the Dominican Republic and Haiti. This final penetration occurred, not because the Wilson administration sought imperialistic advantage or feared immediate European intervention, but rather because intervention and American control seemed the only way to save the Dominican and Haitian peoples from anarchy and sheer starvation.

The Dominican Republic by the summer of 1914 was approaching a condition of anarchy as a result of recent revolutions. Officials in the Latin American affairs division of the State Department argued that only full-scale military occupation would save the Dominican people from chaos. Wilson intervened, first, by trying to persuade the warring chieftains to lay down their arms, agree upon a provisional president, and allow the United States to assume control of the Dominican finances and police force. The Dominican leaders consented to the first two proposals but would not sign a treaty making their country a virtual protectorate of the United States. Wilson decided that the time for drastic action had come when the leader of the strongest rebel band launched a new revolution in 1916. Wilson gave the orders, and American marine and naval forces seized Santo Domingo on May 15, 1916, and took control of the government. And when the Dominican chieftains still refused to ratify the proposed treaty, the American naval commander established a military government on November 29, 1916.

Haitians had also indulged frequently in the revolutionary habit, but they had contrived before 1915 to pay their external debts and escape foreign intervention and control. However, the political situation in the black republic grew so anarchic during 1914 and 1915 that the State Department concluded that American control of Haitian customhouses was the only possible way to remove the incentive to revolution. An excuse for intervention presented itself when a new revolution exploded in June 1915. American marines and bluejackets seized Port-au-Prince on July 28, and the commanding American naval officer took control of the Haitian government on August 9 and compelled the national assembly to elect a pro-American, Sudre Dartiguenave, as president of Haiti. The State Department, moreover, now imposed a treaty—revised to provide not only American supervision of Haitian finances but also establishment of a native constabulary under American control—upon the puppet regime.[8]

To such extremes was the administration of Woodrow Wilson carried by the desire to protect American interests and end the reign of tyranny and anarchy in the Caribbean and Central American regions. The one feature of this policy that prevented it from becoming imperialistic was the idealism that prompted Wilson and especially Bryan to adopt it. Instead of using American diplomatic and military power to promote the exclusive material interests of American citizens, Bryan guarded the interests of the people of Nicaragua, Haiti, or Cuba as vigilantly as he guarded the welfare of the American people. On numerous occasions, for example, he prevented corrupt Latin American politicians from selling special rights and resources to American bankers.

Wilson and Bryan climaxed their hemispheric policy by attempting to unite American republics in a Pan-American Alliance, binding them to respect one another's territorial integrity, guarantee one another's political independence, and settle all disputes by peaceful methods. Practically all the small states approved the proposed pact, and Brazil enthusiastically supported it. Argentina, on the other hand, was not pleased, while Chile was positively opposed to any treaty that would bind her hands in her old border dispute with Peru. As American diplomats were never able to overcome Chile's opposition, Wilson's plans for a hemispheric League of Nations collapsed.

54. Wilson and the Mexican Revolution

The crucial test of New Freedom diplomacy came when Wilson sought to apply a policy of helpfulness through interference in Mexico from 1913 to 1917. The background of the story can be told briefly. The old regime of Porfirio Díaz had been overthrown in 1911 by the reformer Francisco I. Madero. Madero tried to destroy the special privileges of the upper classes and provoked the inevitable counterrevolution. The head of the army, Victoriano Huerta, seized control of the Mexican government on February 18, 1913, and arranged the murder of the deposed president five days later. The Taft administration did not recognize Huerta as provisional president, but Britain, France, Germany, and other powers followed conventional practice in according recognition to the new regime.

This was the situation when Wilson was inaugurated in March 1913. There were appeals from representatives of American investors in Mexico to accord

[8]When Dartiguenave balked at signing away his country's independence, Secretary of State Lansing threatened either to find a new president of Haiti or else to establish complete military government. Dartiguenave signed the treaty on September 16, 1915. It was ratified by the Haitian senate on November 12, 1915, and approved by the United States Senate on February 28, 1916.

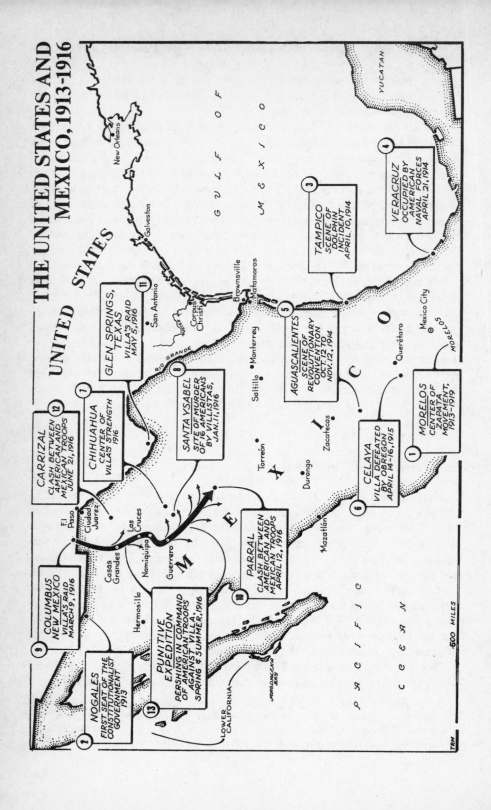

THE UNITED STATES AND MEXICO, 1913–1916

immediate de facto recognition to Huerta's government, but Wilson hesitated because of personal revulsion against Huerta and his "government of butchers." Another development caused him to hesitate further. It was the beginning of an anti-Huerta movement in the northern states of Mexico, led by the governor of Coahuila, Venustiano Carranza. Wilson, therefore, waited to see whether Huerta could consolidate his power.

The American president had decided on a policy by the middle of June 1913. The secretary of state informed Huerta on June 14 that the United States would attempt to mediate between Huerta's government and the followers of Carranza, called Constitutionalists, if Huerta would hold early constitutional elections and agree not to be a candidate for the presidency. President Wilson a short time later recalled the American ambassador from Mexico City and sent John Lind, former governor of Minnesota, to confer with the Mexican leaders. Lind's objectives, in brief, were to obtain Huerta's elimination and the establishment through Wilson's mediation of a constitutional government that the United States could recognize and support.

Wilson of course assumed that the Mexicans would welcome his assistance. The fact was, however, that all factions, Constitutionalists as well as Huertistas, bitterly resented the president's interference and applauded when Huerta rejected Wilson's offer of mediation. Thus rebuffed, Wilson went before a joint session of Congress on August 27, 1913, explained his mediation proposal and Huerta's rebuff, and declared that the United States would adopt a policy of "watchful waiting."

During the next four or five weeks the situation in Mexico seemed to improve. Then Sir Lionel Carden, the new British minister, arrived in Mexico City. Carden was an intimate of S. Weetman Pearson, Lord Cowdray, who had large oil interests in Mexico. As Mexico was then practically the sole source of oil for the Royal Navy, one major objective of British foreign policy was to keep oil flowing from Mexican wells. Wilson suspected that Cowdray controlled Huerta and that Carden was sent to Mexico City to keep Huerta in power. In any event, on October 10, 1913, the day before Carden officially presented his credentials at the presidential palace, Huerta arrested most of the members of the chamber of deputies and inaugurated a full-fledged military dictatorship.

Wilson was so angered by Huerta's usurpation that he abandoned his policy of watchful waiting at once. First, he informed the powers that he would proceed to employ "such means as may be necessary" to depose Huerta. Next, he prepared an angry note to the British foreign office, accusing the British leaders of keeping Huerta in power against his wishes. The note was never sent, but in subsequent correspondence the president made it clear that Britain would have to choose between the friendship of Huerta and that of the United States. In view of the then perilous state of European affairs, the British foreign secretary, Sir Edward Grey, had no alternative but to withdraw support from Huerta.

Wilson now proceeded to his second step. This move involved nothing less than the cooperation of the United States and the Constitutionalists in a war against Huerta, to be followed by the establishment of a new government in Mexico. The president in November 1913 sent an agent to Carranza's camp at Nogales, Mexico, with an offer of cooperation and support. Wilson was surprised and indignant when Carranza replied that the Constitutionalists did not want American support, would oppose with arms the entry of American troops into Mexico, and would proceed to establish their own government in their own way. All that the Constitutionalists desired from the American government, Carranza said, was the privilege of buying arms and ammunition in the United States.

Wounded by Carranza's reply, Wilson withheld aid from the Constitutionalists for two months after the Nogales conference. But as it became increasingly apparent that the revolutionists could never overthrow Huerta without a larger supply of war matériel, Wilson, on February 3, 1914, revoked the arms embargo that Taft had applied. Nonetheless, the speedy triumph of the Constitutionalists that Wilson confidently expected did not occur. In fact, by the beginning of April 1914 Huerta was stronger than he had been before the arms embargo was lifted.

For Wilson this was a catastrophic development, because the United States would now have to use force to fulfill the president's pledge to depose Huerta. Yet how could this be done without provoking war also with the Constitutionalists? There seemed no way out of the dilemma until a trivial incident at Tampico on April 10, 1914, offered an excuse for drastic action. A Huertista colonel arrested the paymaster and several of the crew of the U.S.S. *Dolphin* when they landed their whaleboat behind the lines at Tampico, then under attack by the Constitutionalists. When the Huertista commander in Tampico heard of the incident he at once ordered the release of the American sailors and sent an apology to Admiral Henry T. Mayo, commander of the American fleet off Veracruz.

That would have been the end of the matter had not Mayo rejected the apology and demanded a twenty-one-gun salute to the American flag and had not the president backed up Mayo's demand. Huerta agreed to render the salute, but only provided an American warship returned a simultaneous volley; Wilson drew war plans with his Cabinet and military and naval advisers. Then he went before a joint session of Congress on April 20 and asked for authority to compel Huerta to respect the honor of the United States. Before Congress could act on the president's request, news arrived in Washington of the impending arrival at Veracruz of a German merchant ship, the *Ypiranga,* with a load of ammunition for the Huerta government. Without waiting for congressional sanction, Wilson on April 21 ordered the fleet to occupy Veracruz and prevent the *Ypiranga* from unloading her cargo. Veracruz was in American hands by April 22 after sharp fighting and heavy casualties.

Wilson may have had a full-scale invasion in mind when he began the Veracruz operation, but if he did, unforeseen events soon compelled him to change plans. For one thing, humanitarians in the United States were astonished by the president's belligerence and demanded that he find a peaceful solution. For another, Carranza denounced the Veracruz occupation as wanton aggression and threatened to resist the American forces if they attempted to move against Mexico City.

But how could the United States withdraw without losing face? How could war with Mexico be averted so long as American troops remained on Mexican soil? There seemed to be no answer to these questions until the Argentine, Brazilian, and Chilean envoys in Washington, on April 25, offered to mediate the dispute. In mutual relief Wilson and Huerta accepted the offer. The American and Mexican delegates met at Niagara Falls, Canada, from May 20 until July 2, 1914. As the days passed Huerta's power waned, and the Constitutionalists drove closer to Mexico City. Huerta abdicated on July 15, 1914, after taking one parting shot at the "puritan" in the White House; Carranza and his armies entered Mexico City on August 20.

Huerta's retirement, however, did not signal the beginning of peace in Mexico, for a rupture in the Constitutionalist ranks soon plunged Mexico anew into civil war. The chief cause of the schism was the rivalry between the first chief of the revolution, Carranza, and his most successful general, Francisco, or "Pancho," Villa, who was ignorant and unfit for political leadership. Into this critical and delicate situation the American government moved with alacrity. The president, in August 1914, sent an agent to Mexico to propose a convention of revolutionary leaders and subsequent establishment of a new provisional government which, as the agent later said, "would place Villa in control."[9] Carranza and his generals approved the American plan, and Carranza agreed to retire, provided Villa also gave up his command. That Villa had no intention of withdrawing, however, was evidenced when he declared war on Carranza three weeks before the convention was to meet.

In spite of this evidence of Villa's bad faith, the convention did assemble at Aguascalientes from October 12 through November 12, 1914. Villa controlled a majority and established a provisional government in Mexico City that enjoyed the limited support of the United States for a time. However, Carranza's leading generals, Alvaro Obregón and Pablo Gonzáles, withdrew and joined Carranza in his new headquarters at Veracruz, recently evacuated by the American forces.

Thus the civil war began again between the constructive wing of the revolu-

---

[9]The reasons for the adoption of this policy do no credit to Wilson's and Bryan's judgment. On the one hand, Villa had been depicted in a friendly American press as a genuine social reformer. More important, he had made it clear to Wilson that he would welcome the support and guidance of the United States. On the other hand, Carranza had already demonstrated that under no circumstances would he welcome American advice or reciprocate the friendship that Wilson had earlier proffered.

tion headed by Carranza and the plundering elements under Villa's control. While Villa waited for the Carrancistas to collapse, Carranza broadened his reform program, strengthened his armies, and began a military campaign in January 1915 that drove Villa and his forces northward from the capital. Then Obregón destroyed Villa's offensive power in one great battle at Celaya in April 1915, and the bandit chieftain sought refuge in his native stronghold of Chihuahua.

The swift destruction of Villa's government compelled the Wilson administration to revert to a policy of neutrality in the Mexican conflict. At the same time, the renewal of the civil war set off a vociferous demand in the United States for intervention. For a time Wilson rebuffed these counsels and insisted that Mexicans be allowed to settle their problems in their own way. Gradually, however, his resistance weakened, and, on June 2, 1915, he warned the rival factions to compose their differences or else expect corrective measures by the United States. Two months later, furthermore, Wilson and his new secretary of state, Robert Lansing, called in leading Latin American envoys in Washington to help formulate a plan to eliminate Carranza and create a new provisional government in Mexico.

Events over which Wilson had no control, however, again took over direction of his Mexican policy. First, while Wilson and Lansing talked, Carranza acted. By August 1915 it was evident that Carranza's power was growing daily and that intervention by the United States would provoke a general war with the Mexican people. Second, the United States became embroiled during the summer of 1915 in a serious diplomatic controversy with Germany over the use of submarines against Allied merchant ships. As the possibility of war with Germany increased, Wilson's and Lansing's willingness to risk military involvement in Mexico diminished. Finally, the two American leaders learned that the German government was trying to encourage a war between Mexico and its neighbor in order to lessen American pressure against the unrestricted use of submarines. This revelation caused the Washington government to take a hard second look at plans for intervention.

The only alternative to intervention seemed to be recognition and support of Carranza. Hence Wilson swiftly reversed American policy, persuaded the Latin American envoys to cooperate, and extended de facto recognition to Carranza's provisional government on October 19, 1915. During the next three months relations between the United States and the de facto regime were friendly, and Wilson's troubles would have been at an end had no untoward events occurred. As it turned out, perplexities were just beginning.

The chief troublemaker was Villa, whose evil genius concocted mad schemes to provoke the United States into war. A band of Villistas stopped a train at Santa Ysabel, fifty miles west of Chihuahua City, on January 11, 1916, removed seventeen Americans, and shot sixteen of them on the spot. When this massacre failed to cause American reprisal, Villa made a bold raid on Columbus, New Mexico, on March 9, 1916, burning the town and killing nineteen inhabitants.

At once President Wilson ordered army commanders in Texas to assemble an expedition for the pursuit of Villa. At the same time he sought, and thought that he had obtained, the consent of the leaders of the de facto government for the entry of an American force into Mexican territory. Finally, he sent a punitive expedition, under the command of Brigadier General John J. Pershing, across the border on March 18. The dispatch of the punitive expedition would have provoked no crisis if Villa had been quickly apprehended. However, Villa cunningly led his pursuers deep into Mexico. The punitive expedition had penetrated more than 300 miles into northern Mexico by April 8, 1916, but Villa was still defiantly at large. At this point the expedition halted and gave all appearances of becoming an army of occupation.

The president refused, contrary to advice of his military counselors, to withdraw Pershing's command. He made this fateful decision chiefly because the State Department was not convinced that Carranza was either able or willing to control the bandit gangs that menaced the American border. On the other hand, the Mexican leaders were beginning to suspect that Wilson intended to occupy northern Mexico permanently. As this suspicion grew they gave less attention to pursuing Villa and more to preparing for an inevitable showdown with the United States.

Neither government wanted war, yet a situation was developing that could lead only to hostilities. A skirmish between American and Mexican troops occurred at Parral on April 12 in which forty Mexicans were killed. Such a wave of anger swept over Mexico that Carranza could do nothing less than demand prompt withdrawal of the expedition. The Washington government refused, and Carranza took two steps preparatory to a final reckoning. First, on May 22 he addressed a bitter note to the United States government, accusing it of warlike intentions; second, he ordered his field commanders to resist the American forces if they moved in any direction other than toward the border. Wilson replied by calling practically the entire National Guard to the border on June 18 and by sending a stinging rebuke to Carranza on June 20, declaring that the United States would not withdraw the expedition and warning that any attacks on American soldiers would lead to "the gravest consequences."

The *casus belli* occurred only a few hours after the American note of June 20 was delivered in the Mexican capital. An American patrol tried to force its way through a Mexican garrison at Carrizal in northern Chihuahua. The Mexicans lost thirty men but killed twelve and captured twenty-three Americans. As first reports to Washington told of a treacherous ambush, Wilson demanded the immediate release of the prisoners and prepared a message to Congress asking for authority to occupy northern Mexico, action that could have resulted only in full-scale war. He did not deliver the message because newspapers on June 26 published an account of the Carrizal incident written by an American officer on the spot. It revealed that the Americans had been guilty of an aggressive attack. A wave of revulsion immediately swept through the American people; Wilson was bombarded with appeals for peace from leaders in all walks of life; and war fever passed from Washington almost at once.

The upshot of the Carrizal affair was the eventual settlement of the most troubling phase of the Mexican-American problem. Wilson agreed when on July 4 Carranza suggested the appointment of a Joint High Commission to investigate and recommend. American and Mexican commissioners met from September 6, 1916, through January 15, 1917, and pondered all aspects of the Mexican problem. The Joint High Commission broke up without agreement on January 15, 1917. Now Wilson had to choose between surrendering to Carranza's renewed demand for withdrawal or accepting the possibility of war with Mexico. As events were now inexorably drawing the United States into the European war, the president had no alternative but to yield. The withdrawal was begun on January 27, and a nearly tragic chapter in the history of American foreign relations was happily ended.

The recalling of the punitive expedition and Wilson's de jure recognition of Carranza's new constitutional regime on March 13, 1917, marked a momentous turning point in modern Mexican history. Henceforward the Mexican people could pursue their difficult progress toward democratic institutions free from outside control. Wilson in large measure had made this great opportunity possible. Singlehanded he had prevented the European powers from coming to Huerta's aid, assisted the Constitutionalists in deposing the usurper, and stood off powerful forces in the United States that sought the downfall of the revolution. The pity was that while striving for worthy objectives Wilson interfered so often and in the wrong way that he alienated the friendship of the Mexican people and aroused the deepest suspicions of their leaders.

Chapter 7

The Road
to War, 1914 - 1917

Americans, on the eve of the most frightful holocaust in history up to that time, thought that they were still living in a secure international community, in which a benevolent British sea dominion and a fine world balance of power would operate almost automatically to protect the Monroe Doctrine without a huge American naval and military establishment. Then things suddenly went awry in 1914. German armies destroyed the balance on the Continent; German submarines threatened to destroy British control of the seas. The established international community had collapsed, and Americans found themselves at a crossroads in their history. Upon their reactions to the First World War depended not only the fate of Europe but the destiny of the United States as well.

55. American Neutrality, 1914–1915

To Americans who believed that a general war was virtually impossible, the outbreak of the First World War came, as one North Carolinian wrote in November 1914, "as lightning out of a clear sky." The dominant American reaction in August 1914 was relief that America was far removed from the scene of conflict, coupled with conviction that the United States had no vital stake in the outcome. Even ardent champions of the Allies approved when President Wilson issued an official proclamation of neutrality on August 4 and, two weeks later, urged Americans to be impartial in thought as well as in deed. To be sure, many Americans were unable to follow the president's injunction all the way. The United States was deluged from 1914 to 1917 with propaganda in behalf of the opposing alliances. Probably a majority of thoughtful Americans, concluding that Germany and Austria were primarily responsible for the war's outbreak, desired an Anglo-French victory. However, until 1917, that same majority continued to hope and pray that this country could avoid participation.

The sudden threat and then the outbreak of war in Europe in late July and early August of 1914 set off an economic panic in the United States and compelled the Wilson administration to take drastic steps to protect the domestic economy. For one thing, in order to protect the nation's gold reserve, the administration adopted a policy of discouraging loans by American bankers to the belligerents. The president, however, permitted Secretary Bryan to say that the administration disapproved of private loans to belligerent governments because such loans violated the spirit of neutrality.

Meanwhile, Wilson had also begun negotiations to protect American neutral trade. Since the British soon swept German raiders from the seas and began slowly but inexorably to extend far-reaching controls to prevent neutral trade with the Central Powers, the American government's early difficulties were all with Great Britain. By the end of February 1915, when the British system of maritime controls was severely tightened, the British admiralty had mined the North Sea, laid down a long-range naval blockade of Germany and neutral Europe, and seized American ships carrying certain noncontraband,[1] particularly food, to Italy, Holland, and other European neutrals for transshipment to Germany.

The crucial question during this early period of the war was whether the United States would accept the British maritime system, some aspects of which probably exceeded the bounds of international law (or what neutrals had traditionally considered to be the laws governing war at sea), or whether the United States would insist to the point of war upon freedom of trade with Germany in all noncontraband materials. The reaction of the United States as the principal neutral power was complicated by the inapplicability of many

[1]Under traditional international law, goods during wartime fall into three categories: (1) absolute contraband, that is, materials destined directly for the use of military forces; (2) conditional contraband, that is, goods susceptible of being used by military forces; and (3) noncontraband, that is, food, raw materials, and goods destined only for use by civilians. Under traditional law, a belligerent could seize and confiscate absolute contraband, had to prove that conditional contraband was destined for military forces in order to confiscate it, and was required to allow noncontraband to pass to its enemy.

traditional rules to new weapons such as the mine and the submarine. Wilson's first impulse was to insist sternly upon full respect for American commercial rights. However, his most trusted adviser in foreign affairs, Colonel Edward M. House, persuaded him to avoid provoking a serious crisis. The president acquiesced and allowed the State Department to lodge firm but friendly protests that reserved American rights for future adjudication.

This decision was virtually inevitable. The British did control the seas, and their maritime measures were essentially grounded in the beginning on traditional law and custom. Under British control of the Atlantic, American direct trade with Germany and Austria declined from $169,289,775 in 1914 to $1,159,653 in 1916. During the same period American trade with the Allies increased from $824,800,237 to $3,214,480,547. In short, the United States became virtually an Allied warehouse, from which munitions, food, and other vital raw materials flowed in an increasing stream. This outcome, it should be emphasized, derived from British control of the seas, not from any official American favoritism. Indeed, the United States would have been altogether unneutral had it challenged legitimate use of British sea power.

The Allied-American war trade was not the only consequence of American acquiescence in the British sea measures. The system of international exchange began to collapse as Allied, and particularly British, purchases began to assume enormous proportions in the spring and summer of 1915. As it became evident that continued adherence to Bryan's ban against loans would destroy the only important foreign trade in which Americans could then engage, the administration, including Bryan himself, began gradually to retreat. Bryan opened the door to large-scale loans on March 31, 1915, by declaring that the State Department would not oppose a $50 million "commercial credit" by the House of Morgan to the French government.

Bryan's approval of the French commercial credit partially reversed the State Department's ban on loans. The issue was raised even more squarely when an Anglo-French commission came to the United States in September 1915 to negotiate an unsecured public loan of $500 million. The State Department announced that it had no objections to the loan, thus specifically lifting the Bryan ban, and the United States soon became the arsenal of credit as well as of war materials for the Allies. American bankers advanced an additional $1.8 billion to the Allied governments to finance the war trade during the next eighteen months. Unlike the first Anglo-French public loan, all later loans were secured 100 percent by high-grade American and South American securities, and none was sold by public campaign.

These were some of the ties of trade and credit that bound the United States to the Allies by the autumn of 1915. It is important that we understand why the president approved policies that operated so powerfully to the advantage of one alliance. Perhaps one decisive factor in Wilson's decision to acquiesce in the British maritime system was his conviction, shared by many Americans in 1914 and 1915, that German methods and objectives were morally reprehensible and that the triumph in Europe of imperial Germany, militaristic and expansive, would constitute a potential threat to the security of the United States. We can only surmise that this conviction played a vital role in policy.

We can be more certain that another factor decisively shaped Wilson's neutral policies. It was the fact that he had virtually no choice but to accept British sea measures and allow the United States to become an arsenal of the Allies. The president, roughly speaking, faced the following situation in 1914 and early 1915: On one side, the Germans had used superior land power to overrun Belgium and the industrial areas of France; on the other side, Great Britain had used superior naval power to control the Atlantic and keep open her indispensable sources of supply. In accomplishing these objectives both Germany and Great Britain violated traditional international law to varying degrees but operated within a traditional framework. Because the United States was not prepared to halt the German invasion of Belgium, the president withheld any condemnation of this violation of the European treaty system. Because he had no desire to ensure a German victory, the president acquiesced in the British maritime system. Only if Great Britain had been fighting for objectives that imperiled American security would Wilson have been justified in attempting to deny to the British advantages flowing from their control of the seas.

56. The German Submarine Challenge, 1915

When Germany used a new weapon, the submarine, to challenge British control of the seas, Wilson was compelled to reexamine his whole plan of neutrality. This was necessary because the British and French governments responded to the submarine challenge with a total interdiction of all trade with the Central Powers. Hereafter the United States could no longer acquiesce in the British blockade without impairing friendly relations with Germany, nor acquiesce in the German submarine blockade without impairing friendly relations with the Allies and perhaps also guaranteeing a German victory. In other words, the United States could not be absolutely impartial in these new circumstances; it was bound to give an advantage and impose a disadvantage either way it turned.

The submarine issue arose in such a way, however, as to confuse the American people and their leaders. The German admiralty on February 4, 1915, announced the inauguration of a submarine blockade of the British Isles. All enemy vessels in a broad war zone would be destroyed without warning; even neutral vessels would not be safe because of British misuse of neutral flags. The imperial government, German spokesmen explained, had adopted this extreme measure in retaliation against the British food blockade.

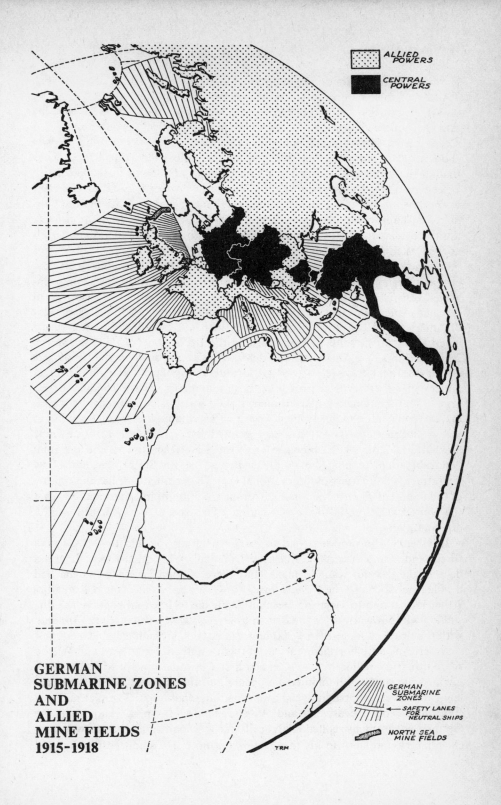

ALLIED
POWERS

CENTRAL
POWERS

GERMAN
SUBMARINE ZONES
AND
ALLIED
MINE FIELDS
1915-1918

GERMAN
SUBMARINE
ZONES

SAFETY LANES
FOR
NEUTRAL SHIPS

NORTH SEA
MINE FIELDS

TRM

Germany would abandon her submarine blockade, they added, if the British abandoned their campaign to starve women and children.

Wilson addressed a note of reply to Berlin on February 10, 1915, warning that the United States would hold Germany to a "strict accountability" for illegal destruction of American ships and lives. At the same time, Wilson endeavored to persuade the British to lift their blockade against food. Even though the submarine blockade was 90 percent bluff at this time, the British agreed to allow foodstuffs to enter Germany, provided that the Germans would give up use of U-boats against merchant shipping. Actually, the German food supply was adequate at this time. The German government insisted, therefore, that the British permit free entry into Germany of raw materials as well as food. The British of course refused.

When the submarine bluff failed to frighten the British, the German government began a general terror campaign of sinking, without warning, unarmed British passenger vessels in the North Atlantic. The great German-American crisis of 1915 revolved entirely around the alleged right of Americans to travel in safety on these British liners. This issue was raised when a submarine sank without warning the British liner *Falaba* on March 28, 1915, and one American was drowned. The president and his advisers during the next five weeks tried to formulate a policy that would protect American rights without provoking a serious crisis with Germany. Bryan argued that the American government should warn its citizens against traveling on belligerent merchantmen and give Germany the same freedom to violate international law that it had granted Britain. Different advice came from Robert Lansing, then counselor of the State Department, and the Joint Neutrality Board, an agency established to advise the State, War, and Navy departments on matters of international law. They contended that the sinking of the unarmed *Falaba* was such a flagrant violation of international law that the United States could not avoid taking a firm stand, even if it provoked a diplomatic crisis.

In essence, the president had to decide whether to yield to the German threat and abandon certain American technical rights on the seas. It was a decision he did not want to make, and there is good evidence that he had decided not to press the *Falaba* case. However, an event occurred on May 7 that forced him to meet the German challenge to freedom of the seas—the sinking without warning of the British liner *Lusitania* off the coast of Ireland, with the death of more than 1,200 noncombatants, including 128 Americans.

Americans were horrified, but few of them wanted to go to war, and Wilson shared their disinclination to fight. His first *Lusitania* note of May 13, 1915, invoked the rights of humanity in appealing to the imperial German government to halt its campaign against unarmed merchantmen. The German foreign office replied evasively, and Wilson renewed his plea. And when the German government replied equivocally for a second time, Wilson was both conciliatory and stern in his third *Lusitania* note. He admitted that subma-

rine operations might be conducted within traditional rules, provided that
U-boat commanders warned their victims and provided for the safety of
passengers and crews. On the other hand, he warned that the United States
would regard a repetition of ruthless sinkings as "deliberately unfriendly."
This was the language of ultimate diplomacy.

So eager was Bryan to avoid doing anything that might conceivably lead
to war that he resigned on June 8, 1915, rather than sign the second *Lusitania*
note. In contrast, Wilson was willing to risk war rather than yield what he
thought was a deeply moral principle—respect for human life even during
wartime. When a submarine sank the White Star liner *Arabic* on August 19,
with the loss of two American lives, the president and his new secretary of
state, Lansing, resolved to force a showdown. This new crisis forced the
German government to reveal that it had issued secret orders to U-boat
commanders on June 6 to spare large passenger liners. It also prompted the
German emperor on August 26 to order total abandonment of unrestricted
submarine operations against all passenger ships. Therefore, the German
ambassador in Washington informed Lansing on September 1 that unresisting
liners would not be sunk without warning and without provision being made
for the safety of passengers and crew.

The *Arabic* pledge preserved the peace and was a major diplomatic triumph for the president. Nonetheless, he could not have been encouraged by
the perilous state of American foreign relations and the signs of disunity and
confusion at home during the summer of 1915. There were numerous revelations of German conspiracies against American neutrality and of German
intrigues to provoke conflict between the United States and Mexico. Such
exposures naturally intensified the anti-German sentiment that had grown by
leaps and bounds since the sinking of the *Lusitania.* On the other hand, the
great mass of Americans were still stubbornly opposed to a belligerent policy.

Meanwhile, the Washington government, after seeming to acquiesce in the
British blockade instituted in March 1915, had made it clear in a note to the
London foreign office on July 14, 1915, that the United States meant to defend
the rights of neutral trade. This was followed by a long and stinging note to
London on October 21. Denouncing the British blockade as "ineffective,
illegal, and indefensible," it seemed to signal the beginning of a firm American
defense of freedom of the seas against all comers.

57. The Diplomacy of Mediation, 1915–1916

It was not easy to know what to do in the face of strong demands at home
both for stern defense of American rights on the seas and preservation of
peace almost at any price. Obviously, the surest way out of this dilemma was
to end the war by Wilson's mediation. Hope for peace ebbed and flowed all

during the period of American neutrality. At Wilson's request, Colonel House went to Europe in January 1915 to explore the possibility of American mediation. He found British officials willing to discuss peace terms, provided that the Germans consented to evacuate Belgium, disarm after the war was over, and give definite guarantees of a future peaceful policy in Europe. But the Germans would make no promises, for they were not yet prepared to face the issue of Belgium's future. House's first peace mission ended in failure.

The German refusal to cooperate for peace and the subsequent submarine controversy and revelations of German intrigues in the United States convinced House that German triumph in Europe would gravely imperil future American security. He had no desire to destroy German power in Europe, for he regarded Germany as a bulwark against Russia. He concluded during the autumn of 1915 that circumstances demanded nothing less than positive action by the United States to end the war and create a new international structure that would safeguard American security. He thought that these goals could be accomplished through cooperation between the United States and the Allied governments in a drive for a reasonable peace.

House first revealed his plan to Wilson in October 1915 and with Wilson's consent broached the matter to Sir Edward Grey, British foreign secretary, soon afterward. Grey replied that the Allies might indeed be willing to consider a negotiated peace if the United States was prepared to join a postwar League of Nations, and Wilson decided to send House to Europe for new talks. In brief, Wilson and House envisaged close Allied and American cooperation in forcing Germany to the peace table. If the Germans refused even to negotiate, the United States would probably enter the war on the side of the Allies. On the other hand, if the German government agreed to negotiate, the United States would cooperate with the Allies at the peace conference in attempting to compel Germany to accept a reasonable settlement. Finally, if Germany withdrew from the conference and renewed hostilities, the United States would probably join the war on the Allied side.

Certainly Wilson and probably House thought of armed intervention only as a last, desperate resort. They knew that there was grave danger of war if they continued to allow the German admiralty indirectly to determine American foreign policy. They thought that the chances of obtaining a reasonable settlement through the president's mediation were good. But, they reasoned, even should the United States have to enter the war under House's plan, the nation would at least be acting on its own volition and in behalf of a cause worth fighting for—a just settlement and an effective postwar international organization. At least Americans would not be fighting merely to vindicate technical rights on the seas.

To carry forward this peace project, House arrived in London on January 6, 1916. After preliminary conferences with Grey and other British leaders, he went to Berlin and Paris, where conversations convinced him that mediation was impossible until the summer campaigns had ended. He was back in

London in February and moved to bring the British to definite accord. House and Grey initialed a memorandum embodying their understanding on February 22, 1916. The president, it said, was ready to move for peace when the Allied governments gave the signal, and—although this was implied by what Grey said and was not included in the document—the Allies presumably would welcome Wilson's mediation according to the plan worked out by Colonel House.

Meanwhile, Wilson and Lansing on the other side of the water had embarked upon a separate diplomatic campaign that nearly wrecked House's negotiation, threatened to draw Germany and the United States into accord, and caused such a controversy in Congress that Wilson almost lost control of American foreign policy. The immediate background was the nearly successful conclusion in January and early February 1916 of Lansing's negotiations with the German government for settlement of the *Lusitania* affair. Even though the Germans were unwilling to admit the outright illegality of the sinking of the liner, they assumed liability for loss of American lives and offered a suitable indemnity.

The issue that set off a diplomatic and political explosion was a larger controversy over armed merchant ships. Months before the submarine challenge was raised, the State Department had issued regulations classifying defensively armed merchant ships as peaceful vessels. But the British not only armed merchant ships during 1915 but also ordered them to attack submarines, and Wilson and Lansing began to wonder whether it was fair to require submarines to surface before they attacked. Convinced that the American people did not want to go to war over the submarine issue, Lansing—with the president's approval—decided to try to find comprehensive understanding with the German government. On January 18, 1916, he sent the Allied governments a proposal for a new modus vivendi to govern maritime warfare. Repeating the German argument that any armed merchant ship was offensively armed in relation to the submarine, it suggested that the Allies disarm their merchant ships. More important, it warned that the American government was considering classifying armed merchantmen as auxiliary cruisers.[2]

Coming at the time when House was in London promoting intimate Anglo-American cooperation for peace, Lansing's modus vivendi struck like a bolt from a clear sky in the British capital. Sir Edward Grey remarked bitterly that the United States was proposing nothing less than destruction of the entire British merchant marine. Colonel House at once perceived the incongruity of his government's proposing a close entente with Great Britain at the very time that it was threatening to adopt a policy that might lead to Britain's defeat. House therefore urged Lansing to hold his proposal in abeyance.

[2]Such action by the United States government would in effect have excluded armed merchantmen from American ports, for under international law belligerent warships could stay only twenty-four hours in a neutral port and could purchase only enough fuel to reach their nearest home port.

Before the secretary of state could withdraw his modus vivendi, however, the German government, on February 10, 1916, announced that its submarines would sink all armed merchant ships without warning beginning on February 29.

Instead of acquiescing, Lansing declared on February 15 that the United States would *not* warn its citizens against traveling on ships armed for limited defense. Democratic leaders in Congress, baffled by this seeming reversal and alarmed by the thought of going to war to protect Americans traveling on armed belligerent merchantmen, went to the White House on February 21 to protest. But Wilson stood firm and declared that he would hold Germany to strict account. News of the president's response provoked panic in the House of Representatives. Democratic members of the foreign affairs committee agreed unanimously to demand prompt action on a resolution offered by Representative Jeff McLemore of Texas, warning Americans against traveling on armed ships, while Democratic leaders in the House visited the president again in the morning of February 25 to warn that the McLemore Resolution would pass by a two-to-one margin. Moreover, Senator Thomas P. Gore of Oklahoma introduced an identical resolution in the upper house soon after Democratic House leaders returned from their conference at the White House.

Wilson acted with customary boldness in this great challenge to his leadership, and he won the tabling of the Gore and McLemore resolutions after a bitter parliamentary struggle. But because he refused for reasons of security to explain his stand, many Democratic leaders began to suspect that he meant to take the country into war. Actually, Wilson had repudiated Lansing's proposed modus vivendi because he realized that he would destroy completely his standing as a mediator among the Allies and give tremendous military advantage to Germany if he insisted upon its adoption.

Events soon gave Wilson an opportunity to force a final reckoning with Germany without raising the issue of armed ships. A submarine torpedoed without warning an unarmed channel packet, *Sussex,* with eighty casualties on March 24, 1916. After agonizing deliberation, Wilson went before a joint session of Congress on April 18 and read the terms of an ultimatum that he had just sent to Berlin: the United States would sever relations if the German government did not abandon its unrestricted submarine operations against all shipping, belligerent and neutral.

Wilson's ultimatum brought to a head a controversy over submarine policy then going on in Germany between the military and civilian branches of the government. Discussion convinced the emperor that the admiralty did not have enough submarines to conduct a successful blockade or to justify bringing the United States into the war. He announced submission to the president's demands on May 1. The German foreign office informed the State Department three days later that henceforth submarine commanders would observe the rules of visit and search before sinking merchant vessels. But the note ended with a warning that Germany reserved freedom of action and might again resort to intensified submarine warfare if the United States did not compel the British to observe international law concerning neutral trade. So complete was the German surrender in this so-called *Sussex* pledge that the tension between the two governments diminished almost at once.

58. The Preparedness Controversy, 1914–1916

The great German-American crisis of 1915–1916 had an impact on the American people that was more powerful than the shock caused by the war's outbreak. Among a small minority it stimulated the conviction that the United States could not safely permit the triumph of German militarism in Europe and the destruction of British sea power. Much more important was the fact that the submarine crisis caused many Americans for the first time to realize that they lived in a chaotic international community; that force, not reason, was the final arbiter in disputes between nations; and that the United States because of its military weakness was practically powerless to affect the outcome of the war in Europe or even to protect its own security. Preparedness advocates were quick to seize the opportunity afforded by the submarine controversy. Beginning in the spring of 1915, they poured out articles and books in a virtual flood.

Wilson knew that he could not continue to oppose preparedness without giving the Republicans a formidable issue for the presidential campaign of 1916. However, it would be inaccurate to say that only political considerations shaped his thinking on the subject after the *Lusitania* crisis. He knew the weaknesses of the American military establishment better than most other men. He knew the disadvantage of dealing from weakness in diplomacy. On July 21, 1915, therefore, he requested his secretaries of war and of the navy to recommend programs that would satisfy the needs of national security.

The general board of the navy proposed adoption of a long-range naval construction program to give the United States equality with Great Britain by 1925. The Army War College proposed a substantial increase in the regular army, scrapping the National Guard, and creation of a volunteer national reserve—a so-called Continental Army—of 400,000 men as the first line of defense. The president presented this as the administration's program in an address on November 4, 1915, and in so doing set off one of the most violent political controversies of the decade.

The issues went deeper than any mere difference of opinion over military policy. The great majority of American progressives were obsessed with a passion for domestic social and economic reform. They believed that wars were always caused by bankers, industrialists, and scheming diplomats. Inevitably they reacted with startled indignation to the president's proposals. To them Wilson was at best a dupe, at worst, a turncoat willing to betray the cause of progressivism and convert the country into an armed camp. Led by Bryan and numerous peace organizations, antipreparedness spokesmen launched a campaign with a powerful appeal to workingmen and farmers.

A group of some thirty to fifty Democrats in Congress, most of them southerners and westerners, formed an antipreparedness bloc to wrest control of policy from the president. Through a member of their group, Claude Kitchin of North Carolina, House majority leader, Democratic antipreparedness congressmen were able to pack the key House military affairs committee when Congress met in December 1915. They were immovable when Secretary of War Lindley M. Garrison urged the most important feature of the army's reorganization plan—abandonment of the National Guard and creation of the new Continental Army. The administration and the House Democratic leaders were in hopeless deadlock by the middle of January 1916. Wilson decided to carry the issue to the people. In an extended speaking tour in late January and early February he urged preparedness as a national cause and pleaded for the Continental Army plan. He returned to Washington on February 4, however, to find his Democratic opponents more inflexible than before. Consequently Wilson yielded to the House leaders in order to obtain any legislation, and this provoked Secretary Garrison to resign on February 10. He was succeeded by the less intransigent Newton D. Baker of Cleveland, a progressive opponent of preparedness.

Garrison's resignation cleared the road, and the House adopted an army reorganization bill on March 23, 1916. It merely increased the regular army from 100,000 to 140,000 men and enlarged and brought the National Guard under control of the War Department. Then came the *Sussex* crisis. As the nation waited for word of peace or war from Berlin, preparedness champions in the Senate pushed through a measure that embodied most of the Army War College's proposals, including a Continental Army. But the *Sussex* crisis had passed by the time the House and Senate conferees resolved their differences in mid-May, and the measure that they had approved embodied mutual concessions. The Army Reorganization bill, which Wilson signed on June 3, 1916, increased the regular army to 11,327 officers and 208,338 men; integrated the National Guard into the national defense structure and increased its authorized strength; and permitted the War Department to establish a number of volunteer summer training camps.

Meanwhile, the naval affairs committees of the two houses had been biding their time. Although most progressives in principle opposed unusual naval expansion, they concentrated their main energies on the army bill. The House on June 2, 1916, approved a bill that ignored the administration's request for a five-year building program but actually provided more tonnage than Secretary of the Navy Josephus Daniels had requested for the first year. The Senate went even further and adopted a bill on July 21 that provided for completion of the five-year building program in three years. Up to this time the president had not interfered in the course of naval legislation. Now he used all his influence to persuade the House leaders to accept the Senate bill. The House capitulated on August 15, 1916, by accepting the important provisions of the Senate measure without altering a word.

The last victory belonged to the antipreparedness radicals in finding new revenues to pay for military and naval expansion. Conservatives proposed to meet the entire cost by a bond issue and increased consumption taxes. Spokesmen of progressive, farm, and labor groups were up in arms, demanding that the wealthy classes, whom they blamed for forcing preparedness on the country, pay the full bill. This ground swell had an immediate impact on the southern and western Democrats who controlled the House ways and means committee. Their measure, adopted by the House on July 10, doubled the normal income tax without lowering exemptions; raised the maximum surtax from 6 to 10 percent; levied a tax of from 1 to 8 percent on gross receipts of munitions manufacturers; imposed a new federal estate tax ranging from 1 to 5 percent; and repealed special consumption taxes that had been imposed in 1914. In the Senate, midwestern progressives like George W. Norris of Nebraska and Robert M. La Follette forced even further changes,[3] so that the Revenue Act of 1916 represented a frank effort to "soak the rich." It was populism and Bryanism finally triumphant—the first important victory in the equalitarian attack on privileged wealth in the United States.

59. The Campaign and Election of 1916

Not since 1910 had the American political scene seemed so confused as during the early months of 1916. The president's preparedness program and his stand on armed ships had nearly disrupted the Democratic party. On the other hand, Republicans were even more divided than their opponents. The eastern wing of the GOP was demanding tremendous military and naval increases, and the eastern leaders, Roosevelt, Elihu Root, and Henry Cabot Lodge, were beginning a fierce denunciation of the president for his allegedly cowardly refusal to defend American rights on the seas and in Mexico. In contrast, the great majority of midwestern Republican voters and leaders bitterly opposed further preparedness and wanted peace even at the price of abandoning rights on the seas.

Democrats closed ranks after Wilson's surrender during the battle over the army bill and after the peaceful settlement of the *Sussex* crisis. It was obvious by the middle of May that there would be no Democratic rupture, although

[3]The Senate increased the surtax to a maximum of 13 percent; levied a new tax on corporation capital, surplus, and undivided profits; increased the estate tax to a maximum of 10 percent; and increased to 12½ percent the maximum tax on munitions manufacturers. All these amendments were accepted by the House.

it was not yet clear what position that party would take on foreign policy during the coming campaign. The key to the future was the alignment of former Progressives—whether they would follow Roosevelt back into the Republican party or would be won to the Democratic party by Wilson's espousal of advanced progressive measures (pp. 122–125).

The chief task before the Republicans was to find a candidate and write a platform that would hold the conservative East without alienating the progressive, pacifistic Midwest and West. At the Republican National Convention that opened in Chicago on June 8, 1916, the party managers rejected Roosevelt, who had made a hard fight for the nomination, and chose instead Charles Evans Hughes, former governor of New York and now an associate justice of the Supreme Court. Adoption of a platform demanding "a straight and honest neutrality" and only "adequate" preparedness was, in the circumstances, an outright repudiation of Roosevelt's demands for a strong policy toward Germany and an effort to appease both the Middle West and the important German-American element. Roosevelt was disgruntled and disappointed, but he was so eager to avoid another four years of what he called Wilson's cowardly infamy that he disbanded his Progressive party and took to the field for Hughes.

The Democrats assembled in national convention in St. Louis on June 14. They dutifully approved the platform that Wilson and his advisers had prepared;[4] and they cheerfully renominated the president on June 15. Otherwise Wilson's plans for the convention went awry. He had planned that the convention should make "Americanism" and patriotism the keynotes of the coming campaign. Instead, the convention gave one long and tremendous ovation for peace, as delegates stormed and demonstrated when speakers extolled Wilson's success in keeping the country out of war.

The campaign that followed was full of strange surprises, but soon a clear pattern of issues emerged. Hughes tried to avoid a straightforward discussion of neutrality and was unable to attack the Democratic reforms of the past three years without seeming reactionary. He finally concentrated his main fire on Wilson's Mexican policy and alleged Democratic inefficiency. Everywhere that he spoke he made votes for Wilson by petty criticisms and failure to offer any constructive alternatives.

Wilson was unable to enter the campaign until September because of a threatened nationwide strike for the eight-hour day by the railroad brotherhoods. He averted this catastrophe by forcing through Congress the Adamson Act, which established the eight-hour day as the standard for all interstate railroad workers. Once this crisis was over, Wilson, on September 23, began a series of speeches that left Republicans dazed. Hughes, thinking that he had

[4]The Democratic platform made an open bid for Progressive support by promising adoption of an advanced program of federal social legislation, endorsed a neutral foreign policy, and commended the administration's program of "reasonable" preparedness. It also endorsed the proposal then being put forward by various groups for the establishment of a postwar League of Nations.

finally discovered an issue, denounced the Adamson Act as a craven surrender to the railroad workers. Wilson replied that the eight-hour day was the goal for which all workers should strive. Hughes denounced the Democrats for lacking a constructive program. Wilson replied by pointing to the most sweeping reform program in the history of the country.

Hughes's straddling and Wilson's bold defense of progressivism caused such a division on domestic issues as the country had not seen since 1896. The left wing of the progressive movement, including many Socialists, single taxers, sociologists, social workers, and intellectuals and their journals, moved en masse into the Wilson ranks. Most of the leaders of the Progressive party repudiated Roosevelt and came out for the president. The railroad brotherhoods, the AF of L, and several powerful farm organizations worked hard for the Democratic ticket. Finally, virtually all important independent newspapers and magazines came to Wilson's support. Thus a new political coalition that included practically all independent progressives came into being during the campaign of 1916 as a result of Wilson's and the Democratic party's straightforward espousal of reform legislation.

To interpret this campaign solely in terms of domestic issues, however, would be to miss its chief development: the fusion of progressivism with the peace cause that the president and his campaigners accomplished. Wilson was profoundly impressed by the peace demonstrations at St. Louis at the very time that he was growing suspicious of the Allies. Unhesitatingly, he took personal command of the peace movement. He charged that the Republicans were a war party and that Hughes's election would mean almost certain war with Mexico and Germany. By implication he promised to keep the country out of war. So overwhelming was the response in the Middle West to the peace appeal that Democratic orators took up the battle cry. "He kept us out of war" became the constant refrain of campaign speeches and the chief theme of Democratic campaign literature.

Early returns on election night, November 7, revealed that Hughes had made nearly a clean sweep of the East and of the eastern Middle West. But the tide turned suddenly in Wilson's favor as returns from the trans-Mississippi West came in. To the core of the Solid South, Wilson added New Hampshire, Ohio, Kansas, Nebraska, North Dakota, Montana, Wyoming, Colorado, New Mexico, Arizona, Utah, Nevada, Idaho, Washington, and California—for a total of 277 electoral votes and a majority of twenty-three. He received 9,129,000 popular votes, as against 8,538,221 for Hughes. It was a gain for the president of nearly 3,000,000 votes over 1912.

The causes of Wilson's breath-taking victory became apparent soon after the returns were in. Democratic promises of continued peace, prosperity, and progressive policies won most independents, a large minority of former Progressives, women voters in the suffrage states, and the left wing element that usually voted the Socialist ticket. The defection to Wilson of some 400,000 persons who had voted Socialist in 1912 was alone sufficient to give the

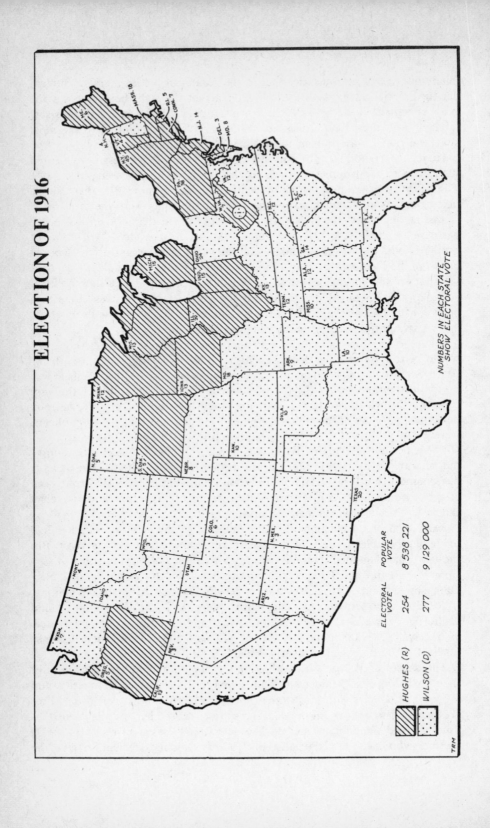

ELECTION OF 1916

	ELECTORAL VOTE	POPULAR VOTE
HUGHES (R)	254	8 538 221
WILSON (D)	277	9 129 000

NUMBERS IN EACH STATE SHOW ELECTORAL VOTE

president a majority in key states like California. These advanced progressives when added to the normal Democratic minority gave Wilson a bare majority and enabled the Democrats narrowly to control Congress for another two years.

60. The United States Enters the War

Let us now go back to the story of American relations with the belligerents where we left it at the end of the *Sussex* crisis. The *Sussex* pledge greatly relieved the tension in German-American relations, and events soon afterward cast a dark shadow over relations between the United States and Great Britain. To begin, Sir Edward Grey made it plain during the spring and summer that the Allies would not welcome the president's mediation so long as they had any hope of military victory. To Wilson and House this was a crushing blow, almost a betrayal; they began to suspect that the Allies desired a vindictive peace, not a righteous settlement. Secondly, American opinion was profoundly shocked by the British army's ruthless suppression of the abortive Irish Easter Rebellion of April 24, 1916. "The Dublin executions," observed the *New Republic,* "have done more to drive America back to isolation than any other event since the war began." Really dangerous Anglo-American tension rose during the summer and autumn as the British intensified their economic warfare in a supreme effort to bring all neutral commerce, even shipping, under their control. Against these new infringements of American neutral rights the State Department protested in menacing language, while the president in September obtained power from Congress to use the armed forces against any nation that discriminated against American commerce.

Wilson could neither take steps to bring the British to book nor launch a peace campaign of his own so long as the nation was in the throes of a presidential campaign. Once the election was over, however, he faced a situation that demanded speedy and decisive action. Both sides were now resolved to use their most desperate weapons to break a deadlock that was consuming manpower and resources at a prodigious rate. For Great Britain this meant further intensification of economic warfare. For Germany it meant revoking the *Sussex* pledge and launching a wholesale campaign against maritime commerce.

To preserve American neutrality in the face of an all-out struggle on the seas would be virtually impossible, and yet that was what the American people wanted Wilson to do. The only way to peace and safety, the president knew, was to bring the war to an end. Yet this would be difficult to achieve in view of continued British hostility to peace negotiations. Wilson obviously had no alternative but to seek peace through cooperation with the German government, which, since the end of the *Sussex* crisis, had been urging him to take leadership in a drive for peace. The president informed House and Lansing on November 14 and 15, 1916, that he had decided to try to end the war. But what would happen, House and Lansing asked, if the Germans agreed to a reasonable settlement and the Allies refused? In that event would not the United States be driven into sympathetic alliance with Germany against the Allies? Wilson replied that he was willing to run this risk. He obviously did not think that it was very great.

While Wilson continued these discussions, civilian and military leaders in Berlin concluded that the success of their recent campaign in Rumania had created a situation favorable to a peace move. They drafted terms that would have assured German mastery of Europe; agreed that Wilson should be used only to force the Allies to the peace table and then ignored during the actual conference discussions; and resolved to begin an all-out submarine campaign if their peace move failed. When Wilson did not move quickly enough, the German government, on December 12, invited its enemies to a peace conference.

Wilson backed up the German overture on December 18 by calling upon the belligerents to define the objectives for which they were fighting. He next undertook highly secret negotiations with the German and British governments looking toward peace. The British Cabinet sent word that it was willing to negotiate on liberal terms, but the German foreign office was evasive and finally informed the president that it did not desire his presence at the peace table. Meanwhile, Wilson went before the Senate on January 22, 1917, to clarify the American position and to explain what kind of a peace settlement the United States would be willing to help enforce. It had to be a peace among equals, he said, a "peace without victory," without indemnities and annexations.

The tragic irony was that the kind of settlement Wilson outlined was possible only if the German leaders were willing to accept a draw and cooperate with Wilson in forcing the Allies to abandon their own equally extreme objectives. Unfortunately, the men in control of the German government did not trust the American president and had abandoned all hope of peace through negotiation. They gave their answer to Wilson's appeal on January 31, 1917: after February 1 submarines would sink without warning all ships, belligerent and neutral, in a broad zone around Great Britain, France, and Italy, and in the eastern Mediterranean. The German admiralty would allow one American ship to sail weekly between New York and Falmouth, England, provided that the ship was suitably marked.

Wilson in response broke diplomatic relations with Germany on February 3, 1917, but he was still hopeful that the Germans would not carry out their threats against American commerce. He continued to pray during the remainder of February that events would not force the nation into war. Meanwhile, demand for protective arming of American ships grew on all sides as more and more ships stayed at their berths and goods began to pile up in warehouses and on wharves. At first Wilson stubbornly refused, saying that the country was not willing to run the risk of war. However, he received a message from Ambassador Walter Page in London on February 25 that removed all his doubts as to German intentions. It was a dispatch transmitting a message, intercepted and deciphered by the British, from the German foreign secretary, Arthur Zimmermann, to the German minister in Mexico City. In the event that Germany and the United States went to war, Zimmermann's message read, the minister should propose to the Mexican government an alliance by which Mexico would join the war against the United States and receive as reward "the lost territory in Texas, New Mexico, and Arizona." Moreover, the minister should request President Carranza to invite Japan to join the new anti-American coalition. Further indication of German intentions came on the same day that Wilson received the Zimmermann telegram, February 25. A submarine sank the British liner *Laconia* without warning off the Irish coast with the loss of American lives.

Wilson on the following day asked Congress for authority, first, to arm American ships for defense and, second, to employ other measures to protect American commerce on the high seas. There was little objection in either house to giving the president authority simply to arm merchantmen. But there was overwhelming opposition to empowering him to wage an undeclared naval war. Wilson tried to force Congress's hand by giving the Zimmermann message to the Associated Press, which published it on March 1. A tremendous surge of anger swept over the country, but a small group of western and southern radicals in the Senate stood firm. Refusing to abdicate the war-making power to the president, this "little group of willful men," as Wilson labeled them, insisted on talking the armed ship bill to death in the closing hours of the Sixty-fourth Congress.

Events from this point on led straight to war. The president announced on March 9 that he would put guns and naval crews on merchant vessels, and then he called Congress into special session for April 16. German submarines on March 18 sank three American merchant vessels with great loss of life. The demand for war, which had heretofore been largely confined to the East, now spread to the South and West. And at this moment of excitement came the first Russian Revolution, which overthrew the autocratic government and established a liberal constitutional regime. To many Americans who had feared Russian anti-Semitism and despotism more than German militarism, the news from Petrograd ended all doubts as to the issues of the war.

The country tottered on the brink of war, but Wilson brooded in hesitation and despair. Yet he finally did accept the decision for war that his advisers were urging upon him. Having moved up the date for the convening of Congress, he went before the joint session on April 2 and asked for a resolution recognizing that a state of war existed as a result of actions of the German government. After recounting the German aggressions against

American neutrality, he tried to find moral justification for leading the American people into this "most terrible and disastrous of all wars." The world, he declared, must be made safe for democracy and led to a universal dominion of righteousness through a concert of free peoples. There was opposition in both houses from antiwar progressives, but the Senate approved the war resolution on April 4, and the House concurred two days later.

Who willed American participation? Radicals and Socialists gave an answer in 1917 that was reiterated many times in the 1930s: The United States had been driven to war by businessmen, bankers, and munitions manufacturers. These enemies of the people had worked in devious ways to protect their profitable trade and enormous investments in an Allied victory. Moreover, this argument went on, Americans had been deceived by cunning propagandists into believing that the Allies were fighting for righteous objectives. The basic trouble, professors of international law added, was that the American government had not been truly neutral.

Obviously no such simple generalizations explain the complex causes for the decision for war in 1917. There is no evidence that bankers and businessmen affected that decision in any important way, and the effect of propaganda has been vastly overrated. In the final analysis it was Wilson, influenced by public opinion and his own conception of right and duty, who made the important decisions that shaped American policy. In the beginning he pursued a course of more or less strict neutrality that favored the Allies because the British controlled the seas. Then, as the British rejected his leadership in his drive for peace in the spring and summer of 1916, the president moved toward a policy of independent mediation. The Germans would have found a friend in the White House eager to join hands with them in 1916–1917 if they had wanted a reasonable settlement and evinced a readiness to cooperate in building a peaceful and secure postwar world.

In view of the pacific state of American public opinion and Wilson's own convictions at the beginning of 1917, it is reasonable to assume that there would have been no war between Germany and the United States had the German government stayed at least technically within the bounds of the *Sussex* pledge. The German leaders knew this, just as they knew that their plan for all-out warfare against commerce would inevitably drive the United States to war. But after much doubt and conflict among themselves, they rejected American friendship and cooperation and chose to run the risks of American belligerency because they did not trust Wilson and had concluded that their only hope lay in a desperate bid for all-out victory. In German hands, in the final analysis, lay the decision for war or peace with America.

Chapter 8

The American Democracy at War

The American people entered the First World War on a Wilsonian note of idealism, not really knowing what the struggle was about or the objectives for which their new friends and enemies were fighting. A recognition of this fact caused President Wilson to attempt to give a moral and altruistic meaning to American participation, to depict intervention in terms of the strong and pure democracy putting on the breastplate of righteousness to do battle for the Lord.

For their earlier refusal to heed all warnings that they had a vital stake in the outcome of the war, the American people paid a fearful price in divisions and doubts and organized efforts to sell the war to them. Nearly fatal was the almost utter lack of readiness for a great military and industrial effort. American unpreparedness and inability to retaliate had been the key factor in the German decision to launch unrestricted submarine warfare in 1917. More important still, the inability of the United States to throw a powerful army without delay into the battle in France prolonged the war and increased the danger of German victory.

In an astonishing manner, however, the American democracy organized for war. The industrial and military mobilization thus hastily accomplished produced the food, materials, ships, and manpower that tipped the balance and broke the deadlock on the western front in 1918. Let us now see how this was done and at what price.

61. An Army to Save the Allies

Neither Wilson nor his military advisers understood the weakness of the Allied military situation in the spring of 1917. Americans had assumed as a matter of course since 1914 that the Allies would win. Most Americans visualized their contribution in terms only of shipping, naval support, credit, and materials even after it was evident that the United States would enter the war. Allied war missions to Washington soon gave different advice.

Wilson and his advisers were shocked when British and French generals revealed that their governments were beginning to draw upon their last reserves. Fortunately, the Army War College had made plans for raising a large American army. The question of how this army should be raised had been hotly debated in Congress during the months preceding the adoption of the war resolution. And administration and army officials, as well as a large segment of thoughtful opinion, had agreed that conscription offered the only rational and democratic method. Even so, the selective service bill, presented to Congress soon after the adoption of the war resolution, set off a bitter struggle in the House of Representatives. Wilson insisted that conscription was essential to victory. In the end he had his way, although there was a hard struggle over age limits and sale of alcoholic beverages at or near army camps. In the measure that Wilson signed on May 18, 1917, the House won its fight to set the minimum age at twenty-one instead of nineteen, as the army demanded, and the Anti-saloon League won another victory over Demon Rum.

Secretary of War Newton D. Baker enlisted state and local officials in making the first registration on June 5, 1917, a nationwide demonstration of patriotism. On that date 9,586,508 men between the ages of twenty-one and thirty-one registered without commotion, riot, or organized resistance. Congress on August 31, 1918, expanded the age limits to include all men between eighteen and forty-five. All told, draft boards registered 24,234,021 men, of whom 6,300,000 were found to be available and 2,810,296 were inducted into the army. In addition, volunteer enlistments in the army, navy, and marine corps brought the total number of men and women under arms by November 1918 to 4,800,000.

For commander of the projected American Expeditionary Force the president and secretary of war turned to Major General John J. Pershing, who had recently commanded the punitive expedition in Mexico. Arriving in Paris on June 14, 1917, to establish the headquarters of the AEF, Pershing quickly

THE UNITED STATES ARMY
IN WORLD WAR I

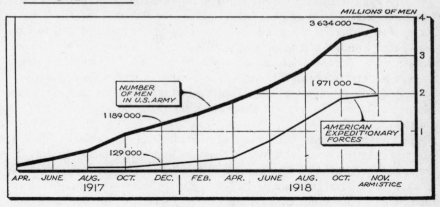

MILLIONS OF MEN

3 634 000

1 971 000

NUMBER
OF MEN
IN U.S. ARMY

1 189 000

AMERICAN
EXPEDITIONARY
FORCES

129 000

APR.   JUNE   AUG.   OCT.   DEC.   FEB.   APR.   JUNE   AUG.   OCT.   NOV.
                1917   1918   ARMISTICE

realized that the Allies were militarily almost bankrupt and obsessed by a passion for defense. He looked forward to the day when he would command a great fresh army that would lead the British and French out of their trenches. Allied military leaders argued that available American troops should be integrated into the existing defensive structure and subordinated to Allied field commanders. However, Pershing stubbornly insisted on preserving the identity and integrity of his command and even demanded a share of the front. The French command gave him the small and quiet Toul sector east of Verdun to defend with his initial force of 14,500 men.

The Germans began a series of heavy blows in October 1917 that pointed up the urgent need of large American reinforcements and forced the Allied governments to unite effectively for the first time. Following a near rout of the Italian armies by the Germans and Austrians came the triumph of the Bolsheviks in Russia, which raised the possibility that Russia would soon withdraw from the war. The Allied prime ministers assembled in extraordinary conference at Rapallo, Italy, in November 1917 and created a Supreme War Council to sit at Versailles and coordinate and direct military operations. During the next few months Pershing and President Wilson were subjected to heavy pressure by British and French leaders to permit American troops, even troops inadequately trained, to be amalgamated into their armies. Pershing refused, promising that he would have an army of a million men in France by the end of 1918.

It seemed, however, that the Germans would win the war before Pershing's reinforcements could arrive. The imperial army hit hard at the British Fifth Army in the valley of the Somme on March 21, 1918, and rolled it back. The Allied leaders and President Wilson hastily elevated Marshal Ferdinand Foch to the post of supreme commander five days later, and Pershing offered his four divisions for use anywhere on the front. The Germans renewed their offensive against the British on April 9, captured enormous quantities of booty and 60,000 prisoners, but failed to break the British lines. The German forces then turned hard against the French on May 27 and pushed to Château-Thierry on the Marne, only fifty miles from Paris. Foch on May 31 sent the American Second Division and several regiments of marines to bolster French colonial troops in this sector, and American troops for the first time participated in an important way. They pushed the Germans back across the Marne at Château-Thierry and cleared the enemy out of Belleau Wood from June 6 to 25.

The German general staff began its last great drive—to break through the Marne pocket between Rheims and Soissons and reach Paris—on July 15. Some 85,000 Americans were engaged in this battle. The German thrust was quickly parried, and the force of the German drive was spent by July 18. Foch then began a counteroffensive against the weak western flank of the German line from the Aisne to the Marne, between Rheims and Soissons. In this engagement, which lasted until August 6, eight American divisions and French troops wiped out the German salient. British and French armies, reinforced by new American divisions, shortly afterward began offensives that did not end until they neared the Belgian frontier in November.

American soldiers began to pour into France in large numbers while Foch was mounting his offensive mainly with British and French troops. The American First Army, 550,000 strong and under Pershing's personal command, was placed in front of the St. Mihiel salient at the southern end of the front on August 10. The Americans pressed forward in the morning of September 12; within three days they had wiped out the German salient and captured 16,000 prisoners and 443 guns. It was the first independent American operation of the war.

The tide was turning rapidly. Pershing had 1,200,000 men, 2,417 guns, and 324 tanks by September 26 and was eager, as he afterward said, "to draw the best German divisions to our front and to consume them." He now hurled his force against the German defenses between Verdun and Sedan. His goal was the Sedan-Mézières railroad, the main supply line for the German forces in this sector. Both sides threw every available man into the battle that raged all during October. The German lines began to crumble on November 1; Americans reached the outskirts of Sedan and cut the Sedan-Mézières railroad on November 7. The American victory in this so-called Meuse-Argonne offensive destroyed a major portion of the German defenses and, coupled with British and French successes in the central and northern sectors, brought the war to an end.

An American tempted to exaggerate his country's contribution to the victory is less inclined to boast when he recalls that only 112,432 Americans died while in service, as compared with 1,700,000 Russians, 1,385,300 Frenchmen, and 900,000 Britons. Belated though it was, the American con-

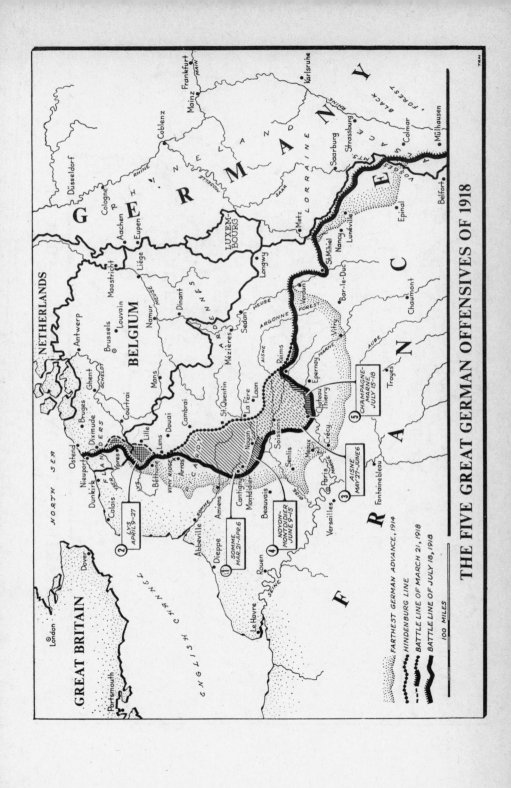

THE FIVE GREAT GERMAN OFFENSIVES OF 1918

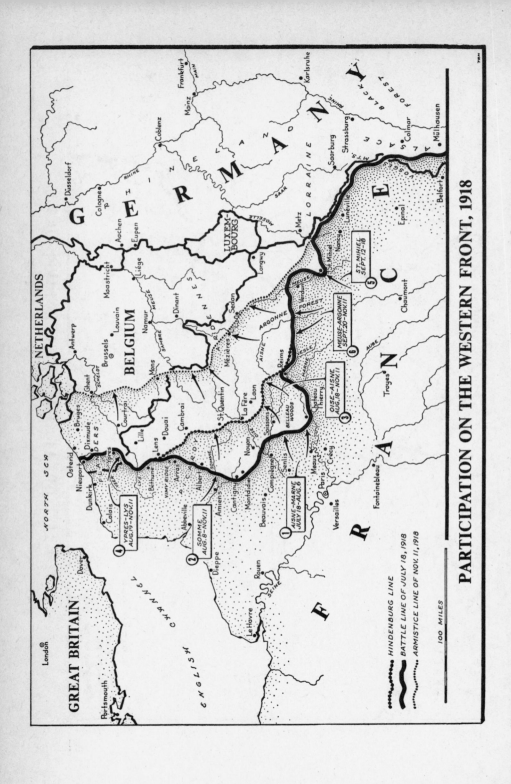

PARTICIPATION ON THE WESTERN FRONT, 1918

| GREAT BRITAIN | NORTH SEA | NETHERLANDS | GERMANY |

NORTH SEA

London

Portsmouth

Dover

Calais
Dunkirk
Ostend
Nieuport

Bruges
Dixmude
Ghent

Antwerp

Brussels

BELGIUM

Maastricht

Louvain

Namur

Liége

Aachen
Eupen

LUXEM-
BOURG

Düsseldorf

Cologne

Mainz

Frankfurt

Coblenz

Karlsruhe

Strassburg

Colmar
Mülhausen

Belfort

Epinal

Chaumont

Troyes

Fontainebleau

Versailles

Paris

FRANCE

Le Havre

Rouen

Dieppe

Abbeville

Amiens

Beauvais

Meaux

Senlis

Compiègne

Noyon

Montdidier

Cantigny

Albert

Arras

Lens

Lille

Douai

Cambrai

St. Quentin

La Fère

Laon

Soissons

Reims

Château-
Thierry

BELLEAU
WOODS

Vimy Ridge

Béthune

Courtrai

Mézières

Sedan

Dinant

Mons

ARGONNE
FOREST

Verdun

St. Mihiel

Nancy

Lunéville

Metz

Longwy

Saarburg

Luneville

Chaumont

① AISNE-MARNE
JULY 18-AUG. 6

② SOMME,
AUG. 8-NOV. 11

③ OISE-AISNE
AUG. 18-NOV. 11

④ YPRES-LYS
AUG. 19-NOV. 11

⑤ ST. MIHIEL
SEPT. 12-16

⑥ MEUSE-ARGONNE
SEPT. 20-NOV. 11

100 MILES

- - - HINDENBURG LINE
••••• BATTLE LINE OF JULY 18, 1918
••••• ARMISTICE LINE OF NOV. 11, 1918

tribution came perhaps in the nick of time to enable the Allies to withstand the last great German assault. On April 1, 1918, at the beginning of the German drive and before the American build-up in France, the Germans had a superiority of 324,000 infantrymen on the western front. By June American reinforcements gave the Allies a majority in manpower. By November the Allied preponderance was more than 600,000 men, enough to overwhelm the German defenses. Americans could rightly say, therefore, that their contribution had at least been decisive.

62. The United States Navy and the War

As U-boats set out in February 1917 to destroy all seaborne commerce, the most dangerous threat to the Allied cause came first not on land but on the seas. The German admiralty had calculated that sinkings at the rate of 600,000 tons a month would bring England to her knees within six months, and it seemed for a time that the promise of the U-boat champions would be fulfilled. All told, submarines destroyed more than 6.5 million tons of shipping during 1917, while all American, Allied, and neutral shipyards combined built only 2.7 million tons. "They will win, unless we can stop these losses —and stop them soon," Admiral Jellicoe, first sea lord of the admiralty, told the American liaison admiral in London, William S. Sims, in mid-April 1917.

The adoption of the war resolution found the American navy ready and eager to join the battle. Secretary Daniels and his staff conferred with British and French admirals on April 10 and 11, 1917, and mapped out a preliminary division of duty. The American navy would defend and patrol the Western Hemisphere, while the British fleet would carry the brunt of the antisubmarine campaign in waters around the British Isles with what help the American navy could spare. American assistance was not long in coming. The first six destroyers reached Queenstown, Ireland, on May 4; there were thirty-five American destroyers stationed at that base by July 5; and 383 American craft were overseas by the end of the war.[1]

The British system of defense against submarines in April 1917 consisted of dispersing sea traffic widely and then channeling merchant ships through heavily patrolled waters around the British Isles. The system created a positive deathtrap for merchantmen, as there simply were not enough ships to patrol the area. To the obvious alternative—the convoy system—British naval planners and masters of merchant ships objected, arguing that convoys were

[1]The administration immediately suspended the large building program authorized by the legislation of 1916 and adopted plans in May 1917 for the construction of 250 destroyers and 400 subchasers.

slow and merchant ships could not stay in formation. But as the submarine toll mounted a minority in the British admiralty joined Secretary Daniels and Admiral Sims in virtually demanding the use of convoys. Even after the feasibility of the plan had been demonstrated in the latter part of May 1917, the British admiralty contended that it did not have enough warships to use the system generally. However, the American reinforcement of destroyers turned the tide in July, and convoys for merchant ships were begun. The intensified antisubmarine campaign and inauguration of the convoy system were the two decisive factors that brought the U-boats under control. Shipping losses fell from 881,027 tons in April to half that figure in December 1917; and British losses never ran above 200,000 tons a month after April 1918.

The American navy's next task was to transport and supply the AEF. The Navy Department had seven troop and six cargo ships, totaling 94,000 tons, on hand on July 1, 1917. By November 1918 it had created a Cruiser and Transport Force of 143 vessels, aggregating 3,250,000 tons, which carried 911,047 soldiers to France. In addition, every available British transport was pressed into service in the Atlantic Ferry when the need for American manpower grew acute in 1918. Slightly more than 1,000,000 soldiers were carried by British vessels. The troop carriers were so fast and closely guarded by naval escorts that only two of them, both British vessels, were sunk on the eastbound voyage.

The American navy, with more than 2,000 vessels and 533,000 officers and men in service at the end of the war, had attained unparalleled size and fighting effectiveness. By November 1918 American ships were patrolling the far reaches of the Western Hemisphere and cooperating with Japanese and British forces in the Far East, while 834 vessels and 200,000 men were either serving in European waters or else transporting troops and supplies to France. By insisting on the adoption of the convoy system, American naval strategists had made a significant contribution to operations that assured an Allied-American victory at sea. By throwing its destroyers into the campaign against the submarines, the American navy perhaps turned the tide against the U-boats in the first Battle of the Atlantic. And by transporting nearly half the AEF and almost all the army's cargo to France, the navy made possible the defeat of Germany in 1918 instead of 1920, as the Allied leaders had originally planned.

63. The Triumph of a Democratic Tax Policy during Wartime

Americans entered the First World War without the slightest conception of the costs of participation. Although predictions as to long-run costs were impossible, two facts became apparent almost at once. First, the structure of international exchange would collapse and the European Allies would be in desperate straits unless Britain and France received huge credits, not a piddling few hundred million dollars. Second, the Revenue Act of March 3, 1917, which had increased taxes only slightly, was grossly inadequate to meet war needs.

Without opposition a somewhat dazed Congress approved the first War Loan Act on April 23, 1917. It authorized the Treasury to issue $2 billion in short-term notes and $5 billion in bonds, $3 billion of which should be lent to the Allies. Congress added subsequent authorizations as the needs of the American and Allied governments grew, so that the government had borrowed $23 billion on a long-term basis by 1920.

Out of the $33.5 billion that is reckoned as the cost of the war to the American people by 1920, therefore, some $23 billion was charged to future generations, and about $10.5 billion was raised by taxes. Determining how much should be borrowed and how much should be raised by taxes set off protracted struggles in Congress. Conservatives of both parties advocated recourse to consumption taxes, borrowing, and perhaps slight increases in income taxes. Progressives and radicals, on the other hand, believed that the wealthy classes, who had allegedly driven the country to war, should be forced to bear practically the entire costs through extraordinary income, inheritance, and excess profits taxes.

Between these two extremes stood the president, the secretary of the treasury, and a large majority of Congress. Secretary McAdoo at first thought that half the costs could be met by taxation; but he revised his figure downward to 35 percent as expenditures skyrocketed. Congressional leaders finally agreed upon a new War Revenue bill, which Wilson signed on October 3, 1917. It imposed a graduated excess profits tax ranging from 20 to 60 percent; increased the normal income tax to 4 percent for individuals and 6 percent for corporations; and increased the maximum surtax to 63 percent. The measure, moreover, increased excise taxes and imposed new ones on luxuries, services, and facilities. Finally, it increased the estate tax to a maximum of 25 percent.

The War Revenue Act of 1917 imposed 74 percent of the financial burden of the war on large individual and corporate incomes alone. Even so, radicals in the Senate denounced the bill as a betrayal of the people because it failed to confiscate all incomes over $100,000. The appalling way in which expenditures mounted during the early months of 1918 convinced Wilson and McAdoo that their radical critics had at least been partially right. The president appeared before a joint session on May 27, 1918, and urged the imposition of additional levies on incomes, profits, and luxuries. Congress's response, the Revenue Act of 1918, approved by the president on February 24, 1919, increased the prevailing tax burden by almost 250 percent and put four-fifths of the load on large incomes, profits, and estates. The normal tax on individual net incomes up to $4,000 was increased to 6 percent, while all net incomes above $4,000 had to pay a normal tax of 12 percent.[2] An additional surtax ranging up to 65 percent brought the total tax on the largest incomes to 77 percent. In addition, the excess profits tax was increased to a maximum of 65 percent.

The effect of the war revenue legislation can best be seen by comparing the fortunes of the wealthy classes with those of other groups during the war period. The average annual real earnings of workers in manufacturing, transportation, and coal mining were 14 percent higher in 1917 than in 1914 and 20 percent higher in 1918 than in 1914. A rapid increase in agricultural prices also brought new prosperity to farmers. The real income, after taxes, of all persons engaged in farming was 25 percent higher in 1918 than in 1915.

It is instructive to contrast these spectacular economic gains by the large majority of low-income receivers with the fortunes of the upper classes during the war period. To be sure, there were notable cases of "swollen" profits among certain industries, particularly munitions, shipbuilding, and steel; and the number of persons reporting incomes—before taxes—of between $50,000 and $100,000 increased from 5,000 in 1914 to 13,000 in 1918. But the gains of the wealthy classes as a whole were far less important than a few sensational figures would indicate. Total disbursements to owners in manufacturing, measured in terms of real income, increased hardly at all from 1913 to 1916. Real income from property increased about 30 percent in 1917 and then fell back in 1918 almost to the level of 1916. But since the recipients of this income from property paid about seven-eighths of the total personal income taxes in 1917 and 1918, it is evident that they suffered a sizable economic loss as a result of the war.

The old picture of the American upper classes fattening on the nation's misery during wartime is, to say the least, overdrawn. The effect of the tax policies shaped by a progressive administration and majority in Congress was greatly to lighten the relative share of the tax burden carried by the overwhelming majority of Americans, and sharply to increase the burdens of that small minority who had paid only slight taxes before 1916. Thus progressives could boast in 1918 that their leaders were putting democracy to work at home with a vengeance, while American soldiers were fighting to save democracy in Europe.

64. The Mobilization of Industry and Agriculture

Preliminary groundwork for a mobilization of industry had been laid before the United States entered the war. Congress in the preparedness legislation

---

[2]This rate applied only for the balance of 1918. For subsequent years the normal rate would be 4 percent on net incomes up to $4,000 and 8 percent on all incomes above that figure.

of 1916 had established a Council of National Defense, composed of six Cabinet members, and the council's working body, the Advisory Commission, made up of business, industrial, railroad, and labor representatives. The council was armed only with limited authority, but it proceeded to take a complete inventory of America's industrial plant and then to establish, on March 31, 1917, a Munitions Standards Board.

This board was soon reorganized as the General Munitions Board and given control over the purchase and supply of ammunition for the armed forces. But the new agency never established its authority over the armed services and the Allied purchasing commissions, and it was evident by the early summer of 1917 that only a central authority, with far-reaching controls, could bring order out of the prevailing chaos. The Council of National Defense abolished the General Munitions Board on July 28, 1917, and created in its place the War Industries Board (WIB) to serve as a clearing house for purchases, allocate raw materials and control production, and supervise labor relations.

The WIB made rapid progress in many fields of industrial mobilization, but it failed to coordinate military purchases because it lacked direct authority over the War and Navy departments. It seemed that the war effort at home was collapsing. The winter of 1917–1918 was terribly severe. Heavy snows blocked the railroads so frequently that there were fuel shortages in the East and a decline in steel production. Rumors of inefficiency led the Senate military affairs committee to begin a searching investigation in December 1917 of the mobilization effort. It revealed a near breakdown in railroad transportation, confusion in the War Department, and failure to provide adequate shelter and clothing for soldiers in cantonments.

The exposures of the Senate military affairs committee led Republicans to demand establishment of a coalition War Cabinet to take direction of the war effort out of the president's hands. Wilson's answer to this challenge to his leadership was as usual bold. He wrote out a measure—the so-called Overman bill—conferring on himself practically unlimited power to organize and direct the nation's resources. As Congress did not adopt the Overman bill until May, the president summoned Bernard M. Baruch, a Wall Street broker with much experience in the WIB, to the White House on March 4, 1918, and made him chairman. Acting under his emergency war powers, the president also granted sweeping new authority to the agency to conserve resources, advise purchasing agencies as to prices, make purchases for the Allies, and, most important, determine priorities of production and distribution in industry.

Gathering about him one hundred of the ablest businessmen in the country, Baruch soon established the WIB as the most powerful agency in the government, with himself as economic dictator of the United States and, to a large extent, of the Allied countries as well. And before many months had passed the board had harnessed the gigantic American industrial machine, mainly by instituting severe controls over the use of scarce materials, particularly steel, and brought such order into the mobilization effort that criticism almost vanished.

An urgent need in the spring of 1917 was an increased flow of food from the United States to provide the margin between life and death for the British, French, and Italian armies and peoples. The president on May 19, 1917, announced inauguration of a food control program under Herbert Hoover, recently director of the Belgian Relief Commission. Hoover's agency at first acted without legal authority as a subcommittee of the Council of National Defense. However, after a lengthy and bitter debate, Congress on August 10, 1917, adopted the Lever Act, giving the president sweeping authority over production, manufacture, and distribution of foodstuffs, fuel, fertilizers, and farm implements. The measure also empowered the president to institute a limited price control over certain scarce commodities. Wilson created the Food Administration on the day that the Lever bill became law and delegated full authority to Hoover.

The most urgent task in the summer of 1917 was production and control of wheat. Bad weather and an epidemic of black stem rust had caused a sharp decline in the American crop in 1916. The domestic supply was nearly exhausted by January 1917, and the price of wheat was skyrocketing. The Lever Act fixed a minimum price of $2.00 a bushel in order to stimulate production; and the Food Administration, on August 30, 1917, offered to buy the 1917 crop at $2.20 a bushel and established the United States Grain Corporation to purchase and distribute wheat. But 1917 was another poor wheat season, and stocks of bread grains abroad fell below the danger point in early 1918. Only by loyal cooperation from American housewives and the severest economies and controls was Hoover able to find enough wheat to carry Britain and France through the winter. Nature was more bountiful in 1918, and the bumper wheat crop of that year assured a plentiful supply of bread. The Food Administration's second major objective was increased production of hogs, as pork was another important staple in the Allied diet. When Hoover's agency began its work in the spring of 1917, the slaughtering of hogs was running 7 to 10 percent below the figure for the corresponding period in 1916. The Food Administration solved the problem in November 1917 by setting hog prices so high—at $15.50 per hundredweight—that farmers (and hogs) outdid themselves and nearly doubled production in 1918 and 1919.

For over-all accomplishment with a minimum of confusion and direct controls the Food Administration rivaled the reorganized WIB under Baruch's direction. By appealing to American pride and patriotism Hoover persuaded people to tighten their belts on meatless and breadless days. Consequently, the United States was able to export 12,326,914 tons of food in 1917–1918 and 18,667,378 tons in 1918–1919, as compared with an average for the three prewar years of 6,959,055 tons.

65. Shipping and Railroads

The British prime minister, David Lloyd George, told a group of Americans in London a few days after the United States entered the war: "The absolute assurance of victory has to be found in one word, ships, in a second word, ships, and a third word, ships." And so it seemed, as submarines took a fearful toll, nearly 900,000 tons of shipping, in that gloomy April of 1917. The Washington administration, however, promised "a bridge of ships" and chartered the Emergency Fleet Corporation, a subsidiary of the United States Shipping Board, on April 16 to build ships faster than submarines could sink them.

The government's shipbuilding program began with great fanfare but soon ran afoul of adversities. In the end it was the most important failure of the American war effort. The heads of the Shipping Board and the Emergency Fleet Corporation quarreled so violently that small progress had been accomplished by July 1917. The president removed them both and gave full power to Edward N. Hurley, energetic chairman of the Federal Trade Commission. Moving with great speed, Hurley began construction of new shipyards along the Atlantic coast; they contained ninety-four shipways and were supposed to produce 15 million tons of shipping. But the Emergency Fleet Corporation had delivered only 465,454 tons of new shipping by September 1918, while the first ship from the corporation's largest shipyard—at Hog Island, near Philadelphia—was not delivered until December 3, 1918.

Meanwhile, the Shipping Board had moved in more fruitful directions to marshal an American merchant marine. First, it seized and put into service ninety-seven German ships in American harbors, totaling more than 500,000 tons. Second, Hurley on August 3, 1917, commandeered for the Shipping Board the 431 ships, totaling 3 million tons, then under construction in private shipyards. Finally, in March 1918, he seized over half a million tons of Dutch shipping then in American ports. Through purchase, seizure, and requisition, the Shipping Board by September 1, 1918, had acquired the large fleet without which the AEF could never have been transported and supplied.

Organization of American railroads was assumed during most of 1917 by a voluntary Railroads War Board. It worked in cooperation with the Council of National Defense to divide traffic and move troops and army supplies. Struggling under an extraordinary burden and lacking any unified control, the railroads seemed near collapse in December 1917, when snows blocked lines and cold weather froze switches and impeded the operation of terminals. Conditions in the eastern freight yards and ports were nearly chaotic by Christmas. Therefore, the president on December 28, 1917, put all railroad transportation under the control of a United States Railroad Administration headed by William G. McAdoo. By controlling traffic on a rational, nation-wide scale, spending more than $500 million for long-needed improvements

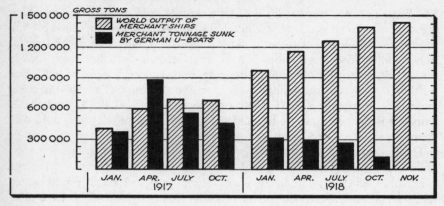

SUBMARINE SINKINGS AND SHIPBUILDING
JANUARY, 1917 TO NOVEMBER, 1918

and equipment, and subordinating passenger traffic to war needs, the Railroad Administration created an efficient national transportation system that met fully the demands of the great military effort of 1918.

66. Government and Labor during Wartime

In no area of public policy was the Wilson administration's determination to reinforce democracy at home during wartime better illustrated than in the field of labor policy. The president and his advisers rejected proposals to conscript labor and refused to allow the machinery of the labor market to regulate wages and hours. Instead, they embarked upon what soon became a comprehensive program designed to guarantee full utilization of manpower without depriving labor of rights and living standards that it had already won.

Like most other wartime policies, the labor program evolved slowly in response to need, experience, and the administration's maturing social conscience. The War and Navy departments had the most immediate and the largest interest in uninterrupted production and could wield direct power over manufacturers and contractors. They moved quickly into the field of labor relations during the first months of the war. There was still a need for unified policies and national direction of the labor administration. Hence the president established the National War Labor Board (WLB) on April 8, 1918, as a supreme court for labor controversies. Under the joint chairmanship of Frank P. Walsh, a distinguished labor lawyer, and former President William H. Taft, the WLB heard 1,251 cases affecting 711,500 workers. Lacking any statutory authority, the board enforced its rulings through the president's war powers. For example, when the Smith & Wesson Arms factory at Springfield, Massachusetts, refused to accept the WLB's decision, the War Department simply commandeered the plant. On the other hand, when workers in the munitions factories in Bridgeport, Connecticut, threatened to strike rather than accept the board's award, the president wrote a sharp letter to the Machinists' union at Bridgeport, telling members that they could either work or fight.

The members of the WLB soon discovered that they were actually more a policy-making than an arbitral body; yet they often had to decide labor policies on a basis of insufficient information and without knowing the needs of the country as a whole. To fill the need for a scientific agency to determine general policies, President Wilson created the War Labor Policies Board in May 1918. Under the direction of Felix Frankfurter the new agency undertook the gigantic task of surveying the whole labor field, standardizing wages and hours, and giving a central direction to the flow of labor. One result was the establishment in the Department of Labor of a United States Employment Service that registered over 5 million workers and placed 3.7 million of them in vital industries.

This, then, was the administrative machinery that mobilized American manpower and inaugurated the most significant and far-reaching social experiment in the history of the United States to that time. In general, the government threw its war power to labor's side and accomplished such sweeping social gains as to warrant the conclusion that a virtual revolution was effected during wartime. A few particulars will illustrate the generalization. All the various administrative boards, for example, recognized and protected the right of workers to organize and bargain collectively. As a result, total membership of the AF of L grew from 2,072,702 in 1916 to 3,260,168 in 1920. Secondly, the administration compelled the adoption of the eight-hour day when it was possible to do so without disrupting industrial operations. The result was a sharp decline in the hours of labor, from an average of 53.5 per week in 1914 to 50.4 in 1920, while the proportion of wage earners in manufacturing who worked 48 hours or less a week rose from 11.8 percent in 1914 to 48.6 percent in 1919. Thirdly, the War and Navy departments and various labor boards worked diligently to improve conditions of labor and prevent exploitation of women and children by manufacturers with government contracts. Moreover, when the Supreme Court in 1918 invalidated the Child Labor Act of 1916, Congress responded immediately by levying a prohibitive 10 percent tax on products manufactured in whole or in part by children under fourteen. Fourthly, the federal administrators attempted to guarantee all workers under their jurisdiction a living wage, that is, an income sufficient to provide a minimum of health and decency. In the face of a 50 percent increase in the cost of living from 1914 to 1918, such a program involved heroic efforts to keep wages abreast of the rising level of prices. Because of full employment and the vigilance of the war labor agencies, however, the average annual real income of labor increased 14 percent above the prewar level in 1917 and 20 percent above the prewar level in 1918.

These efforts involved such federal intervention as few progressives had dreamed of before 1917. Under the spur of war necessity, an advanced element in the administration had demonstrated that public control of hours, wages, and working conditions could be effected without enslaving workers or causing undue hardship on management. The experiment was abandoned after the war, to be sure, but a precedent for future action in another dire emergency had been established.

67. Public Opinion and the War

At the outset there was a profound division in public sentiment over American participation in the war. It is impossible to estimate the extent of opposition to the war resolution soon after its adoption. Probably a majority reluctantly accepted it as the only solution, but there were millions of Americans—Socialists, extreme radicals, many progressives, and tens of thousands of German and Irish Americans—who still believed that American intervention was the work of an unneutral president and great evil forces that abetted him.[3]

To convert this hostile opinion and educate all citizens to an understanding of American objectives, Wilson, only a week after the adoption of the war resolution, created the Committee on Public Information with George Creel, a progressive journalist from Denver, as head. One of Creel's first official acts was the establishment of a voluntary press censorship that worked remarkably well. He next turned to the more difficult task of making Americans war-conscious; before the war had ended he had mobilized 150,000 lecturers, writers, artists, actors, and scholars in the most gigantic propaganda campaign in American history.

As a consequence an official line was sold to the American people. One side of the propaganda glorified American participation in terms of an idealistic crusade to advance the cause of freedom and democracy throughout the world—a concept that the president reiterated in 1917 and 1918. The other side portrayed the German menace in the most lurid colors, in terms of the Hun attempting to despoil Europe and extend his dominion to the Western Hemisphere. Although the Creel Committee rejected the cruder atrocity stories, it appropriated and spread many of the official Allied atrocity charges.

The Creel Committee's efforts to make Americans war- and security-conscious came at a time when they were already distraught by rumors of disloyalty, espionage, and sabotage. The result of Creel's propaganda, and even more of the agitation of irresponsible volunteer organizations like the

---

[3]The Socialist party before its suppression was the only important organization that opposed the war effort. Socialist mayoralty candidates in 1917 polled 22 percent of the popular vote in New York City, nearly 34 percent in Chicago, 44 percent in Dayton, Ohio, and 25 percent in Buffalo —an impressive indication of the extent of popular feeling against participation.

National Security League and the American Protective League, was to stimulate such an outbreak of war madness as the country had never before witnessed. Most of the hysteria was turned against German-Americans, all things German, and the antiwar radicals and progressives. Each state had a committee of public safety, with branches in every county and city; and in many areas these committees were not much better than vigilante groups. It was they who conducted reigns of terror against German-Americans, especially in Montana, Minnesota, and Wisconsin. La Follette, as the leader of the progressives who voted against the war resolution, was burned in effigy in Madison, expelled from the Madison Club, and publicly censured by most of the faculty of his beloved University of Wisconsin. The climax came when the Minnesota Public Safety Committee demanded his expulsion from the Senate.

As one historian has shrewdly observed, the majority of Americans in their hatred of things German lost not only their tolerance but their sense of humor as well. Statues of heroes like Von Steuben and Frederick the Great were taken from their pedestals. Many states forbade the teaching of German or church services conducted in German. Sauerkraut was renamed "liberty cabbage," German measles, "liberty measles." The crowning blow came when Cincinnati ruled pretzels off free lunch counters in saloons.

68. Civil Liberties during Wartime

All governments try to protect themselves against enemies from within as well as from without during extreme crises. To Wilson and other administration leaders it was an absurd situation when the federal government could force men to fight and give their lives for their country and yet could not punish persons who attempted to obstruct the war effort or gave aid and comfort to the enemy without violating the law of treason.[4] The president's answer to opponents of the war was the Espionage Act of June 15, 1917. It provided imprisonment up to twenty years and/or a fine up to $10,000 for persons who willfully made false reports to help the enemy, incited rebellion among the armed forces, or attempted to obstruct recruiting or the operation of the draft. An equivalent of censorship appeared in a section empowering the postmaster general to deny the use of the mails to any matter which, in his opinion, advocated treason, insurrection, or forcible resistance to the laws of the United States. Postmaster General Albert S. Burleson of Texas had been a staunch supporter of Wilson's policies, but he was neither tolerant nor discriminating in judgment, and he used his vast new power to establish a

[4]Several Civil War statutes, still on the books in 1917, prohibited conspiracies to resist recruiting and persuade men to resist the draft; but these laws did not affect individuals. The only statute applying to individuals was the treason law, which applied only to treasonable acts, not utterances, and was extremely difficult to enforce.

capricious censorship. For example, he banned the *American Socialist* from the mails soon after the passage of the Espionage Act. Two other leading Socialist publications, *The Masses* and Victor Berger's daily *Milwaukee Leader,* fell under the Texan's ban in August and October 1917.

In effect the Espionage Act became a tool to stamp out dissent and radical, but never conservative, criticism. As one authority has observed, "It became criminal to advocate heavier taxation instead of bond issues, to state that conscription was unconstitutional though the Supreme Court had not yet held it valid, to say that the sinking of merchant ships was legal, to urge that a referendum should have preceded our declaration of war, to say that war was contrary to the teachings of Christ. Men have been punished for criticising the Red Cross and the Y.M.C.A."[5] A movie producer, Robert Goldstein, was sentenced to prison for ten years for displaying a movie about the American Revolution that allegedly incited hostility against an associate of the United States. The most famous case involved Eugene V. Debs, the leader of the Socialist party. Debs expressed his frank revulsion at the war in a speech before a Socialist convention in Canton, Ohio, on June 16, 1918. He was speedily brought to trial and sentenced to a term of ten years in federal prison.

In all fairness it should be said that the administration was not responsible for the excesses of this legal witch hunt. Indeed, President Wilson courageously headed off a movement to have so-called traitors tried and punished by military courts. The excesses were the outcome largely of the hysteria and maelstrom of hatred that converted district attorneys, judges, and juries into persecutors of a dissenting minority. Federal judges in the North had stood forthrightly, although usually vainly, during the Civil War in defense of civil liberties against encroachments by the military commanders. However, the federal courts provided no effective defense during the First World War against the momentary madness of the majority. None of the sedition cases reached the Supreme Court until after the war was over. But in *Schenck* v. *United States,* 1919, Justice Oliver Wendell Holmes, speaking for a unanimous court, upheld the Espionage Act. Schenck had admittedly counseled resistance to the draft. In ordinary times, Holmes said, such action would have been legal. In wartime, however, Congress had power to prevent utterances that might constitute a "clear and present danger" and provoke evils that Congress had a right to prevent.

The government's power over thought and utterance was inevitably gradually enlarged, not diminished, as the war progressed. The Trading-with-the-Enemy Act of October 6, 1917, empowered the president to censor all international communications and gave the postmaster general sweeping powers of censorship over the foreign-language press in the United States. Still

[5]Zechariah Chafee, Jr., *Freedom of Speech in the United States* (Cambridge, Mass., 1941), p. 51.

the attorney general claimed that he lacked a means to check disloyalty and asked Congress for broader authority. Congress moved again in April and May 1918, but not so much in response to the attorney general's request as in reaction to two developments that had shaken the country during preceding months.

The first of these was the government's suppression of the Industrial Workers of the World, a left-wing union which, as we have seen, functioned mainly among western lumbermen, miners, and agricultural workers. The IWW conducted a violent campaign during the first eight months of 1917 against the copper companies, especially the Anaconda in Montana and Arizona. The production of vital copper began to decline precipitously, and the Justice Department moved swiftly. Federal agents raided IWW offices throughout the West on September 5, 1917, and arrested the union's leaders. Nearly one hundred of them were subsequently tried, convicted, and imprisoned.

The second development was the mounting of war hysteria during the preceding winter, especially in states like Montana and Minnesota, where the IWW and German-Americans were an important element. The Montana legislature met in special session in February 1918 to consider the crisis; and Governor Samuel V. Stewart signed a criminal syndicalism act on February 21. It prohibited any language calculated to bring the American Constitution, form of government, flag, or armed forces into disrespect or contempt.

Spurred by appeals from the West, Congress succumbed to the clamor for legislation against sabotage and sedition. The Sabotage Act, approved April 20, 1918, was aimed at the IWW and made willful sabotage of war materials, utilities, and transportation facilities federal crimes. The Sedition Act, signed by the president on May 16, 1918, was modeled after the Montana statute and supported chiefly by senators from the Rocky Mountain states. The Espionage Act had empowered the government to punish seditious utterances only if it could prove that injurious consequences would result directly from such utterances. The Sedition Act, in contrast, extended the power of the United States over speech and printed opinion, regardless of consequence. It forbade disloyal, profane, scurrilous, or abusive remarks about the form of government, flag, or uniform of the United States, or any language intended to obstruct the war effort in any way. In addition, the postmaster general was empowered to deny the use of the mails to any person who, in his opinion, used the mail service to violate the Sedition Act.

All told, 2,168 persons were prosecuted and 1,055 were convicted under the Espionage and Sedition acts, sixty-five for threats against the president, and only ten for actual sabotage. But this reckoning gives little indication of the extent to which suppression of dissent was carried out by organized groups who lynched, whipped, tarred and feathered, or otherwise wreaked vengeance on labor radicals, German-Americans, or any persons suspected of disloyalty. In retrospect, the war hysteria seems the most fearful price that the American people paid for participation in the First World War.

Chapter 9

The Great Crusade
Ends in a Separate Peace

We can see in retrospect that the participation of the United States in the First World War restored a preponderance of strength to the Atlantic powers, but that Britain and France were more severely weakened by the war than was Germany. We can also see that a future preponderance of the Atlantic community depended upon the continued active participation of the United States in the western coalition. In other words, the future peace of the world depended upon the willingness of the American people to maintain a new Anglo-French preponderance of power, at least until a genuine world concert could come into being.

Wilson and perhaps a majority of thoughtful Americans realized this fact in 1919 and 1920. Many Americans, however, were unprepared to assume the duties of leadership that circumstances seemed to demand. When the Paris Peace Conference gave birth, not to a Wilsonian millennium, but to a settlement that seemed to embody many of the old evils that they had fought to destroy, American crusaders by the thousands turned into cynics and wished only to abandon Europe to an inevitable self-destruction. But this disillusionment over the Treaty of Versailles was not the only factor in the rejection by the American people of leadership in world affairs. Historic and powerful isolationist sentiments revived in full force once the war was over and provided an ideological frame of reference to which opponents of the treaty could appeal. Old anti-British animosities found a more virulent expression for having been suppressed during the war, while various national groups rebelled against aspects of the treaty. But the most fatal and decisive development was the manner in which the question of a peace settlement was subordinated, by Democrats and Republicans alike, to partisan ambitions. This was the factor chiefly responsible for the failure of the treaty in the United States.

The story we are about to relate has about it many elements of high tragedy. A concert of free peoples and the greatest aggregation of military power the world had yet seen ended in bitter and inglorious rupture, and a chain of events was set in motion that led to the Second World War.

69. The Formulation of the Liberal Peace Program

The formulation of the liberal peace program illustrates the way in which thoughtful minorities affect the course of history. Groups of intellectuals and humanitarians in all western European nations not long after the outbreak of the war began to study prevention of future wars. Their remedy called for open diplomacy, an end to antagonistic balances of power, no postwar indemnities or annexations, self-determination for subject nationalities, democratic control of foreign policies, freedom of the seas, and disarmament on land. Their suggestions were causing a tremendous ferment by the spring of 1916. An American counterpart was the League to Enforce Peace, organized in June 1915. It numbered among its leaders former President Taft, President A. Lawrence Lowell of Harvard, and Hamilton Holt, editor of the *Independent,* and it proposed a powerful international organization to preserve peace.

The most important moment in the peace movement came when Wilson espoused the league idea and the liberal peace program. The president had refused before 1916 to make any public comment on the causes of the war or proposals for a settlement. But in a speech before the League to Enforce Peace in Washington on May 27, 1916, he came out boldly in support of American participation in a postwar association to maintain freedom of the seas and the territorial integrity of its members. When this momentous declaration evoked much favorable comment and little criticism, Wilson incorporated the league concept in the Democratic platform and made it a leading issue in the ensuing presidential campaign of 1916.

Encouraged by a favorable popular response, Wilson next conjoined the league concept to the liberal peace program in his "Peace without Victory" speech to the Senate on January 22, 1917. He reaffirmed his belief that the American people were prepared to join a postwar League of Nations and help maintain peace. He went further, however, and for the first time outlined in general terms the kind of peace that the American people would be willing to help enforce. It was a settlement giving independence to the Poles and autonomy to oppressed nationalities, guaranteeing freedom of the seas, and substituting a world community of power for the old system of a divided Europe. This would be a peace without great indemnities and annexations, except—and this could only be inferred from the address—perhaps to return Alsace-Lorraine to France and give Russia access to the Mediterranean.

There can be no doubt that Wilson believed that this was the only kind of peace worth fighting for because it was the only kind of peace that would endure. Yet he let the opportunity pass to obtain such a settlement when he might have won it most easily—during the anxious two months before the American war resolution. Failing to use American intervention as a bargaining weapon for peace objectives that the United States could approve, he permitted the country to drift into war merely to defend highly questionable maritime rights.

His second mistake was nearly as damaging. Wilson from the beginning of American belligerency insisted on maintaining the fiction that the United States was carrying on a private war with Germany, as an associate but not an ally of the Entente, presumably free to withdraw when it had won its objectives. This thinking was unrealistic, for after April 6, 1917, the United States and the Allied countries had to make war together, win together, and make peace together.

This became apparent soon after the American declaration of war, when the president and Allied leaders first discussed a possible settlement. Certainly after his talks with the British foreign secretary, Arthur Balfour, in late April 1917, Wilson knew the terms of some of the secret treaties that the Allied governments had concluded for the division of German and Austro-Hungarian territory and colonies. He knew also that he faced an inevitable showdown on the whole subject of peace terms. On several occasions he attempted to broach the subject with the British and French and was diverted from his efforts by warnings that such talk would cause a fatal division in the face of the impending German onslaught on the western front. Wilson comforted himself with the thought that he could *force* Britain and France to accept his terms after the war was over. "By that time," he predicted, "they will among other things be financially in our hands."

Unable, as he thought, to come to definite agreement with the Allied governments and acting in response to demands at home and abroad for a clear statement of war aims, Wilson launched his own campaign for a liberal and just peace settlement. The opening note of this campaign, the Fourteen Points address, came in response to the direst catastrophe that had befallen the Allies since the beginning of the war. The Bolsheviks overthrew the socialistic Kerenesky government in November 1917, appealed to war-weary peoples to put an end to the fighting, and announced their intention to expose the Allied governments by publishing their secret agreements on war aims. Failing to receive any response to these moves, the Bolsheviks opened separate peace negotiations with Germany.

Some answer had to be made. The American people, Wilson said, would not fight for "any selfish aim on the part of any belligerent." After trying vainly to persuade the Interallied Conference in Paris to formulate a reply, Wilson set himself independently to the task on January 5, 1918. Three days later he went before a joint session of Congress to announce the peace program for which the United States and the Allies were fighting. It was enumerated in fourteen points. The first five were general and called for open diplomacy, freedom of the seas "alike in peace and in war," removal of artificial trade barriers, reduction of armaments, and an "absolutely impartial adjustment of all colonial claims." Point 6 demanded the evacuation of Russia by German forces and self-determination for the Russian peoples. Points 7 and 8 called for German evacuation of Belgium and France and proposed the return of Alsace-Lorraine to France. Point 9 called for the readjustment of Italy's boundary along the clear line of nationality. Point 10 called for autonomy for the subject nationalities of Austria-Hungary. Point 11 called for the evacuation and restoration of Rumania, Serbia, and Montenegro. Point 12 called for autonomy for the subject peoples of the Ottoman empire. Point 13 called for the creation of a free and independent Poland with access to the sea. For the end the president saved the capstone, Point 14: "A general association of nations . . . affording mutual guarantees of political independence and territorial integrity to great and small states alike."

The Fourteen Points at once became the great manifesto of the war. Enthusiastically received by liberal and labor groups in the United States and the Allied countries, the outlined peace program also had a powerful appeal to the German people. Wilson had promised, not the destruction of Germany, but the welcoming of a democratized Reich into the new concert of power. Although the Allied leaders used the Fourteen Points as a weapon of war, they gave no indication that they were willing to adopt them, verbatim, as a basis for peace. Nonetheless, Wilson intensified his campaign for a liberal peace all during the spring and summer of 1918.

70. Armistice: 1918

Wilson's opportunity to take command of armistice negotiations arose as a result of the weight of the Allied-American offensive on the western front that began in July 1918. General Ludendorff, one of the German supreme commanders, demanded on September 29 and October 1 that the imperial civil authorities obtain an armistice immediately. A new chancellor, Prince Max of Baden, a liberal antimilitarist, was at this moment in process of forming a new government. When the high command warned that the army could not hold long enough to permit protracted negotiations, Prince Max appealed to President Wilson on October 3 for an armistice based on the Fourteen Points and subsequent Wilsonian pronouncements.

There were demands for driving straight to the Rhine, but Wilson resolved to end the fighting, provided an effective German surrender could be obtained. Actually, Ludendorff and the other German leaders hoped to use the supposedly simple Wilson to win the respite that they needed in order to prepare defense of the Fatherland. Wilson's reply to Prince Max's appeal revealed that the president understood German purposes. The United States was ready to consider peace negotiations, Wilson wrote on October 8, but only if the Central Powers would evacuate Belgium and France and give adequate guarantees that they would not resume hostilities—in other words, if Germany was prepared to admit defeat. Furthermore, Wilson added, he would negotiate only with a responsible, legitimate civilian government, not with the military masters of Germany.

Prince Max replied on October 12, assuring Wilson that he spoke in the name of the German people, accepting the Fourteen Points, and suggesting that a mixed commission be established to supervise the evacuation of France and Belgium. The president responded on October 14. Rejecting the suggestion of a mixed commission, he made it clear that the only kind of armistice that he would approve was one that guaranteed the present supremacy of the American and Allied armies. This note fell like a bolt in Berlin. The German commanders were now all for fighting to the last man. At the same time, it was evident that the morale of the German people was destroyed beyond repair, and the civilian government finally took control. Prince Max informed Wilson on October 20 that Germany accepted the president's conditions.

Convinced that the German peace appeal was sincere, Wilson replied on October 23 that he would transmit that appeal to the Allied governments and discuss with them the question of an armistice. Agreement on the military and naval terms had been reached by the evening of November 4 by the Supreme War Council, the Interallied Naval Council, Colonel House, representing President Wilson, and the British, French, and Italian premiers. In the meantime, events were transpiring within Germany that made acceptance of almost any terms by the German authorities inevitable. Wilson's message of October 23 to Prince Max had contained the hint that a German republic would fare better at the peace conference than an imperial Germany. Feeling in civilian and military circles reached such a point that the emperor abdicated and fled to Holland on November 8. The lowering of the imperial standards so shattered the army's morale that Germany was afterward incapable of waging even a purely defensive war.

Meanwhile, discussions in the Allied camp had brought Allied and American differences over peace terms sharply into the open. Believing that he had now or never to win Allied approval of his peace program, Wilson sent

Colonel House to Paris to force a showdown with the Allied premiers. At the first conference on October 29 the Allied spokesman claimed that they did not know what the Fourteen Points were. House read them. David Lloyd George, the British prime minister, refused point blank to accept Point 2 regarding freedom of the seas; the French and Italian leaders concurred. House replied that the president might feel compelled to lay the matter before the American people and make a separate peace if his colleagues refused to accept the Fourteen Points. He reiterated this warning on the following day and headed off a whole host of French and Italian objections.

The Allied leaders surrendered for the moment in the face of this threat, but not until the president had agreed that the British might reserve freedom of action on Point 2, and that the Germans should be told that they would be required to pay reparations for all civilian damages caused by their aggression. The Supreme War Council approved the compromise on November 4. On the following day Wilson informed the German government that Marshal Foch was ready to receive its representatives. German delegates met the French marshal and a British naval representative in Foch's headquarters in a railroad car in Compiègne Forest on November 8. At 5:15 on the morning of November 11 they signed articles providing for a rapid withdrawal of the German armies beyond the right bank of the Rhine, surrender of a huge quantity of matériel and 150 submarines, and withdrawal of the German surface fleet to the Baltic.

71. Preliminaries to the Peace Conference

The president would need the full support of the American people in the months following the armistice if he was to win the peace settlement that he had set his heart upon. But he could have overwhelming support at home only if he continued to be the spokesman of the entire country, of Republican moderates as well as Democrats of good will. In this situation, which demanded adroit and national leadership, Wilson so failed to unite the country that it was doubtful whether he spoke for a majority of his people when the peace conference opened.

He made his first mistake even before the guns were silenced on the western front, at the close of the hotly contested off-year congressional campaign. Importuned on all sides by Democratic congressional and senatorial nominees for individual endorsements such as he had given many times before, Wilson decided to issue a blanket appeal to the country. Instead of asking voters to elect candidates who would support him regardless of party affiliation, he made a frankly partisan appeal for a Democratic Congress on October 25, 1918. "The return of a Republican majority to either House of the Congress," he said, "would . . . certainly be interpreted on the other side of the water as a repudiation of my leadership." It was an invitation to disaster. By attempting to make political capital out of foreign policy, Wilson outraged the numerous Republicans whose support had made his war measures possible and threw the question of the peace settlement into the arena of partisan discussion. Even worse, Wilson had declared that he would stand repudiated in the eyes of the world if the people did not vote the Democratic ticket. He had asked for a vote of confidence when he should have known that such a vote is impossible in the American constitutional system.

It is ironical that Wilson's appeal probably had little effect on the outcome of the elections on November 6. Other factors—business resentment against high taxes, disaffection of western wheat farmers because the administration had put ceilings on wheat prices and allowed cotton prices to rise uncontrolled, all the large and petty irritations that stemmed from the war, and the normal inclination of a majority to vote Republican—these, rather than Wilson's ill-timed and futile appeal, accounted for the Republican victory.[1]

Whether or not he stood repudiated by his own people, President Wilson had to proceed. He went ahead unperturbed, sustained by the conviction that he was the representative, not only of the great majority of Americans, but of forward-looking people everywhere. Wilson announced on November 18, 1918, that he would go to the peace conference in Paris as head of the American delegation. Believing as he did that only he could prevail against the forces of greed at Paris, and that the fate of the liberal international program depended upon his presence at the peace conference, Wilson thought that he had no choice in the matter. He went to Paris because stern duty called him there, and whether his decision was a mistake is at least debatable.

Wilson's choice of the peace commissioners was, as things turned out, more obviously a blunder. The commissioners, in addition to the president, were Colonel House, Secretary of State Lansing, General Tasker H. Bliss, a member of the Supreme War Council, and Henry White, an experienced Republican diplomat. They were all able men, but circumstances demanded more than mere ability. Other considerations aside, political necessity demanded appointment of a peace commission that was broadly representative, for Wilson would fail in the critical period after the peace conference if he could not command the support of the Senate and a large minority of Republicans. Wilson understandably ignored the Senate, because he knew that he would have to include Henry Cabot Lodge of Massachusetts, who would be the new chairman of the foreign relations committee, if he appointed any senators at all. Personal relations between the president and Senator Lodge were already so bad that Lodge's appointment was out of the question. On the other hand, it is difficult to understand why Wilson ignored certain other prominent Republicans, notably William H. Taft, who might have worked loyally with

[1] In the next, or Sixty-sixth, Congress, the Republicans would outnumber the Democrats in the House of Representatives 237 to 190 and have a majority of 2 in the Senate.

him at Paris. The answer lies perhaps in Wilson's growing realization that the important work would, perforce, have to be done by the heads of government at the conference, and in his belief that he would need a group of advisers whom he could trust absolutely. But by refusing to take prominent Republicans to Paris, Wilson offended the great body of moderate Republicans and lent credibility to the charge then current that he intended to maintain an exclusive Democratic monopoly on peacemaking.

72. The Versailles Compromise

Wilson, the peace commissioners, and a large body of technical experts sailed from New York aboard the *George Washington* on the morning of December 4, 1918. The American delegation, Wilson told the experts assembled on board, would be the only disinterested spokesman at the conference; the Allied leaders did not even represent their own people. "Tell me what's right and I'll fight for it," he promised. The situation in Europe did not, however, portend easy sailing for one who wished merely to fight for the right. England was in the throes of a parliamentary campaign that found Lloyd George and his Conservative-dominated coalition obliged to give hostages to the aroused passions of the electorate. The French were in a state of postwar shock and clamoring for fearful retribution. Italians expected compensation for their losses in the form of large accretions of Austrian territory. Germany was torn by revolt, and the old Austro-Hungarian Empire had already crumbled. Moreover, the meeting place of the conference, Paris, was a hotbed of anti-German hatred. The crippling terms that the Germans had imposed on the Russians in the treaty of Brest-Litovsk in March 1918 could be used to put aside arguments in favor of greater leniency. At the same time, consideration of long-term issues was handicapped by the immediate fears of the spread of bolshevism into central and even western Europe. As has often been said, bolshevism was the ghost that stalked the peace conference. As for Russia, the situation in that country was in so much flux on account of a civil war raging between the Bolsheviks and their enemies, called Whites, that it would be difficult if not impossible for Wilson and Allied leaders to try to vindicate Wilson's earlier demand in his Fourteen Points Address for absolute self-determination for the Russian people. All through the early months of 1918, Wilson had sternly vetoed fantastic Anglo-French proposals for intervention in Russia to reestablish the eastern front. Under intense Allied pressure, Wilson, in August 1918, had reluctantly dispatched about 5,000 troops to join British forces at Murmansk to guard military supplies there against possible capture by the Germans. He had also sent a force of some 10,000 men under General William S. Graves to Vladivostok to keep the door of escape open for a sizable Czech army fleeing eastward from the Bolsheviks. Incidentally, this force was also to keep an eye on the Japanese, who sent some 73,000 troops into Siberia.

The British and French later sent large forces into Russia to bolster the Whites—action that proved in the end to be totally futile. But beyond this limited action which we have already described, Wilson would not go. Throughout the peace conference he stoutly rejected all proposals for cooperative military Allied-American intervention in Russia. The Russian people, he insisted, should be given the right to settle their own problems in their own way. Moreover, while avowing his hostility to revolutionary communism, he also said that the Russian Revolution was an authentic social and economic revolt against centuries-old oppression and injustice, and that it would be impossible to turn it back by military force.

Wilson first made triumphal tours of Paris, London, and Rome. He then returned to Paris on January 12, 1919, for discussions with the Allied leaders, who made plans for the first plenary session that met six days later. So unwieldy was the conference that important questions were referred to a Council of Ten representing Great Britain, France, Italy, the United States, and Japan, while the detail work was divided among sixty commissions on which the small nations were represented. In order to hasten the conference's work, the Council of Ten was abolished on March 24, and the so-called Big Four—Wilson, Lloyd George, Premier Georges Clemenceau of France, and Prime Minister Vittorio Orlando of Italy—began a long series of private discussions. At the same time, the Council of Five, consisting of the foreign ministers of the five great powers, was established to discuss matters of subordinate importance.

A treaty for Germany had been hammered out and presented to the government of the new German republic by the end of April. The German foreign secretary appeared before a plenary session to receive the treaty on May 7; the German delegates presented a comprehensive reply on May 29; the German National Assembly at Weimar approved the treaty on June 23. The formal ceremony of signing was held on June 28, 1919, in the Hall of Mirrors of the Versailles Palace, where the German empire had been proclaimed forty-eight years before.

This chronology ignores the thousand small details and the writing of treaties with other Central Powers. What concerns us most at this point, however, is what Wilson accomplished at Paris. How did his liberal peace program fare, in spite of the high passions that pervaded the deliberations? The answer is that Wilson accomplished less than he fought for and a great deal more than his critics later admitted. The Versailles treaty was a compromise between the Fourteen Points and what the Allied, and especially the French, peoples demanded.

The foremost problem was security against future German aggression in the West. Foch and Clemenceau proposed to tear the west bank of the Rhine from Germany and create buffer states under French control. Wilson resisted

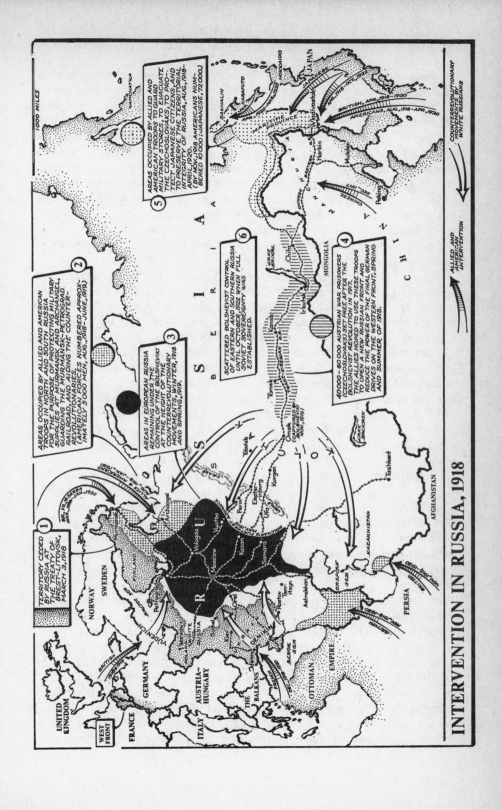

INTERVENTION IN RUSSIA, 1918

1000 MILES

1. TERRITORY CEDED BY RUSSIA AT THE TREATY OF BREST-LITOVSK, MARCH 3, 1918

2. AREAS OCCUPIED BY ALLIED AND AMERICAN TROOPS IN NORTH AND SOUTH RUSSIA FOR THE PURPOSE OF PROTECTING MILITARY SUPPLIES AT MURMANSK AND ARCHANGEL, GUARDING THE MURMANSK-PETROGRAD RAILROAD, AND AIDING THE COUNTER-REVOLUTIONARIES. (AMERICAN FORCES NUMBERED APPROXIMATELY 5,000 MEN, AUG., 1918-JUNE, 1919.)

3. AREAS IN EUROPEAN RUSSIA REMAINING UNDER THE CONTROL OF THE BOLSHEVIKI AT THE HEIGHT OF THE COUNTER-REVOLUTIONARY MOVEMENTS, WINTER, 1918 AND SPRING, 1919.

4. 40,000 - 60,000 AUSTRIAN WAR PRISONERS (CZECHOSLOVAKS) SET FREE AFTER THE BOLSHEVIST REVOLUTION IN 1917. THE ALLIES HOPED TO USE THESE TROOPS TO OPEN A NEW RUSSIAN FRONT AND REDUCE THE POWER OF THE FINAL GERMAN DRIVES ON THE WESTERN FRONT, SPRING AND SUMMER OF 1918.

5. AREAS OCCUPIED BY ALLIED AND AMERICAN TROOPS, TO EVACUATE THE CZECHOSLOVAKS, TO PROTECT JAPANESE CITIZENS, AND TO PRESERVE THE TERRITORIAL INTEGRITY OF RUSSIA, AUG., 1918- (BY NOV. 1918 AMERICANS NUMBERED 10,000 ; JAPANESE, 72,000.)

6. SCATTERED BOLSHEVIST CONTROL OF EASTERN RUSSIA UNTIL OCTOBER, 1922 WHEN FULL SOVIET SOVEREIGNTY WAS ESTABLISHED.

ALLIED AND AMERICAN INTERVENTION

COUNTERREVOLUTIONARY WHITE RUSSIANS

UNITED KINGDOM
WEST FRONT
FRANCE
GERMANY
NORWAY
SWEDEN
ITALY
AUSTRIA-HUNGARY
THE BALKANS
OTTOMAN EMPIRE
PERSIA
AFGHANISTAN
CHINA
MONGOLIA
JAPAN

SIBERIA
KAZAKHSTAN

Moscow
Petrograd
Vologda
Archangel
Murmansk
Kazan
Samara
Tsaritsyn
Astrakhan
Rostov
Perm
Ekaterinburg
Ufa
Kungur
Omsk
Tomsk
Tobolsk
Krasnoyarsk
Irkutsk
Kansk
Chita
Vladivostok
Harbin
Mukden
Peking
Tashkent

BRITISH, APR. 1918-1920
AMERICANS, AUG. 1918-APR. 1920
JAP. 1918-OCT. 1922
CHINESE, DEC. 1917

this demand with Lloyd George's assistance. Instead, France had to be satisfied with the return of Alsace-Lorraine, which was in accord with the principle of self-determination and the Fourteen Points; the permanent demilitarization and a fifteen-year occupation by Allied forces of the west bank of the Rhine; and an Anglo-French-American treaty of mutual defense against Germany. It was this promise of a triple defensive security treaty that persuaded Clemenceau to abandon his demand for the creation of buffer states in the Rhineland. Finally, the German army and navy were so severely limited in size that a future German war of aggression was to be impossible. On the whole, Wilson, Lloyd George, and Clemenceau succeeded in erecting an intelligent defensive structure which, if maintained in full vigor, might have preserved the peace of Europe. Certainly it did not violate the Fourteen Points in any important way.

Secondly, Wilson found the spokesmen of Britain, the British Dominions, Japan, and Italy determined that Germany should not recover her overseas colonies. In the face of their inflexible position, he gave in, but not without gaining important concessions. For one thing, although Japan received title to German economic rights in Shantung Province, she promised to return that province to the political control of China. For another, the former German colonies were not awarded outright to new masters, but were made mandates of the League of Nations and given in responsible trusteeship to Great Britain, the Dominions, and Japan. Whether this arrangement represented the "absolutely impartial adjustment of all colonial claims" that Wilson had demanded in Point 5 would in large measure depend upon the development of the mandate system. We can now see that approval of the mandate system marked the end of western colonialism.

A third major problem was the creation, without violating unduly the principle of self-determination, of a Polish state that would have access to the sea and include former German and Austrian territory inhabited mainly by Poles. Wilson and Lloyd George stood firm against Clemenceau and the Polish representatives to win a settlement that vindicated the Fourteen Points. Poland was given a corridor to the Baltic, while Danzig, her outlet to the sea, was made a free city under the administration of the League of Nations.

The fourth important issue—how much Austrian territory Italy should receive—involved the validity of the secret Treaty of London of 1915. It had brought Italy into the war and promised her the Trentino, the Austrian Tyrol, and a strip of the Dalmatian coast. Wilson was impressed by the plea that control of the Brenner Pass in the Tyrol was absolutely essential to Italian security. He therefore agreed that this area, which contained 200,000 Germans, should go to Italy. The Italians also demanded a long strip of the Dalmatian coast, including the important port of Fiume. Wilson passionately objected, going so far as to appeal to the Italian people over the heads of their government. He argued that Fiume was the only possible outlet to the sea for the new state of Yugoslavia, and he pointed to the Treaty of London, which awarded the port to Yugoslavia. He won his case by main force.

In the struggle over the fifth great issue, reparations, Wilson made his most important concessions. He had agreed during the prearmistice negotiations that Germany should be compelled to pay for all civilian damages incurred by the Allied countries during the war—alone this would be a staggering sum. At the conference he agreed that Germany should also be forced to bear the cost of separation allowances and pensions for Allied veterans. Although he was ill at the time and acted through Colonel House, the president later approved Article CCXXXI of the treaty, in which Germany acknowledged legal responsibility for all losses incurred by the Allied governments and peoples during the war. Wilson agreed, besides, that the Allies might occupy the Rhineland until the potentially astronomical reparations bill was finally paid. Nor was this all. In compensation for wanton destruction of French mines by the retreating German armies, France was given ownership of the mines in the Saar Province of Germany, and the territory was to be governed by a League of Nations commission for fifteen years. The people of the Saar might vote to join the Fatherland at the end of that period. Finally, the treaty compelled the Germans to pay to Britain, France, and Belgium twenty billion gold marks' worth of reparations in kind—merchant shipping, coal, livestock, and the like. In Wilson's defense it should be said that first, he argued consistently in favor of setting a fixed sum for the reparations bill and adjusting it to Germany's capacity to pay; second, he knew that the terms of the reparations were impossible and would have to be revised in the near future —as they were; and third, he gave in to the terms of the reparations only under duress.

In Wilson's mind, the first, last, and overriding issue was the establishment of an international organization to create a concert of world power and preserve the peace. He insisted from the outset of the conference that the covenant, or constitution, of the League of Nations be firmly embedded in the treaty, and that execution of the treaty be entrusted to the League. Clemenceau was not opposed to the League, but he contended that the organization would be helpless to maintain peace unless it had a powerful army and navy at its command. Convinced that such a proposal was politically impossible, Wilson and the British delegates created a League that would depend upon the wholehearted support of its leading members for its effectiveness. As Clemenceau thought that he had obtained security for his beloved France by other means, he was willing to let Wilson write any kind of covenant he desired.

Wilson must have looked back over his labors at Paris and remembered the tense sessions, the bitter complaints of Orlando, the barbed remarks of Clemenceau, and the compromises that he inevitably had had to make. He was nonetheless certain that he had helped to write a treaty and create a postwar peace structure that would endure. He knew that the treaty was not perfect, but he was sure that time would heal many wounds, and that the United

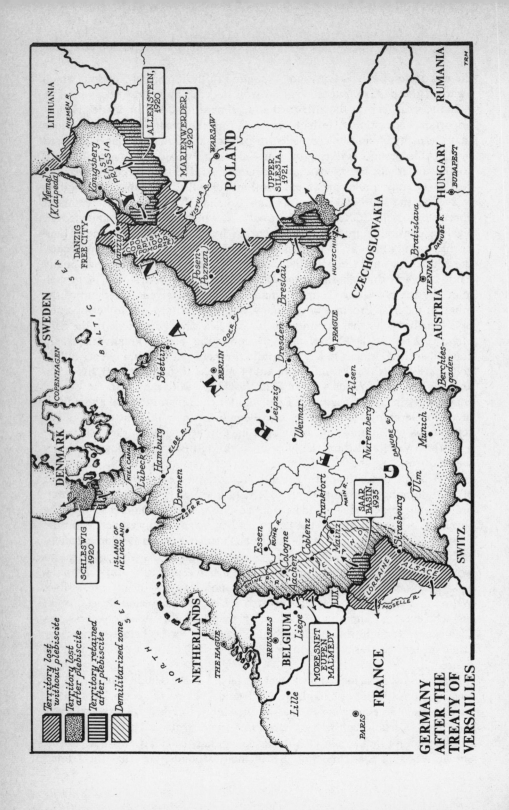

GERMANY AFTER THE TREATY OF VERSAILLES

States could obtain modifications within the League of Nations. Moreover, he had high hopes that the new international order that he had helped so significantly to create would be one in which a reformed capitalism, purged of atavistic imperialism and led by the United States, would offer an irresistible alternative to the Communist demand for a new order to be achieved through the warfare and dictatorship of the proletariat.

Critics, contemporary and historical, have castigated Wilson in general for failing to win the liberal peace program at Paris, in particular for bargaining all his Fourteen Points away in order to win a League of Nations. Such criticism can come only from one who has never bothered to read the Fourteen Points, for that document was actually honored more in the observance than in the breach. Wilson's chief failures—on the colonial question and reparations—were perhaps inevitable. But the damage done was not irreparable, given forceful American leadership in the League of Nations and the reparations commission. Wilson failed to vindicate the principle of freedom of the seas only because he finally realized during the conference that freedom of the seas was a part of the old system of neutrality, and that neutrality would be impossible in future wars. As he said, there could be no neutrals in the new system of collective security.

Wilson's critics, not content with exaggerating his failures, have also minimized his difficulties. He did not write the treaty alone but in collaboration with three astute and determined negotiators. To be sure, Wilson could have withdrawn from the conference, as on one occasion he seriously threatened to do. But the results of American withdrawal would have been even worse than an unsatisfactory settlement. Furthermore, Wilson's difficulties at Paris were compounded by virulent opposition to his peace program in the United States. Senator Lodge, for example, did not lighten the president's burdens by writing to Clemenceau that Wilson did not speak for the American people, who, Lodge declared, desired a harsh and punitive settlement.

Finally, the historian must ask what kind of a peace treaty would have been written if Wilson had not been at Paris and had not won British support for most of his principles. Wilson and Lloyd George together prevented the dismemberment of Germany in the west and compelled a redrawing of the map of Europe that did not unnecessarily violate the principle of self-determination. As the spokesman of the only disinterested nation represented at the conference, Wilson emerged from the fiery trial with the greatest stature precisely because he was able to accomplish so much in spite of stupendous obstacles.

73. First Phases of the Treaty Fight

There were signs long before the end of the Paris Peace Conference that Wilson would encounter strong opposition in the Senate if he insisted on incorporating the covenant of the League in the treaty. The president returned briefly to Washington in the latter part of February 1919 and conferred with the members of the House and Senate foreign relations committees in an effort to meet the rising criticism. Many senators, he learned, objected because the covenant contained no explicit recognition of the Monroe Doctrine, did not specifically exclude internal affairs from the jurisdiction of the League, and made no provision for the right of a member nation to withdraw. On March 4, 1919, just before Wilson was to return to France, moreover, Senator Lodge presented to the upper house a round robin drawn up by Republican leaders warning that the covenant, "in the form now proposed," was unacceptable. It was signed by thirty-nine senators or senators-elect, considerably more than the one-third plus one necessary to defeat ratification. Back in Paris, Wilson obtained changes in the covenant to meet all the criticisms noted above. The president returned to the United States on July 8 and formally presented the treaty to the Senate two days later. "Our isolation was ended twenty years ago," he declared. "There can be no question of our ceasing to be a world power. The only question is whether we can refuse the moral leadership that is offered, whether we shall accept or reject the confidence of the world."

Wilson spoke confidently of the great new role of "service and achievement" that lay ahead for the American people, whose destiny had been disclosed by the very hand of God. His poetic phrases, however, suggested a unanimity that did not exist. No one could yet say how large a part of the population critics of the treaty represented, but they were already well organized and exceedingly vociferous by this time. Leading the opposition was a small group of extreme isolationists in the Senate, chief among whom were Hiram W. Johnson of California, William E. Borah of Idaho, and James A. Reed of Missouri. These irreconcilables, as they were called, were convinced that membership in the League would violate wise historic policy, and they pledged themselves to keep America free from the entanglements of Europe.

Perhaps even more bitterly opposed to the treaty were the so-called hyphenates, their newspapers, and their chief journalistic allies, the Hearst publications. German-Americans protested that the treaty was a base betrayal of the Pre-Armistice Agreement. Italian-Americans were sulking over Wilson's refusal to award Fiume to Italy. But the most virulent opposition came from the Irish-Americans. They were up in arms because Wilson had refused to press the cause of Irish independence at Paris or throw the support of the United States behind the Irish rebellion then in progress.

These opponents were powerful, but the president might yet have triumphed if all Americans who believed in the liberal international program had stood together. Unfortunately for Wilson, such a solid phalanx did not materialize. In the first place, many cautious liberal internationalists—like Elihu Root and Henry L. Stimson, who put their faith in international law and arbitration—feared that Wilson was going too far too fast in breaking with ingrained American traditions. In the second place, many independent progressives and radicals, who had followed Wilson during the war and shared his noble dream of a new world order, drew back in revulsion when the terms of the treaty were published. "The European politicians who with American complicity have hatched this inhuman monster," exclaimed the *New Republic,* the leading liberal internationalist journal, "have acted either cynically, hypocritically, or vindictively." The *Nation* and other liberal journals were equally bitter.

The greatest obstacles to ratification of the treaty, however, were personal and partisan rivalries and prejudices, old traditions of apartness, and the absence in 1919 and 1920 of any popular conviction that membership in the League was essential to American security. Germany had been decisively beaten and disarmed; Russia was in chaos. No war clouds darkened the horizon; no nation menaced the peace and security of the United States. Men might warn of the perils of the future, but who would believe them when it was obvious there could never be another war?

After Wilson presented the treaty to the Senate, the vortex of the struggle over ratification shifted to the upper house, which in the past had upset the plans of many presidents. A fairly distinct alignment was already evident by midsummer of 1919. There were sixteen bitter-end isolationists, mainly Republicans, who would vote against the treaty in any form so long as it contained the covenant. They were a small minority, but they dominated the foreign relations committee and were able to influence the committee's chairman, Lodge, by their frequent threats to bolt the Republican camp. On the other hand, at least forty-three of the forty-seven Democrats would follow Wilson's lead, while the great majority of the forty-nine Republicans favored ratification after making certain reservations to safeguard American interests. Most of these were what were called strong reservationists. Thus considerably more than the necessary two-thirds in the Senate favored ratification of the treaty and membership in the League. The main task of statesmanship in the months ahead would be to find common ground upon which this preponderant majority could stand.

Much, of course, would depend upon the ability of leaders of both parties to suppress partisan ambitions and prejudices and pull together for the common good. The Republican leader in the Senate was Henry Cabot Lodge, a Boston Brahmin, long an intimate of Theodore Roosevelt, and a man of some intellect. Although he had supported a postwar League in 1915 and 1916, Lodge reversed himself after Wilson linked the League plan with the concept of a "peace without victory." Exactly where he stood on the League of Nations in the summer of 1919, it is impossible to say. One historian has recently suggested that Lodge was not an irreconcilable but rather that he was intent upon taking leadership in the treaty struggle out of Wilson's hands and winning credit for ratification for himself and the Republican party.

Lodge's position was, admittedly, extraordinarily difficult. As leader of his party in the Senate he had to preserve some semblance of harmony among the three Republican factions—the irreconcilable isolationists, a small group of so-called mild reservationists, and the large majority who favored strong reservations. Naturally he was buffeted about and appeared all things to all men. But never during the treaty fight or afterward did he act like a sincere friend of the League or a statesman who was able to exalt the national interest above his consuming personal hatred of Wilson and the Democratic party. On the contrary, moving from one calculated step to another, he acted as if his chief purpose was to embarrass the president and prevent ratification of the treaty.

Public sentiment in July 1919 was running so strongly in favor of the treaty that Lodge knew that he could not defeat it outright. Thirty-two state legislatures and thirty-three governors had endorsed the League. Leaders of the League to Enforce Peace were now actively campaigning for unconditional ratification, and a poll of the nation's press indicated that an overwhelming majority of newspapers favored American membership in the League. It was evident to the Massachusetts senator, therefore, that he must work indirectly —first, by packing the foreign relations committee with enemies of the League; second, by appending such strong reservations to the covenant that the president would refuse to accept them.

Meanwhile, Lodge desperately needed time to allow the opponents of the League to agitate. Time he easily obtained, by reading aloud all of the 264 pages of the treaty, which consumed two weeks, and then by holding public hearings on the treaty for another six weeks. In the meantime, the bitter-enders, liberally supplied with funds by the steel manufacturer Henry C. Frick and the banker and aluminum monopolist Andrew W. Mellon, flooded the country with anti-League propaganda.

Opponents of the treaty were gaining momentum by September 1919. At the same time, a series of convulsive strikes had diverted Wilson's attention and prevented him from giving his customary leadership to the League forces. It is true that he had appeared before Lodge's committee on August 19 and conferred individually with some twenty Republican senators, in an effort to detach them from their party. But the more he conferred with senators the more he realized that the situation was passing out of his control. In these circumstances Wilson decided upon bold steps. First, he announced on September 3 that he would not oppose interpretive reservations that did not impair the integrity of the covenant or require new diplomatic negotiations. Second, he decided to carry his fight for the League to the people. He would purify the wells of public sentiment poisoned by the irreconcilables; he would tell the people the truth about their stake in preserving peace through the League of Nations.

No act of his public career so dramatically demonstrated Wilson's sincerity as his decision to undertake this campaign. His health had been poor since he had suffered what was perhaps a slight stroke at Paris. He was now weak and exhausted, and his physician warned that a long speaking tour might take his life. He gladly took the risk, however, thinking that he could arouse such a ground swell of support for the League that his senatorial opponents could not resist it. He traveled more than 8,000 miles through the Middle and Far West for three weeks in September and delivered some thirty-seven addresses. The strain on his meager physical resources was great, but the total effect of his outpouring to the people of the West was magnificent. The deeper Wilson moved into the West the larger and more enthusiastic the crowds became. In fact, the irreconcilables were so alarmed by the president's triumphal procession that they sent their two best speakers, Senators Johnson and Borah, to trail him.

The effects of the strain began to tell on Wilson even before the tour was half over. He began to have blinding headaches and to show signs of exhaustion. He delivered one of his longest and most important speeches at Pueblo, Colorado, on September 25. "It always seems to make it difficult for me to say anything, my fellow citizens, when I think of my clients in this case," he exclaimed. "My clients are the children; my clients are the next generation. . . . I intend to redeem my pledges to the children; they shall not be sent . . . [to France]." After this address the president was so near collapse that his physician canceled the remaining speeches and sped the presidential train straight to Washington. Wilson suffered a stroke on October 2, 1919, that paralyzed the left side of his face and body, and for days his life hung in a precarious balance.

74. The Triumph of Partisanship

Meanwhile, the battle in the Senate had begun when the foreign relations committee reported the treaty on September 10, 1919, with forty-five amendments and four reservations. The Democrats defeated all the amendments with the help of some twelve Republican "mild reservationists." Thereupon Lodge, on November 6, presented for his committee a series of fourteen reservations. Most of them merely underlined existing provisions of the covenant and provided that the United States could take no action in important matters without the consent of Congress. The fourth reservation reserved control over all domestic affairs exclusively to the United States; the fifth removed all questions arising under the Monroe Doctrine from the jurisdiction of the League; the sixth declared that the United States withheld assent from the articles of the treaty relating to Shantung. The most important reservation, the second, had been suggested by Elihu Root on June 21, 1919. It asserted that the United States assumed no obligations under Article X of the covenant to preserve the territorial integrity or political independence of any country, interfere in controversies between nations, or use its armed forces to uphold any article of the treaty for any purpose, unless Congress by joint resolution so provided. The Senate approved twelve of Lodge's reservations, including the second, after a bitter partisan battle, and then two others were added.

The next move was up to the ailing president and his Democratic colleagues in the Senate. Colonel House and other friends of the League begged Wilson either to compromise on Lodge's terms or else to accept the Senator's reservations entirely, if that was necessary to get the United States into the League. Gilbert M. Hitchcock of Nebraska, Democratic leader in the Senate, was allowed to visit Wilson in his sickroom on November 7 and 17. He found the president determined never to surrender and disposed to compromise only on his own terms—by accepting reservations that he thought did not impair the obligations of the United States under the covenant. Furthermore, in a public letter to Hitchcock, actually drafted by Hitchcock, Wilson declared on November 18 that the Lodge reservations provided for nullification, not ratification, of the treaty. He virtually ordered Democratic senators to vote against them.

The first showdown came when the Senate voted on the treaty on the following day, November 19, 1919. On a resolution to ratify with the Lodge reservations, the irreconcilables combined with a nearly solid Democratic phalanx to defeat ratification by a vote of fifty-five nays to thirty-nine ayes. A Democratic resolution to ratify without any reservations failed immediately afterward by a vote of fifty-three nays to thirty-eight ayes.

It was apparent from the two test votes that seventy-seven senators, considerably more than the necessary two-thirds, favored ratification with or without reservations. What chance was there for compromise between the two factions? It was clear after the first Senate vote that Lodge would never surrender and that Wilson would have to compromise largely on the Senator's terms if he wanted ratification. Colonel House advised the president to wash his hands of responsibility and let the Senate decide; William J. Bryan urged immediate ratification, even with reservations, and most Democratic senators privately agreed. The French and British leaders were, if anything, more frightened by the prospect of the treaty's defeat than were Wilson's friends. The British government sent Sir Edward Grey (now Viscount Grey of Fallodon), former foreign secretary, as a special ambassador to Washington to plead for compromise. The president, however, refused to see Grey and was angered when the viscount later issued a public statement declaring that the League would fail without the United States, and that the Allies would accept the Lodge reservations without requiring a reopening of negotiations.

Public sentiment in the United States, moreover, refused to accept the Senate's vote on November 19, 1919, as final. Leaders of the League to Enforce Peace, now called the League of Free Nations Association, appealed for ratification with necessary reservations; newspaper spokesmen were up in arms. Leaders of twenty-six organizations representing some 20 million members on January 13 and February 9, 1920, demanded that Lodge and Wilson compromise their differences. But the weary man in the White House paid scant heed to this ground swell, if, indeed, he knew much about it. He tried to find some constitutional way to challenge his senatorial foes to resign and go before their constituents on the issue of the League. In this plan he would have resigned if his opponents were returned to the Senate. Failing for technical reasons to work this out, Wilson made another proposal in a public letter to Democrats assembled at a Jackson Day dinner in Washington on January 8, 1920. He was certain, Wilson asserted, that the overwhelming majority of Americans desired prompt ratification without crippling reservations. If, however, the Senate refused thus to ratify, then the presidential election of 1920 would be a "great and solemn referendum" in which the voters could decide the issue. Public opinion now turned decisively against the president who had put himself in the position of being the chief obstacle to a solution.

In the face of what seemed to be an overwhelming demand at home and abroad for ratification, the Senate agreed to reconsider and began debate anew in mid-February 1920. While Democratic leaders tried desperately to find common ground with the Republicans, the president, now vastly improved in health and mental vigor, hurled blast after blast at the Lodge reservations and even intimated that he would refuse to proclaim the treaty if the Senate adopted them. The treaty came up for vote on March 19. One reservation, favoring Irish independence, had been added by the Democrats in an effort to embarrass Lodge, while the second reservation regarding Article X had been made even more sweeping than before.

Practically all Democratic senators desperately wanted to accept the reservations. But a majority of them were literally too afraid of Wilson to oppose him; and twenty-three Democrats joined the irreconcilables to defeat approval by a vote of thirty-five nays to forty-nine ayes. A change of only seven Democratic votes would have put the United States in the League of Nations! To end the state of hostilities, Congress adopted a joint resolution on May 15, 1920, repealing the war resolutions against Germany and Austria-Hungary and reserving to the United States all rights under the Treaty of Versailles. Wilson vetoed this resolution on May 27, declaring that he would not be party "to an action which would place ineffable strain upon the gallantry and honor of the United States."

It was the end, although the tragedy was prolonged during the "great and solemn referendum" that was no referendum at all. Who was responsible for American refusal to enter the League of Nations and for the "ineffable stain" of a separate peace? Certainly Lodge and his Republican friends shared a large measure of guilt for one of the most tragic episodes in American history. Had they been less interested in the election of 1920 and more concerned with their country's good they would have suppressed personal and partisan ambitions and met the champions of the League halfway. In addition, the irreconcilables, who used every device to defeat ratification, shared a large part of the blame, for the unscrupulous propaganda that some of them put forth helped to confuse the public about the implications of American membership in the League.

On the other hand, Wilson, too, was partly responsible. Perhaps because of his hatred for Lodge, perhaps because he believed to the end that the people would force the Senate to his terms, perhaps because his illness had impaired his judgment, he also refused to compromise. He ignored the advice of his best counselors and threw away the only possible chance for ratification. He therefore shared responsibility for breaking the heart of the world. Finally, those Democratic senators who voted against ratification with reservations out of fear of Wilsonian wrath served neither the national interest nor the cause of international peace.

Whatever the causes for the great betrayal of 1919–1920, the consequences remained. The American people were perhaps not yet ready to assume leadership in world affairs, but their leaders denied them an opportunity even to learn the duties of leadership or to grow in wisdom and experience. More important were the catastrophic effects of the American rejection on the infant League and on the future development of European politics. Given American leadership in the postwar era, the League might have developed into the association of free peoples of which its founders had dreamed, and it might have become more efficient in dealing with the maladjustments of European society.

Chapter 10

Demobilization and the Triumph of Normalcy, 1918-1920

All postwar periods in American history have been times when partisanship runs at fever pitch and passions generated by the war drive people to acts of violence. So it was during the years following the armistice, as war hysteria found new victims in "Reds," foreigners, Jews, Negroes, and Catholics. As if further to confuse the domestic scene, labor unrest during 1919 and 1920 was at its highest peak since the 1890s. Politically, the postwar era was marked by extraordinary partisanship. Centering at first on the struggle over ratification of the Versailles treaty, this partisan conflict culminated in 1920, when a reunited Republican party smashed the Wilsonian progressive coalition and swept into control of the federal government. The election results were convincing evidence that the people were determined to put an end to the division of control in the federal government and to return, as the Republican candidate in 1920 said, to "normalcy," to the good days of prosperity and peace.

75. Demobilization, 1918–1920

Just as it had adopted the war resolution without any earlier effective preparation for a great war effort, the American government found itself on November 11, 1918, without any plan for demobilization and reconstruction. Indeed, the sudden and unexpected German collapse came at a time when American leaders were planning, not for peace, but for an invasion of Germany in 1919.

The president aptly described the manner in which demobilization took place in his Annual Message to Congress in December 1918: "The moment we knew the armistice to have been signed we took the harness off." And that is about what happened. The AEF was brought home and quickly demobilized. Various war agencies began to wind up their affairs. For example, the War Industries Board, refusing to believe there were any problems of demobilization that the business world could not solve, abandoned its control of industry once the fighting stopped. "The magnificent war formation of American industry was dissipated in a day," writes the board's chief historian.

Everyone, it seemed, expected the country to return quickly to normal without benefit of governmental controls and planning. However, by the time that Wilson returned from Paris for the first time, in February 1919, prices were rising fast, and large-scale unemployment and industrial conflict seemed inevitable. Unable to obtain legislation from the lame-duck session, Wilson prepared for the impending crisis as best he could. Calling governors and mayors to the White House on March 3, he warned them of the dangers ahead. In addition, he established an Industrial Board to coordinate the efforts of various governmental purchasing agencies to hold the line on prices. The Industrial Board, however, had neither statutory authority nor prestige in the business world. It disbanded in May 1919, after the Railroad Administration refused to permit it to fix prices for steel.

For the most part, therefore, the administration was powerless to meet the larger problems of postwar inflation, business readjustment, and industrial conflict. On the other hand, the period 1919–1920 was not as chaotic or unproductive as this generalization might suggest. For one thing, there were specific problems of demobilization so urgent that Congress could not ignore them. For another, the last two years of the Wilson era witnessed congressional approval of significant measures that brought several phases of the progressive movement to final culmination.

The first requirement was the most urgent—to provide funds to liquidate the war effort at home, care for wounded soldiers and sailors, bring the AEF back from France, and provide relief for Europe. In spite of demands for immediate tax reduction, the lame-duck session courageously adopted a War Revenue bill in February 1919 that increased the tax burden, especially on business and the upper classes. (For the provisions of this measure see pp. 187–188.)

The second problem was the disposition of the railroads still being operated by the Railroad Administration at the beginning of 1919. While McAdoo recommended a five-year experiment in public operation and Congress deliberated during the summer of 1919, the so-called Plumb Plan, suggested by Glenn E. Plumb, a lawyer for the brotherhoods, to nationalize the railroads and give the workers a share in their management and profit gained the support of the AF of L and the railroad workers. Wilson took no part in the controversy over the Plumb Plan. He simply announced on December 24, 1919, that he would return the railroads to their owners on March 1, 1920, unless Congress decided otherwise.

Congress responded with the Transportation Act of 1920, drafted largely by two midwestern progressive Republicans, Representative John J. Esch of Wisconsin and Senator Albert B. Cummins of Iowa, and approved February 28, 1920. The Transportation Act was perhaps the most significant measure of the immediate postwar era because it marked the complete fulfillment of the movement for thoroughgoing federal control of railroads. Stopping only short of nationalization, the act gave the ICC complete control over rates, even those set by state commissions; authorized the ICC to supervise the sale of railroad securities and expenditure of the proceeds; permitted railroads to pool traffic in the interest of economy; and empowered the ICC to consolidate existing lines into a limited number of systems.

A third issue was disposition of the huge fleet of merchant vessels that the Shipping Board had purchased, confiscated, or built during and after the war. No one wanted to junk a merchant marine that totaled some 15 million tons by 1920; yet Congress was unwilling to embark upon a long-range program of public operation. A compromise solution was embodied in the Merchant Marine Act of 1920. It directed the Shipping Board to sell as many vessels as possible to corporations of predominantly American ownership and authorized the federally owned Merchant Fleet Corporation to open new shipping lines and operate surplus vessels. As it turned out, the Shipping Board's low prices on easy terms and guarantees against operational losses to private firms lured considerable private capital into the shipping industry and kept a sizable merchant marine afloat in the 1920s. By 1930 the privately owned American merchant marine totaled over 7 million tons.

Four measures—the General Leasing and Water Power acts of 1920 and the woman's suffrage and prohibition amendments—rounded out the postwar legislative program and revealed that the reform spirit was by no means dead. The General Leasing Act empowered the secretary of the interior to lease public lands containing mineral and oil deposits to private parties on terms that safeguarded the public interest. The Water Power Act established a Federal Power Commission, composed of the secretaries of war, the interior, and agriculture. It could license the building and operation of dams and hydroelectric plants on navigable rivers and nonnavigable streams in the public domain. We will reserve our discussion of national prohibition for a later chapter. The point here is that Congress acted promptly and, it thought, effectively to implement what many progressives hailed as the greatest triumph for morality since the abolition of slavery. Another important objective of the progressive movement, woman's suffrage, also came to fruition at this time. Congress approved the Nineteenth Amendment, which forbade denying the right to vote on account of sex, in June 1919; it was ratified in August 1920. (For details of the struggle for women's rights, see pp. 59–61.)

76. Postwar Inflation and Labor Troubles

Leaders in Washington and the states prepared during the early months of 1919 as best they could to cope with the mass unemployment that they thought would follow demobilization. The crisis that they anticipated never came. Instead, a boom got under way during the summer of 1919, and industrial production was well above the wartime peak by the following October. In face of what seemed to be insatiable demand, prices began rising in the spring of 1919 and continued to mount until the autumn of 1920. The cost of living rose to 77 percent above the prewar level in 1919 and to 105 percent above the prewar level in 1920.

The postwar inflation's chief significance lay in the fact that it combined with other forces to set off an unprecedented outbreak of labor troubles. All told, during 1919 there were 2,665 strikes involving more than 4 million workers, as organized labor fought to preserve wartime gains and embarked upon ambitious new projects of unionization.

The wave of strikes began four days after the armistice, when the Amalgamated Clothing Workers in New York and Chicago struck for the forty-four-hour week and a 15 percent wage increase. Victory for the union was followed by adoption of the new wage and hours scale in the entire clothing industry. Then in rapid succession followed a general strike in Seattle and strikes by textile workers in New England and New Jersey, telephone operators in New England, telegraph operators throughout the country, the printers' union, the longshoremen of New York, and switchmen in the Chicago railroad yards. Practically all these strikes, and hundreds of others, succeeded, and organized labor was able not only to hold its own against rising prices but also to win an increase in real income.

This outbreak of industrial unrest, however, occurred at a time when the American people were disturbed by a new hysteria—the so-called Red scare. Most of the strikes of 1919 were waged successfully in spite of a growing popular suspicion that they were being provoked by Communist agents and would culminate in a general labor uprising. On the other hand, organized labor's most important effort in 1919, the AF of L's drive to win collective bargaining in the steel industry, ran afoul of the Red hysteria.

The United States Steel Corporation had stood since 1901 as the chief barrier to unionization of the basic industries. Encouraged by the friendly attitude of federal authorities and what they thought was a sympathetic public opinion, the AF of L convention directed its executive committee in June 1918 to undertake "one mighty drive to organize the steel plants of America"—the first attack in a new general offensive against the mass industries. The union's president, Samuel Gompers, appointed a National Committee for the Organizing of the Iron and Steel Industry on August 1, with William Z. Foster, a left-wing syndicalist, as secretary.

Foster and his committee organized the steel workers all during late 1918 and early 1919, and the reorganized steel workers' union claimed a membership of 100,000 by June 1919 and was ready to test its strength in battle. Although the union included a minority of the steel workers, no impartial observer could doubt that it voiced the protests of the overwhelming majority against old and rankling grievances. Steel workers lived everywhere under the tyranny of petty bosses, and even mild complaints often brought prompt dismissal. Moreover, about half the iron and steel employees worked from twelve to fourteen hours a day, an additional quarter worked between ten to twelve hours daily, and a minority worked twenty-four hours a day every other Sunday.[1] Wage rates were so low in 1919 that 60 percent of all steel workers and their families lived below or barely above a minimum subsistence level.

Union officials presented their demands—recognition, the eight-hour day, "an American living wage," and reinstatement of workers discharged for union activities—to Judge Elbert H. Gary, head of United States Steel, in August 1919. Gary refused to negotiate, and some 343,000 workers in the plants of United States Steel went on strike on September 22. Three days later the walkout spread to plants of Bethlehem Steel. The ensuing struggle was marked by widespread violence in which eighteen strikers were killed, by the use of state and federal troops to prevent picketing, and by stern suppression of civil liberties in all strike districts except West Virginia. Perhaps the most significant aspect of the conflict was management's use of new propaganda techniques learned during the war. By raising and reiterating the false alarm of Bolshevism, management and the vast majority of newspapers diverted public attention from the workers' grievances to the false issue of communism. As a result the workers lost the support of public opinion in this most crucial battle.

With a large segment of public opinion and most state officials arrayed against them, the strikers could not win, for the steel companies had emerged from the war with full treasuries and resources adequate for a long struggle. The first break came when United States Steel officials imported tens of thousands of strikebreakers and put them to work under military guard. For

---

[1] The average work week in the steel industry in 1919 was 68.7 hours, as compared with a work week of 67.6 hours in 1910.

example, the large United States Steel works at Gary, Indiana, were operating at 75 percent capacity by November. The struggle dragged on into January 1920, when it was officially ended by the unconditional surrender of the AF of L.

While the steel strike was getting under way a police strike in Boston gave further evidence of deep social unrest and incidentally catapulted an obscure governor of Massachusetts into the vice-presidency of the United States. The police of Boston, like most other public employees during the postwar inflation, were struggling to survive on prewar salaries. When city authorities refused to raise wages and correct other grievances, the policemen's organization, the Boston Social Club, obtained a charter as an AF of L local in August 1919 and threatened to strike. A hastily appointed Mayor's Citizens' Committee was conciliatory and proposed a settlement that would have granted most of the union's demands, except recognition. The police commissioner, however, not only rejected the proposed settlement but also summarily dismissed nineteen leaders of the local.

Thus goaded, the policemen abandoned their posts on September 9, 1919. A volunteer force was unable to control the gangs of looters that menaced the city, and Governor Calvin Coolidge called out the Boston companies of the National Guard and took personal command. The strike was quickly broken; the rebel policemen were dismissed; and a new police force was assembled. And when Gompers appealed to Coolidge to persuade the Boston authorities to reinstate the strikers, the governor replied with a cryptic rebuke that made him at once nationally famous: "There is no right to strike against the public safety by anybody, anywhere, anytime."

The last important strike of the immediate postwar era, the short-lived bituminous coal strike of November 1919, was notable in that it provoked the first test of strength between the federal government and the new president of the United Mine Workers of America (UMW), John L. Lewis. Of all workers in the country bituminous miners probably had the best grounds for discontent. The UMW had concluded a no-strike agreement—the so-called Washington Agreement—with the Fuel Administration in August 1917. Although anthracite miners later received substantial wage increases, bituminous miners received none. Meeting in Indianapolis in September 1919, the UMW adopted a bold program demanding immediate abrogation of the Washington Agreement, a six-hour day and five-day week, and wage increases to 60 percent. And when the operators refused to negotiate until the Washington Agreement had expired, Lewis called a nationwide bituminous strike for November 1. Meanwhile, Attorney General A. Mitchell Palmer had tried vainly to persuade the UMW to cancel the strike order, which, he claimed, was in violation of the Lever Act.

Faced with a complete shutdown of the mines, Palmer obtained one injunction on November 8 from the federal district court in Indianapolis ordering Lewis and other UMW officials to cease all strike activity. Shortly afterward he obtained another injunction commanding union officials to cancel their strike order by November 10. "We cannot fight the government," Lewis declared as he called off the strike. Nonetheless, the miners refused to go back to work until the government, a month later, ordered an immediate 14 percent wage increase and established an arbitration commission to consider the union's demands. The commission, after extended hearings, awarded the miners another 27 percent increase in pay without changing the hours of work.

77. The First Red Scare

The triumph of the Bolshevik revolution in Russia in November 1917, the ensuing spread of communism into Germany, Hungary, and other parts of Europe, and especially the formation in Moscow on March 2, 1919, of the Third International, or Comintern, as it came to be known, dedicated to stimulating immediate world proletarian revolution, set off a wave of new hysteria in the United States. No other development of the postwar era so well reflected the insecurity of the American people as their reactions to fantastic rumors of an equally fantastic Bolshevik uprising in their midst.

An early sign of the excited state of public opinion was the trial of Victor Berger, Socialist congressman from Milwaukee, for conspiracy under the Sedition Act. Reelected to the House in November 1918 after his indictment, Berger was tried in Chicago in the following December, convicted, and sentenced to prison for twenty years. He was released on bail pending appeal (the government finally dropped all charges against Berger in 1922), but denied his seat in the lower house when Congress met in special session in May 1919. Reelected in a special election in December 1919, Berger was again denied his seat in January 1920.[2]

Berger's conviction was the first manifestation of hysteria that developed in response to a series of events during the following months into the first Red scare. Workers in Seattle staged a general strike on February 6, 1919, that brought industry to a standstill and seriously crippled operation of utilities and transportation services. Asserting that the strike was the work of Bolsheviks and the IWW, Mayor Ole Hanson trumpeted that it was the first step in a nationwide workers' uprising. At the same time, committees of the United States Senate and the New York legislature began investigations of Bolshevik activities, while the Justice Department rounded up fifty-three alien Communists on the West Coast on February 11 and shipped them to New York for deportation. A week later a naturalized citizen was quickly acquit-

[2]He was reelected to the House in 1922, seated promptly when Congress convened, and served until his death in 1929.

ted in Indiana for killing an alien who had shouted, "To hell with the United States!"

The climax came with the discovery in April of a plot to assassinate governors, judges, Cabinet members, and other public officials. A large bomb was found in Mayor Hanson's mail on April 28; the following day the maid of Senator Thomas W. Hardwick of Georgia had her hands blown off when she opened a package in the senator's Atlanta home. Immediate investigation in the New York Post Office uncovered sixteen bomb packages addressed to such persons as Attorney General Palmer, Postmaster General Burleson, Justice Oliver Wendell Holmes, J.P. Morgan, and John D. Rockefeller. Some twenty other explosive devices were discovered elsewhere in the mails. In addition, later in the spring the residences of Attorney General Palmer, two judges, and others were partially destroyed, with loss of two lives, by bombs in eight cities. The guilty parties, probably a few anarchists, were never apprehended.[3]

Popular retaliation came quickly and indiscriminately. The California legislature outlawed membership in organizations that advocated use of violence. In the wake of the investigations of its Lusk Committee, the New York legislature enacted similar, if less drastic, legislation.[4] Some four hundred soldiers and sailors invaded the offices of the New York *Call*, a Socialist daily, and beat up several May Day celebrants. In other parts of New York, and in Boston and Cleveland, there were clashes between May Day paraders and servicemen and police. The most serious outbreak occurred in the lumber town of Centralia, Washington, on Armistice Day. Members of the newly organized American Legion attacked the local headquarters of the IWW, and four of the attackers were killed in the ensuing fracas. In swift reprisal enraged townspeople lynched one of the defenders; police officials raided IWW headquarters throughout the state, arresting more than one thousand leaders of the union; and eleven IWW members involved in the Centralia affair were soon afterward convicted of murder and sentenced to long prison terms.

Scare headlines and sensational newspaper reports magnified these events and stimulated a widespread public alarm,[5] and never was a great nation so afraid of phantom invaders and so agitated by groundless fears. Any threat

[3]The worst bombing occurred more than a year later, in September 1920, when a wagonload of explosives was set off in front of the offices of J. P. Morgan & Company in New York City. Thirty-eight people were killed, more than 200 were injured, and property damage ran to more than $2 million.

[4]Vetoed by Governor Alfred E. Smith, the New York anti-Communist bill was reenacted and signed by Smith's Republican successor in 1921.

[5]One good index of the state of public opinion was the adoption by state legislatures in 1919 and 1920 of laws outlawing display of the Red flag, prohibiting membership in organizations that advocated the violent overthrow of the government, and forbidding seditious utterances. Thirty-four states and two territories enacted such statutes in 1919; two states adopted such legislation in 1920.

would have had to come from the newly organized Communist parties, the alleged spearheads of the revolution. One of them, the Communist Labor party, breaking away from the national Socialist convention in Chicago, was formed on August 31, 1919. It had between 10,000 and 30,000 members by the end of the year. Another, the Communist Party of America, was organized on September 1. It had a membership of between 30,000 and 60,000 by the end of 1919.

The danger of social upheaval in 1919 now seems exceedingly remote in view of the extreme weakness of these parties of the Left. The Wilson administration, however, acted as if the menace were dire and launched such a campaign against civil liberties as the country had not witnessed in peacetime since 1799. The organizer and leader of this campaign was the attorney general, A. Mitchell Palmer of Pennsylvania, who thought that he had a good chance to become the next resident of the White House. Palmer not only set the entire Federal Bureau of Investigation to work ferreting out Communists and boring into their organizations, but he also urged Congress to adopt a measure that went so far as to punish persons guilty even of inciting sedition.

When Congress refused to enact Palmer's sedition bill, the attorney general struck out on his own private campaign. The Labor Department had rounded up some 249 known Russian Communists and shipped them to Finland on December 21, 1919. But Palmer was after bigger game. Without informing the secretary or assistant secretary of labor of his plan, Palmer obtained warrants for the arrest of some three thousand alien members of the Communist and Communist Labor parties from a subordinate official in the Labor Department. Thousands of federal agents and local police executed a gigantic simultaneous raid on Communist headquarters throughout the country on the night of January 2, 1920. Some four thousand persons, many of them non-Communists and American citizens, were hurried off to jails and bull pens in thirty-three major cities in twenty-three states. Persons visiting prisoners in Hartford, Connecticut, were arrested on the ground that they, too, must be Communists.

Eventually one-third of the victims were released for lack of evidence. American citizens suspected of membership in a Communist party were turned over to local authorities for indictment and prosecution under state syndicalism laws. But for the aliens it was a different story. Outraged by Palmer's procedure, Assistant Secretary of Labor Louis F. Post took charge of the deportation proceedings and saw that justice was done. Only 556 aliens, all of them proved members of the Communist party, were deported.

Palmer continued to warn of gigantic Red plots, but he executed no more raids. The scene now shifted to the states, with investigations by the Lusk Committee of the New York legislature and the subsequent expulsion of five Socialist members of the New York Assembly on April 1, 1920, for no crime except membership in the Socialist party; the arrest and conviction of two anarchists, Nicola Sacco and Bartolomeo Vanzetti, for the alleged murder of a paymaster in a South Braintree, Massachusetts, shoe factory; and the growth everywhere of demands for conformity. As we shall see in a later chapter, the postwar era bequeathed to the 1920s a heritage of hatred and hysteria that permeated and disturbed every aspect of life and thought.

78. Troubled Race Relations

This summer of the first Red scare was also a time of tribulation for American Negroes, as postwar intolerances found yet other victims and another form of expression. Tensions burst into the most awful outbreak of interracial warfare in the history of the United States. Let us look first at the causes of this violence on America's most troubled social frontier.

To begin with, a decline in immigration from a little over 1,218,000 in 1914 to 327,000 in 1915 created a scarcity of unskilled labor and stimulated the first large-scale migration of Negroes from the southern countryside to northern and midwestern industrial centers. This stream of black workers swelled in response to increased demands in 1917 and 1918. The nearly half million Negroes who went to the North found no warm welcome awaiting them. Forced to crowd into the worst areas, they became the object of the suspicion and hatred of white unskilled workers, most of them immigrants themselves, who resented Negro competition and mores.

At the same time, Negro-white relations were considerably worsened by the Negroes' participation in the war. Some 400,000 Negroes served in the armed forces, about half of them overseas where they were accorded an equality they had never known in their native South. White southerners were terrified at the thought of so many Negro men learning the use of firearms and the ways of equality. They were prepared in 1919 to use the rope and the faggot to remind returning Negro veterans that the Great Crusade had been no war for racial democracy in the South.

Thirdly, while the war heightened anti-Negro sentiments in both the North and South, the Negro people of America and their spokesmen were beginning to demand higher wages, immunity from violence, and larger participation in politics. Most important, their participation in the war effort had given them a new sense of pride in their own race. The National Association for the Advancement of Colored People, now under control of a militant element, was especially active during the war. One of the NAACP's leaders, William E. B. Du Bois, convoked a Pan-African Congress in Paris during the peace conference to speak for Negroes throughout the world.

These tensions burst into wholesale violence in the South as white men resorted to traditional weapons to intimidate Negro communities. Lynchings increased from thirty-four in 1917 to sixty in 1918, and to more than seventy in 1919. Ten Negro veterans, several of them still in uniform, were lynched in 1919; fourteen Negroes were burned publicly. Southern white terrorism also found expression in a form more ominous than these individual acts of violence—in the rapid spread, especially through the Southwest, of the newly revived Ku Klux Klan, about which more will be said later. The Klan grew during 1919 from insignificance into a thriving organization of more than 100,000 members with cells in twenty-seven states. Defying law enforcement officials, hooded Klan night riders flogged, tarred, and hanged their victims in many southern and southwestern communities.

Even worse travail awaited Negro Americans in the outbreak of the most fearful race riots in American history.[6] They began in July 1919 in Longview, Texas, and spread a week later to the nation's capital, where mobs composed principally of white servicemen pillaged the Negro section. The worst riot broke out in Chicago on July 27, 1919, after an altercation between whites and Negroes on a Lake Michigan beach. Mobs roamed the slum areas of the city for thirteen days, burning, pillaging, and killing, with the National Guard unable to subdue them. Fifteen whites and twenty-three Negroes were dead when it was over; 178 whites and 342 Negroes were injured; and more than 1,000 families were homeless. During the next two months major riots broke out in Knoxville, Omaha, and Elaine, Arkansas, and the final count by the end of 1919 revealed some twenty-five riots, with hundreds dead and injured and property damages running into the millions.

Negroes and liberal whites were dismayed and reacted in varied ways. The NAACP and other militant Negro groups counseled resistance and undertook a public campaign against lynching. It culminated in the passage by the House of Representatives of the first antilynching bill in 1921. This measure was endorsed by twenty-four governors and an overwhelming northern opinion, but it was defeated by a southern filibuster in the Senate. The most significant reaction in the South was the first substantial awakening of the southern conscience and the organization in Atlanta in 1919 of the Commission on Interracial Cooperation. It would become the spearhead of a growing southern liberal movement in the 1920s and 1930s.

The mass of Negroes, however, were not inspired by antilynching campaigns or encouraged by the beginning of an organized southern effort to combat racial intolerance. They had demonstrated a new militancy during the riots by fighting back courageously and often effectively in self-defense. They were also ready to follow a leader who was proud of his race. Such a black was Marcus Garvey, a Jamaican, who organized his Universal Negro Improvement Association in 1914 and moved to New York City two years later. Garvey urged Negroes to be proud of their race and culture and follow him back to Africa to build a "free, redeemed and mighty nation." In the racial

[6]That is, in the postwar period. There had been a serious race riot in East St. Louis, Illinois, in July 1917.

upheaval of the postwar years Garvey's schemes stimulated visions of a grand new destiny in the minds of countless Negroes. Claiming 4 million followers in 1920 and 6 million in 1923, Garvey proclaimed himself provisional president of an African Empire in 1921 and raised funds to buy a Black Star steamship line and carry his people home. The empire crumbled in 1923, however, when Garvey was convicted in federal court of using the mails to defraud and sentenced to the Atlanta penitentiary for a five-year term. American Negroes, obviously, would not go back to Africa, but the fact that so many of them rallied to Garvey's standard was evidence of important stirrings of black racial self-respect.

79. The Election of 1920

Politicians began their quadrennial preparations for the coming presidential campaign during this season of social conflict and racial unrest. It was obvious by the beginning of 1920 that any passable Republican candidate would win the presidency, and there was much activity in the GOP camp. However, the commanding figures who had led the party since 1900 were absent or in retirement. Into the fight for leadership, therefore, rushed a number of lesser dignitaries. General Leonard Wood, who had inherited most of the following of Theodore Roosevelt, who had died in 1919, made the most formidable campaign for the Republican nomination. Wood was forthrightly independent of party bosses, intensely nationalistic, and a champion of universal military training. Nearly as popular was Frank O. Lowden, former congressman and governor of Illinois in 1920, who had the support of the business and farm interests of the Middle West. On the periphery were Senator Hiram W. Johnson of California, vainly trying to rally the old insurgents; Senator Robert M. La Follette of Wisconsin, always a hopeful but never a successful contender; Herbert Hoover, who announced that he was a Republican and would accept the nomination; and a number of favorite sons, including the nondescript Warren G. Harding of Ohio.

The outcome was, therefore, by no means certain when the Republicans met in national convention on June 8, 1920. The Wood and Lowden managers battled fiercely to a standstill during the first four ballots on Friday, June 11. Fearing an impasse, Chairman Henry Cabot Lodge adjourned the convention at seven o'clock, in order, he said, to give the leaders a chance to think. Managers and leaders had little time for reflection during the ensuing hectic hours. The Wood leaders tried unsuccessfully to win the Johnson delegates and refused to make entangling alliances with party bosses and oil lobbyists. At the same time, another group was gathering in the suite of National Chairman Will H. Hays at the Blackstone Hotel. It included Hays and a clique of powerful senators and their allies, among them Lodge, Senator Frank B. Brandegee of Connecticut, George Harvey, caustic New York editor, and other party regulars. They wanted, not Wood or Lowden, but a president whom they could control. Their opportunity to name the candidate seemed to be at hand on account of the Wood-Lowden deadlock.

The senatorial clique in the now legendary "smoke-filled" room in the Blackstone continued their search all during the evening of Friday, June 11. They settled upon Senator Warren G. Harding of Ohio, a party hack who met all the qualifications of a perfect dark horse. Harding had many friends, particularly among delegates to the convention, and no enemies in the party; he had voted for the Lodge reservations, and, most important, was thought to be controllable. The decision was made and relayed to other party leaders by eleven o'clock on Friday night. Harvey called Harding to the smoke-filled room at about two o'clock on Saturday morning, told him of the decision, and asked if there was any reason why the party should not nominate him. After meditating privately in an adjoining room for ten minutes, Harding returned to reply that there was no reason why he should not be president.

The senatorial clique was, of course, proceeding on the assumption that the Wood and Lowden forces would never combine. As it turned out, it was a safe enough gamble. The deadlock continued for four more ballots on Saturday morning, June 12, until Chairman Lodge recessed the convention in the early afternoon. Then, while the Wood and Lowden managers negotiated to no avail, Harvey and the senatorial clique, for reasons that are still obscure, tried to rally the party behind Will Hays. The effort failed, and Harding was nominated on the tenth ballot soon after the convention reassembled Saturday afternoon. The main reason seems to have been that leaders and delegates realized that he was the one candidate who could now be nominated without a grueling, disruptive battle. For vice-president the senatorial clique had settled upon Senator Irvine L. Lenroot of Wisconsin. However, the weary delegates in an unexpected burst of independence nominated Governor Calvin Coolidge, hero of the recent Boston strike.

The Republican platform gave notice of the GOP's intention to destroy Wilsonianism and all its works. It promised tariff increases, tax reductions, immigration restriction, vigorous aid to farmers, and, by implication, an end to further federal social legislation. On the issue of the League the framers made room both for irreconcilables and Republican League men. The platform condemned Wilson's League but approved membership in the World Court and "agreement among nations to preserve the peace of the world."

Meanwhile, the Democrats had been engaged in a preconvention contest even more confused than the struggle that preceded the Republican convention. The chief cause of the Democratic uncertainty was the president himself, for Wilson acted very much like a receptive if silent candidate after his partial recovery during the early months of 1920. He dismissed Secretary of State Lansing and took charge of the government in February. He attended well-publicized Cabinet meetings and took long rides in his automobile. And just before the Democratic convention met in June he called photographers to the White House and gave an important interview to Louis Seibold of the New York *World.* All available evidence indicates that the president hoped that he might be chosen to lead a campaign for the League of Nations, and that he intended, if elected, to resign once the treaty had been ratified.

Wilson's potential candidacy cast a long shadow over the aspirations of his son-in-law, William G. McAdoo, the chief contender for the Democratic nomination. As a gesture of filial respect, McAdoo "withdrew" from the race on the same day, June 18, that Wilson's interview appeared in the New York *World.* McAdoo's strongest rival was the attorney-general, A. Mitchell Palmer, who was still beating drums for Americanism. Among the favorite sons, Governor James M. Cox of Ohio had the greatest potential strength, even though President Wilson thought that his candidacy was "a joke." Three times elected governor of a doubtful state, Cox had an excellent progressive record, had survived the Republican victory of 1918, and was more acceptable to the city bosses than McAdoo or Palmer because of his opposition to prohibition.

Because of the division in the Wilsonian ranks, the Democratic convention that opened at San Francisco on June 28 was no less confused than its Republican counterpart. As events turned out, Wilson had no influence over the convention's choice. He had made plans to have his name presented and his nomination effected by acclamation once a deadlock occurred. But this stratagem was never executed because a group of the president's close friends met in San Francisco on July 3–4 and agreed that a third nomination would kill both Wilson and the Democratic party. The Irish bosses who controlled the delegations from Massachusetts, New York, New Jersey, Indiana, and Illinois held the balance of power and, in the end, named the candidate in the same manner that the senatorial clique had done at Chicago, or at least had tried to do until events took control out of their hands. The McAdoo and Palmer forces fought to a standstill for thirty-seven weary ballots. Palmer released his delegates on the thirty-eighth ballot; but as most of them went to Cox, a McAdoo drive fizzled, and Cox was named on the forty-fourth roll call on July 5. Cox's choice for running mate was Franklin D. Roosevelt of New York, assistant secretary of the navy, a prominent Wilsonian and League supporter.

Meanwhile the convention had adopted a platform that sidestepped the prohibition question, extended sympathy to Ireland, and promised tax reductions and independence for the Philippines. On the all-important League issue the platform was at the same time straightforward—reflecting Wilson's demands—and evasive—reflecting the arguments of Democrats who wanted to accept the Lodge reservations. We advocate immediate ratification of the treaty without crippling reservations, the platform declared; but we do not "oppose the acceptance of any reservations making clearer or more specific the obligations of the United States to the League associates."

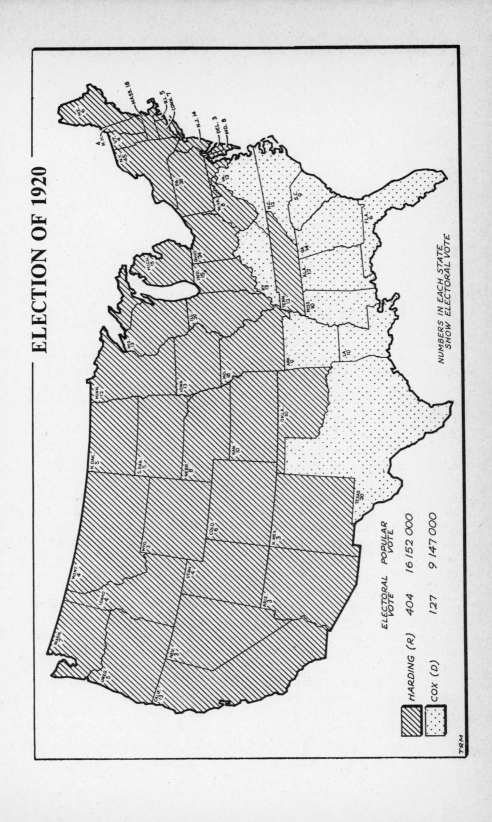

ELECTION OF 1920

NUMBERS IN EACH STATE
SHOW ELECTORAL VOTE

	ELECTORAL VOTE	POPULAR VOTE
HARDING (R)	404	16 152 000
COX (D)	127	9 147 000

TRM

In spite of the convention's straddle, Cox and Roosevelt labored heroically during the ensuing campaign to make the election a "great and solemn referendum" òn the League and to warn voters that the reactionary business interests would control the government if Harding won. Harding's managers, on the other hand, wisely decided that the less that he said the better his chances would be. Hence Harding made no long tours like Cox, but rather he stayed at home in Marion, Ohio, and greeted delegations on his front porch. It was impossible to judge from his sonorous homilies just where Harding stood on any specific issue. Isolationists were certain that he would keep the country out of the detested League. In contrast, a group of thirty-one distinguished pro-League Republicans, including Charles Evans Hughes, Elihu Root, and Herbert Hoover, assured voters that Harding's election was the first necessary step in ratification with reservations.

Harding's ambivalent speeches and the statement of the thirty-one so confused the voters that it is doubtful if the League was even an important issue in the campaign. It was evident long before election day that the Republicans were capitalizing on an accumulation of grievances going back all the way to the progressive legislation of 1916 and the adoption of the war resolution. The disparate elements opposed to Democratic policies—the Irish- and German-Americans, Negroes, industrialists and businessmen in rebellion against high taxes and policies favorable to labor, champions of civil liberty, independent progressives outraged by the treaty and the Palmer raids, and midwestern and Plains farmers then undergoing a severe depression—moved en masse into the Republican camp.

The result of the combining of the dissident elements with the normal Republican majority was the most smashing electoral triumph since the re-election of James Monroe in 1820. Harding received 16,152,000 popular votes, or 61 percent of the total; he won all the states outside the South, for an electoral vote of 404; and he even broke the Solid South by carrying Tennessee. With only 9,147,000 popular and 127 electoral votes, Cox was the worst beaten Democratic candidate since Stephen A. Douglas. The Republican sweep in the senatorial and congressional contests—there would be Republican majorities of 22 in the Senate and 167 in the House in the next Congress—was nearly as impressive as Harding's own majority.

This landslide did not signify a repudiation of the League but rather revealed the confusion and growing popular apathy over that issue. It did not signify a repudiation of progressivism or any great collapse of idealism among the people. It signified, rather, the triumph of the combined forces of dissent and protest. Wilson had created a majority Democratic coalition in 1916 composed principally of Southerners, middle and far western antiwar progressives and farmers, independents, and workingmen throughout the country. Wilson's policies after 1916 consistently alienated independents, antiwar progressives, and, most important, western farmers. By destroying the Wilsonian coalition in 1920, these groups not only registered their protests against

Wilson's alleged betrayal of their interests, they also destroyed the only political alliance capable of carrying on progressive policies in a systematic way. And unwittingly they turned the next administration over to their traditional enemies—the business elements who once again were in control of the Republican party.

Suggested
Additional Reading

1. American Politics from Theodore Roosevelt through Woodrow Wilson

A. *Aspects of the Progressive Revolt*

For the origins and immediate background, see Charles A. Barker, *Henry George* (1955); Chester McA. Destler, *Henry Demarest Lloyd and the Empire of Reform* (1963); Sidney Fine, *Laissez Faire and the General Welfare State* (1956); and Harold U. Faulkner, *Politics, Reform, and Expansion, 1890–1900* (1959). We now have a number of general accounts of varying quality and different emphases, the best of which is Robert H. Wiebe, *The Search for Order, 1877–1920* (1967). Among the others are Richard Hofstadter, *The Age of Reform* (1955); Samuel P. Hays, *The Response to Industrialism, 1885–1914* (1957); Eric F. Goldman, *Rendezvous with Destiny* (1953); Harold U. Faulkner, *The Quest for Social Justice, 1898–1914* (1931); Benjamin P. De Witt, *The Progressive Movement* (1915); Russell B. Nye, *Midwestern Progressive Politics* (1951); C. Vann Woodward, *Origins of the New South, 1877–1913* (1951); Jack T. Kirby, *Darkness at the Dawning: Race and Reform in the Progressive South* (1972); and Hugh C. Bailey, *Liberalism in the New South* (1969). Significant phases are illuminated by James H. Timberlake, *Prohibition and the Progressive Movement, 1900–1920* (1963); Samuel P. Hays, *Conservation and the Gospel* of Efficiency: The Progressive Conservation Movement, 1890–1920 (1959); L. E. Fredman, The Australian Ballot: The Story of an American Reform (1968); Robert H. Wiebe, Businessmen and Reform: A Study of the Progressive Movement (1962); Samuel Haber, Efficiency and Uplift: Scientific Management in the Progressive Era (1964); and Mark H. Haller, Eugenics: Hereditarian Attitudes in American Thought (1963).

Still the classic accounts of the progressive revolts in the cities and states are Lincoln Steffens, The Shame of the Cities (1904) and The Struggle for Self-Government (1906), which should be read with The Autobiography of Lincoln Steffens (1931). The secondary literature on urban and state progressivism and problems is growing by leaps and bounds. For general introductions to the former, see Charles N. Glaab, The American City (1963); Blake McKelvey, The Urbanization of America, 1860–1915 (1963) and The Emergence of Metropolitan America, 1915–1966 (1968); Frank M. Stewart, A Half-Century of Municipal Reform: The History of the National Municipal League (1950); Mel Scott, American City Planning since 1890 (1969); and John W. Reps, The Making of Urban America: A History of City Planning in the United States (1965).

Among the particular studies that highlight urban reform are James B. Crooks, Politics & Progress: The Rise of Urban Progressivism in Baltimore, 1895 to 1911 (1968); Zane L. Miller, Boss Cox's Cincinnati: Urban Politics in the Progressive Era (1968); Melvin G. Holli, Reform in Detroit: Hazen S. Pingree and Urban Politics (1969); William D. Miller, Memphis during the Progressive Era, 1900–1917 (1957); and George S. Reynolds, Machine Politics in New Orleans, 1897–1926 (1936). Joel A. Tarr, A Study in Boss Politics: William Lorimer of Chicago (1971), makes a strong case for the social usefulness of the city boss.

Excellent state studies include Ransom E. Noble, Jr., New Jersey Progressivism Before Wilson (1946); George E. Mowry, The California Progressives (1951), which should be supplemented by Olin C. Spencer, Jr., California's Prodigal Sons: Hiram Johnson and the Progressives, 1911–1917 (1968), and Michael P. Rogin and J. L. Shover, Political Change in California: Critical Elections and Social Movements, 1896–1966 (1970); David P. Thelen, The New Citizenship: Origins of Progressivism in Wisconsin, 1885–1900 (1972); Robert S. Maxwell, La Follette and the Rise of the Progressives in Wisconsin (1956); Herbert F. Margulies, The Decline of the Progressive Movement in Wisconsin, 1890–1920 (1968); Stanley P. Caine, The Myth of a Progressive Reform: Railroad Regulation in Wisconsin, 1903–1910 (1970); Carl H. Chrislock, The Progressive Era in Minnesota, 1899–1918 (1971); Irwin Yellowitz, Labor and the Progressive Movement in New York State, 1897–1916 (1965); Richard M. Abrams, Conservatism in a Progressive Era: Massachusetts Politics, 1900–1912 (1964); Sheldon Hackney, Populism to Progressivism in Alabama (1969); Albert D. Kirwan, The Revolt of the Rednecks: Mississippi Politics, 1876–1925 (1951); Raymond H. Pulley, Old Virginia Restored: An Interpretation of the Progressive Impulse (1968); and Allen W. Moger, Virginia: Bourbonism to Byrd, 1870–1925 (1968). Prohibition was often an important aspect of progressivism on the state level. There are studies on Tennessee by Paul E. Isaac, on Virginia by C. C. Pearson and J. Edwin

Hendricks, on Alabama by James Benson Sellers, on North Carolina by Daniel J. Whitener, and on California by Gilman M. Ostrander.

Among the biographies of city and state leaders, some of the following range far beyond the scope of this section: Alpheus T. Mason, *Brandeis: A Free Man's Life* (1946); Melvin I. Urofsky, *A Mind of One Piece: Brandeis and American Reform* (1971); Belle C. and Fola La Follette, *Robert M. La Follette* (2 vols., 1953); Aubrey L. Brooks and H. T. Lefler (eds.), *The Papers of Walter Clark* (2 vols., 1948–1950); Joseph L. Morrison, *Josephus Daniels: The Small-D Democrat* (1966); Dewey W. Grantham, *Hoke Smith and the Politics of the New South* (1958); Oliver H. Orr, Jr., *Charles Brantley Aycock* (1961); William Larsen, *Montague of Virginia, The Making of a Southern Progressive* (1965); Richard Lowitt, *George W. Norris, The Making of a Progressive* (1963); G. Wallace Chessman, *Governor Theodore Roosevelt: The Albany Apprenticeship, 1898–1900* (1965); Robert F. Wesser, *Charles Evans Hughes: Politics and Reform in New York, 1905–1910* (1967); Nancy Joan Weiss, *Charles Francis Murphy, 1858–1924: Respectability and Responsibility in Tammany Politics* (1968); Robert M. Crunden, *A Hero in Spite of Himself: Brand Whitlock in Art, Politics, & War* (1969); Jack Tager, *The Intellectual as Urban Reformer: Brand Whitlock and the Progressive Movement* (1968); William B. Hixson, Jr., *Moorefield Storey and The Abolitionist Tradition* (1972); Rupert N. Richardson, *Colonel Edward M. House: The Texas Years, 1858–1912* (1964); William D. Miller, *Mr. Crump of Memphis* (1964); Edwin R. Lewinson, *John Purroy Mitchel, The Boy Mayor of New York* (1965); J. Joseph Huthmacher, *Senator Robert F. Wagner and the Rise of Urban Liberalism* (1968); and William F. Holmes, *The White Chief: James Kimble Vardaman* (1970). Daniel Levine, *Varieties of Reform Thought* (1964), dealing with Jane Addams, Samuel Gompers, Robert M. La Follette, and others, is an important contribution.

We are now well on the way toward a comprehensive history of the social justice movement. Don D. Lescohier, "Working Conditions," and Elizabeth Brandeis, "Labor Legislation," in John R. Commons *et al., History of Labour in the United States* (4 vols., 1918–1935), Vol. III, contain much of the basic information. Robert H. Bremner, *From the Depths: The Discovery of Poverty in the United States* (1956), is a rich and eloquent general account, which should be supplemented by his brief *American Philanthropy* (1960). Roy Lubove, *The Professional Altruist: The Emergence of Social Work as a Career, 1880–1930* (1965) and *The Struggle for Social Security, 1900–1935* (1968), are important studies, as is Allen F. Davis, *Spearheads for Reform: The Social Settlements and the Progressive Movement, 1890–1914* (1967). On child labor reform, see Walter I. Trattner, *Crusade for Children* (1970); Jeremy P. Felt, *Hostages of Fortune: Child Labor Reform in New York State* (1965); and Elizabeth H. Davidson, *Child Labor Legislation in the Southern Textile States* (1939). Excellent biographies of the social justice leaders are Daniel Levine, *Jane Addams and the Liberal Tradition* (1971); John C. Farrell, *Beloved Lady: A History of Jane Addams' Ideas on Reform and Peace* (1967); Josephine C. Goldmark, *Impatient Crusader: Florence Kelley's Life Story* (1953); Dorothy R. Blumberg, *Florence Kelley: The Making of a Social Pioneer* (1966); Louise C. Wade, *Graham Taylor: Pioneer for Social Justice, 1851–1938* (1964); Walter I. Trattner, *Homer Folks: Pioneer in Social*

Welfare (1968); and Hugh C. Bailey, *Edgar Gardner Murphy: Gentle Progressive* (1968). (The Social Gospel movement is covered in Section 4-D of this bibliography.)

On the muckrakers, there is a rich literature: Cornelius C. Regier, *The Era of the Muckrakers* (1932); Louis Filler, *Crusaders for American Liberalism* (1939); Harold S. Wilson, *McClure's Magazine and the Muckrakers* (1971); Daniel Aaron, *Men of Good Hope* (1951); Lloyd R. Morris, *Postscript to Yesterday* (1947); David Mark Chalmers, *The Social and Political Ideas of the Muckrakers* (1964); John E. Semonche, *Ray Stannard Baker: A Quest for Democracy in Modern America, 1870–1918* (1969); Robert C. Bannister, Jr., *Ray Stannard Baker: The Mind and Thought of a Progressive* (1966); and Peter Lyon, *Success Story: The Life and Times of S. S. McClure* (1963). The writings of the muckrakers and the literature of revolt are discussed in Chapter 3 of this volume.

We still have no general history of intellectual progressivism, but see Henry S. Commager, *The American Mind* (1950); Charles Forcey, *The Crossroads of Liberalism: Croly, Weyl, Lippmann and the Progressive Era, 1900–1925* (1961); Benjamin G. Rader, *The Academic Mind and Reform: The Influence of Richard T. Ely in American Life* (1966); Jean B. Quandt, *From the Small Town to the Great Community: The Social Thought of Progressive Intellectuals* (1970); John Adam Moreau, *Randolph Bourne: Legend and Reality* (1966); Richard Hofstadter, *The Progressive Historians: Turner, Beard, Parrington* (1968); and Daniel M. Fox, *The Discovery of Abundance: Simon N. Patten and the Transformation of Social Theory* (1967). Eric F. Goldman, *Rendezvous with Destiny* (1953), and Alpheus T. Mason, *Brandeis: A Free Man's Life* (1946), also provide valuable insight. For the most important contributions by the intellectual progressives, see Chapter 3 of this volume.

The struggle for women's rights and woman suffrage, long neglected by professional historians, can now claim an imposing literature: Eleanor Flexner, *Century of Struggle, The Woman's Rights Movement in the United States* (1959); Aileen S. Kraditor, *The Ideas of the Woman Suffrage Movement, 1890–1920* (1965); Mildred Adams, *The Right to Be People* (1967); Andrew Sinclair, *The Emancipation of the American Woman* (1966); William L. O'Neill, *Everyone Was Brave: The Rise and Fall of Feminism in America* (1969), *The Woman Movement: Feminism in the United States and England* (1969), and *Divorce in the Progressive Era* (1967); Alan P. Grimes, *The Puritan Ethic and Woman Suffrage* (1967); David M. Kennedy, *Birth Control in America: The Career of Margaret Sanger* (1970); and Anne Firor Scott, *The Southern Lady* (1971).

The literature on socialism and left wing unionism is large and excellent: David A. Shannon, *The Socialist Party of America: A History* (1955); Donald D. Egbert and S. Persons (eds.), *Socialism and American Life* (2 vols., 1952); Howard H. Quint, *The Forging of American Socialism* (1953); Ira Kipnis, *The American Socialist Movement, 1897–1912* (1952); James Weinstein, *The Decline of Socialism in America, 1912–1925* (1967); John H. M. Laslett, *Labor and the Left: A Study of Socialist and Radical Influences in the American Labor Movement, 1881–1924* (1970); Henry F. Bedford, *Socialism and the Workers in Massachusetts, 1886–1912* (1966); Robert Laurence Moore, *European Socialists and the American Promised Land* (1970); Melvyn Dubofsky, *We Shall Be All: A History of the Industrial Workers of the World*

(1969); Robert L. Tyler, *Rebels of the Woods: The I.W.W. in the Pacific Northwest* (1967); Ray Ginger, *The Bending Cross: A Biography of Eugene Victor Debs* (1949); and Kent and Gretchen Kreuter, *An American Dissenter: The Life of Algie Martin Simons* (1969).

B. The Republican Era, 1901–1913

George E. Mowry, *The Era of Theodore Roosevelt, 1900–1912* (1958), has filled the need for a good, concise political history of the Republican era. The first four volumes of Mark Sullivan, *Our Times: The United States, 1900–1925* (6 vols., 1926–1935), are racy and informative. Gabriel Kolko, *The Triumph of Conservatism: A Reinterpretation of American History, 1900–1916* (1963), and James Weinstein, *The Corporate Ideal in the Liberal State: 1900–1928* (1968), are provocative Marxist interpretations of the period. For other general studies, see Horace S. and Marion G. Merrill, *The Republican Command, 1897–1913* (1971); James Holt, *Congressional Insurgents and the Party System, 1909–1916* (1967); and Norman M. Wilensky, *Conservatives in the Progressive Era: The Taft Republicans of 1912* (1965).

For legislative issues, battles, and policies, see Frank W. Taussig, *Tariff History of the United States* (1931); Albro Martin, *Enterprise Denied: Origins of the Decline of American Railroads, 1897–1917* (1971), a highly revisionist study; Sidney Ratner, *American Taxation* (1942); M. Nelson McGeary, *Gifford Pinchot, Forester-Politician* (1960); Elmo P. Richardson, *The Politics of Conservation: Crusaders and Controversies, 1897–1913* (1962); Alpheus T. Mason, *Bureaucracy Convicts Itself: The Ballinger-Pinchot Controversy of 1910* (1941); James R. Penick, *Progressive Politics and Conservation: The Ballinger-Pinchot Affair* (1968); Hans Thorelli, *The Federal Antitrust Policy* (1954); William Z. Ripley, *Railroads: Rates and Regulation* (1912); Gabriel Kolko, *Railroads and Regulation, 1877–1916* (1965); Paul P. Van Riper, *History of the United States Civil Service* (1958); and Oscar E. Anderson, Jr., *The Health of a Nation: Harvey W. Wiley and the Fight for Pure Food* (1958).

The general biographical literature of this period grows increasingly richer. Henry F. Pringle, *Theodore Roosevelt, A Biography* (1931), long the standard, has been supplanted by William H. Harbaugh, *Power and Responsibility: The Life and Times of Theodore Roosevelt* (1961). Significant additions to Rooseveltian biography are G. Wallace Chessman, *Theodore Roosevelt and the Politics of Power* (1968), and Willard B. Gatewood, Jr., *Theodore Roosevelt and the Art of Controversy: Episodes of the White House Years* (1970). However, no student should overlook Elting E. Morison and John M. Blum (eds.), *The Letters of Theodore Roosevelt* (8 vols., 1951–1954), and John M. Blum, *The Republican Roosevelt* (1954), for new information and insights. Henry F. Pringle, *The Life and Times of William Howard Taft* (2 vols., 1939), covers the entire period and beyond.

For other political leaders in this period, see Philip C. Jessup, *Elihu Root* (2 vols., 1938); Richard W. Leopold, *Elihu Root and the Conservative Tradition* (1954); Merlo J. Pusey, *Charles Evans Hughes* (2 vols., 1951); Carolyn W. Johnson, *Winthrop Murray Crane: A Study in Republican Leadership, 1829–1920* (1967); John A. Garraty, *Henry Cabot Lodge (1953);* Francis B. Simkins, *Pitchfork Ben Tillman* (1944);

Richard Lowitt, *George W. Norris, The Making of a Progressive* (1963); John Braeman, *Albert J. Beveridge: American Nationalist* (1971); A. Bower Sageser, *Joseph L. Bristow: Kansas Progressive* (1968); Hermann Hagedorn, *Leonard Wood* (2 vols., 1931); Elting E. Morison, *Turmoil and Tradition: A Study of the Life and Times of Henry L. Stimson* (1960); Paul W. Glad, *The Trumpet Soundeth: William Jennings Bryan and His Democracy, 1896–1912* (1960); Paola E. Coletta, *William Jennings Bryan: Political Evangelist, 1860–1908* (1964); and Louis W. Koenig, *Bryan: A Political Biography* (1971). George E. Mowry, *Theodore Roosevelt and the Progressive Movement* (1946), and Kenneth W. Hechler, *Insurgency: Personalities and Politics of the Taft Era* (1940), are excellent for the rise of the insurgents and the rupture of the GOP. J. Rogers Hollingsworth, *The Whirligig of Politics: The Democracy of Cleveland and Bryan* (1963), relates the fortunes of the Democratic party during this period of Republican ascendancy.

C. *The Wilson Era*

The only general works on the period 1912–1921 are Frederick L. Paxson, *The American Democracy and the World War* (3 vols., 1936–1948); and Arthur S. Link, *Woodrow Wilson and the Progressive Era* (1954). For aspects of domestic history, see Henry Parker Willis, *The Federal Reserve System* (1923); and J. Laurence Laughlin, *The Federal Reserve Act* (1933), for the background and writing of the Federal Reserve bill; John D. Clark, *The Federal Trust Policy* (1931), for the writing of the Clayton and Federal Trade Commission bills; and Stephen B. Wood, *Constitutional Politics in the Progressive Era: Child Labor and the Law* (1968), for the two child labor acts of the Wilson administration. George B. Tindall, *The Emergence of the New South, 1913–1945* (1967), discusses the relation of the South to Wilsonian policies. A. L. Todd, *Justice on Trial: The Case of Louis D. Brandeis* (1964), is a good account of the fight over the confirmation of Brandeis's appointment to the Supreme Court. Graham Adams, *Age of Industrial Violence, 1910–1915: The Activities and Findings of the United States Commission on Industrial Relations* (1966), is excellent on this subject.

The American home front during the war is treated by Seward W. Livermore, *Politics Is Adjourned: Woodrow Wilson and the War Congress, 1916–1918* (1966); Frederick Palmer, *Newton D. Baker: America at War* (2 vols., 1931); and Daniel R. Beaver, *Newton D. Baker and the American War Effort, 1917–1919* (1966). Arthur S. Link (ed.), *The Impact of World War I* (1969), reprints some of the significant articles on this subject. Bernard M. Baruch, *American Industry in War* (1941), discusses the problems of industrial mobilization. For special studies, see Alexander D. Noyes, *The War Period of American Finance, 1908–1925* (1926); Charles Gilbert, *American Financing of World War I* (1970); Walker D. Hines, *War History of American Railroads* (1928); Edward N. Hurley, *The Bridge to France* (1927); Frank M. Surface and R. L. Bland, *American Food in the World War and Reconstruction Period* (1931); George Creel, *How We Advertised America* (1920); James R. Mock and C. Larson, *Words that Won the War: The Story of the Committee on Public Information, 1917–1919* (1939); George T. Blakey, *Historians on the Home-front: American Propagandists and the Great War* (1971); Frank L. Grubbs, Jr., *The*

Struggle for Labor Loyalty: Gompers, the A.F. of L., and the Pacifists, 1917–1920 (1968); Melvin I. Urofsky, *Big Steel and the Wilson Administration* (1969); Joan M. Jensen, *The Price of Vigilance* (1968); and H. C. Peterson and Gilbert C. Fite, *Opponents of War, 1917–1918* (1957).

There is a growing literature on demobilization and the politics and problems of the immediate postwar era. Mark Sullivan, *Our Times: The United States, 1900–1925* (6 vols., 1926-1935), Vols. V and VI; Frederick L. Paxson, *The American Democracy and the World War* (3 vols., 1936–1948), Vol. III; Frederick Lewis Allen, *Only Yesterday, An Informal History of the Nineteen-Twenties* (1931); William E. Leuchtenburg, *The Perils of Prosperity, 1914–1932* (1958); and Preston W. Slosson, *The Great Crusade and After, 1914–1928* (1930), are all good introductions. James R. Mock and E. Thurber, *Report on Demobilization* (1944), is more detailed. For good studies of the race riots from 1917 to 1920, see Elliott M. Rudwick, *Race Riot at East St. Louis* (1964); Charles F. Kellogg, *NAACP: A History, Volume I: 1909–1920* (1967); William M. Tuttle, Jr., *Race Riot: Chicago in the Red Summer of 1919* (1970); and Arthur I. Waskow, *From Race Riot to Sit-In* (1966). David Brody, *Labor in Crisis: The Steel Strike of 1919* (1965), is superb. For the Red scare, see Zechariah Chaffee, Jr.'s indispensable *Free Speech in the United States* (1941); Robert K. Murray, *Red Scare: A Study in National Hysteria, 1919–1920* (1955); Stanley Coben, *A. Mitchell Palmer: Politician* (1963); Theodore Draper, *The Roots of American Communism* (1957); William Preston, Jr., *Aliens and Dissenters: Federal Suppression of Radicals, 1903–1933* (1963); Robert L. Friedheim, *The Seattle General Strike* (1964); and Woodrow C. Whitten, *Criminal Syndicalism and the Law in California, 1919–1927* (1969).

William T. Hutchinson, *Lowden of Illinois* (2 vols., 1957); Frank Freidel, *Franklin D. Roosevelt: The Apprenticeship* (1952); James M. Cox, *Journey Through My Years* (1946); Robert K. Murray, *The Harding Era: Warren G. Harding and His Administration* (1969); and Randolph C. Downes, *The Rise of Warren Gamaliel Harding, 1865–1920* (1970), are all informative about the presidential campaign of 1920; but see especially the fine general study by Wesley M. Bagby, *The Road to Normalcy: The Presidential Campaign and Election of 1920* (1962). J. Joseph Huthmacher, *Massachusetts People and Politics, 1919–1933* (1959), and Franklin D. Mitchell, *Embattled Democracy: Missouri Democratic Politics, 1919–1932* (1968), are pioneering state studies.

The most voluminous and sometimes the best literature on the Wilson era are the biographies and memoirs of the leaders of that period. Arthur Walworth, *Woodrow Wilson* (2 vols., 1958), is a good personal biography. Arthur S. Link, *Wilson: The Road to the White House* (1947), *Wilson: The New Freedom* (1956), *Wilson: The Struggle for Neutrality, 1914–1915* (1960), *Wilson: Confusions and Crises, 1915–1916* (1964), and *Wilson: Campaigns for Progressivism and Peace, 1916–1917* (1965), cover the public career from 1902 to 1917 in some detail. Arthur S. Link, *Woodrow Wilson, A Brief Biography* (1963); John M. Blum, *Woodrow Wilson and the Politics of Morality* (1956); and John A. Garraty, *Woodrow Wilson* (1956), are brief studies. Arthur S. Link *et al.* (eds.), *The Papers of Woodrow Wilson* (1966–   ), will soon reach the gubernatorial period. Meanwhile, for Wilson's speeches and public papers the student may consult Ray S. Baker and William E. Dodd (eds.), *The Public Papers of Woodrow Wilson* (6 vols., 1925–1927), and John Wells Davidson (ed.), *A Crossroads of Freedom: The 1912 Campaign Speeches of Woodrow Wilson* (1956). An indispensable source is Charles Seymour (ed.), *The Intimate Papers of Colonel House* (4 vols., 1926–1928). For biographies of men active in the Wilson era, see John M. Blum, *Joe Tumulty and the Wilson Era* (1951); Frank Freidel, *Franklin D. Roosevelt: The Apprenticeship* (1952); Monroe L. Billington, *Thomas P. Gore: The Blind Senator from Oklahoma* (1967); C. H. Cramer, *Newton D. Baker, A Biography* (1961); Margaret L. Coit, *Mr. Baruch* (1957); Stanley Coben, *A. Mitchell Palmer: Politician* (1963); Lawrence W. Levine, *Defender of the Faith, William Jennings Bryan: The Last Decade, 1915–1925* (1965); Paolo E. Coletta, *William Jennings Bryan: Progressive Politician and Moral Statesman, 1909–1915* (1969) and *William Jennings Bryan: Political Puritan, 1915–1925* (1969); and Richard Lowitt, *George W. Norris: The Persistence of a Progressive* (1971).

D. *The Supreme Court and Social and Economic Policy*

Charles Warren, *The Supreme Court in United States History* (2 vols., 1937); William F. Swindler, *Court and Constitution in the Twentieth Century* (2 vols., 1969–1970); Alfred H. Kelly and W. A. Harbison, *The American Constitution* (1963); and Paul L. Murphy, *The Constitution in Crisis Times, 1918–1969* (1972), are excellent surveys. Louis B. Boudin, *Government by Judiciary* (2 vols., 1932), focuses on the Supreme Court and social and economic legislation. Biographies of leaders in the Court for this period include Merlo J. Pusey, *Charles Evans Hughes* (2 vols., 1951); Alpheus T. Mason, *Brandeis: A Free Man's Life* (1946); and Max Lerner (ed.), *The Mind and Faith of Justice Holmes* (1943).

2. The United States and Its World Relations, 1900–1920

A. *General*

Samuel F. Bemis and Robert H. Ferrell (eds.), *The American Secretaries of State and Their Diplomacy* (17 vols., 1927–1967); Foster R. Dulles, *America's Rise to World Power, 1898–1954* (1955); George F. Kennan, *American Diplomacy, 1900–1950* (1951); Norman A. Graebner (ed.), *An Uncertain Tradition, American Secretaries of State in the Twentieth Century* (1961); Robert E. Osgood, *Ideals and Self-Interest in America's Foreign Relations* (1953); Selig Adler, *The Isolationist Impulse* (1959); H. C. Allen, *Great Britain and the United States* (1955); William Appleman Williams, *The Roots of the Modern American Empire* (1969); Julius W. Pratt, *Challenge and Rejection: The United States and World Leadership, 1900–1921* (1967); E. Berkeley Tompkins, *Anti-Imperialism in the United States, 1890–1920* (1970); Sandra R. Herman, *Eleven Against War: Studies in American Internationalist Thought, 1898–1921* (1969); and Warren F. Kuehl, *Seeking World Order: The United States and Interna-*

tional Organization to 1920 (1969), are good surveys for readers deficient in background. However, the best general work is Richard W. Leopold, *The Growth of American Foreign Policy* (1962).

B. *Colonial Administration and the United States and Europe and Asia,*
   1900–1914

Julius W. Pratt, *America's Colonial Experiment* (1950), is a splendid survey of the rise, governing, and decline of the American colonial empire. It may be supplemented with Edward J. Berbusse, *The United States in Puerto Rico, 1898–1900* (1966); David A. Lockmiller, *Magoon in Cuba: A History of the Second Intervention, 1906–1909* (1938); Allan Reed Millett, *The Politics of Intervention: The Military Occupation of Cuba, 1906–1909* (1968); W. Cameron Forbes, *The Philippine Islands* (2 vols., 1928); and Charles C. Tansill, *The Purchase of the Danish West Indies* (1932).

We lack any general study of American relations with Europe from 1900 to 1914. Howard K. Beale, *Theodore Roosevelt and the Rise of America to World Power* (1956); Walter V. and Marie V. Scholes, *The Foreign Policies of the Taft Administration* (1970); John A. Garraty, *Henry Cabot Lodge* (1953); Richard W. Leopold, *Elihu Root and the Conservative Tradition* (1954); Philip C. Jessup, *Elihu Root* (2 vols., 1938); Henry F. Pringle, *Theodore Roosevelt, A Biography* (1931) and *The Life and Times of William Howard Taft* (2 vols., 1939); William H. Harbaugh, *Power and Responsibility: The Life and Times of Theodore Roosevelt* (1961); Tyler Dennett, *John Hay* (1933); and Allan Nevins, *Henry White: Thirty Years of American Diplomacy* (1930), are all valuable for the diplomacy of the Roosevelt-Taft period. Bradford Perkins, *The Great Rapprochement: England the United States, 1895–1914* (1968); Richard R. Heindel, *The American Impact on Great Britain, 1898–1914* (1940); Charles S. Campbell, Jr., *Anglo-American Understanding, 1898–1903* (1957); Alexander E. Campbell, *Great Britain and the United States, 1895–1903* (1961); and Clara E. Schieber, *The Transformation of American Sentiment toward Germany, 1870–1914* (1923), are excellent particular studies.

In contrast to the paucity of general works on American-European relations from 1900 to 1914 stands a large body of general literature dealing with the United States and the Far East during the same period. A. Whitney Griswold, *The Far Eastern Policy of the United States* (1938); Edwin O. Reischauer, *The United States and Japan* (1965); and John K. Fairbank, *The United States and China* (1958); are the best surveys, but George F. Kennan, *American Diplomacy, 1900–1950* (1951), and Louis J. Halle, *Dream and Reality: Aspects of American Foreign Policy* (1958), make some provocative observations. For important monographs on Japanese-American relations, see Raymond A. Esthus, *Theodore Roosevelt and Japan* (1966); T. Dennett, *Roosevelt and the Russo-Japanese War* (1925); John A. White, *The Diplomacy of the Russo-Japanese War* (1964); Eugene P. Trani, *The Treaty of Portsmouth: An Adventure in American Diplomacy* (1969); Thomas A. Bailey, *Theodore Roosevelt and the Japanese-American Crisis* (1934); and Charles E. Neu, *An Uncertain Friendship: Theodore Roosevelt and Japan, 1906–1909* (1967). For special studies on Chinese-

American relations, see Herbert Croly, *Willard Straight* (1924); Paul A. Varg, *Missionaries, Chinese, and Diplomats* (1954) and *The Making of a Myth: The United States and China, 1897–1912* (1968); Jerry Israel, *Progressivism and the Open Door: America and China, 1905–1921* (1971); Thomas J. McCormick, *China Market: America's Quest for Informal Empire* (1967); Charles Vevier, *The United States and China, 1906–1913* (1955); and Nemai S. Bose, *American Attitude and Policy to the Nationalist Movement in China (1911–1921)* (1970). L. Ethan Ellis, *Reciprocity, 1911* (1939), relates Taft's ill-fated effort to win a reciprocal trade agreement with Canada. The most concise survey of Wilson's Far Eastern policy before 1917 is in Arthur S. Link, *Woodrow Wilson and the Progressive Era* (1954), but see also his *Wilson: The New Freedom* (1956) and *Wilson: The Struggle for Neutrality, 1914–1915* (1960).

C. The United States and Latin America, 1900–1920

Samuel F. Bemis, *The Latin American Policy of the United States* (1943), covers the entire period and is the best general survey. For general works on the United States and the Caribbean, see Wilfrid H. Callcott, *The Caribbean Policy of the United States, 1890–1920* (1942); Dexter Perkins, *Hands Off: A History of the Monroe Doctrine* (1941), *The Monroe Doctrine, 1867–1907* (1937), and *The United States and the Caribbean* (1947); Howard C. Hill, *Roosevelt and the Caribbean* (1927); and Dana G. Munro, *Intervention and Dollar Diplomacy in the Caribbean, 1900–1921* (1964). Dwight C. Miner, *The Fight for the Panama Route* (1940), and William D. McCain, *The United States and the Republic of Panama* (1937), are good for the Panama incident. Arthur S. Link, *Woodrow Wilson and the Progressive Era* (1954), *Wilson: The New Freedom* (1956), *Wilson: The Struggle for Neutrality, 1914–1915* (1960), *Wilson: Confusions and Crises, 1915–1916* (1964), and *Wilson: Campaigns for Progressivism and Peace, 1916–1917* (1965), have the best accounts of Wilson's Caribbean and Mexican policies, but for specialized works on the United States and Mexico, see Howard F. Cline, *The United States and Mexico* (1953); Peter Calvert, *The Mexican Revolution, 1910–1914: The Diplomacy of Anglo-American Conflict* (1968); Kenneth J. Grieb, *The United States and Huerta* (1969); Robert E. Quirk, *An Affair of Honor: Woodrow Wilson and the Occupation of Veracruz* (1962) and *The Mexican Revolution, 1914–1915: The Convention of Aguascalientes* (1960); and Clarence E. Clendenen, *The United States and Pancho Villa* (1961).

D. The First Road to War, 1914–1917

Among the general studies, Charles Seymour, *American Diplomacy during the World War* (1934) and *American Neutrality, 1914–1917* (1935); Ernest R. May, *The World War and American Isolation* (1959); and Edward H. Buehrig, *Woodrow Wilson and the Balance of Power* (1955), are the best. Charles Seymour (ed.), *The Intimate Papers of Colonel House* (4 vols., 1926–1928), includes materials indispensable to understanding Wilson's policies. Arthur S. Link, *Woodrow Wilson and the Progressive Era,* (1954), is a useful summary, but see particularly Link's much fuller account in *Wilson:*

The Struggle for Neutrality,1914–1915 (1960), *Wilson: Confusions and Crises, 1915–1916* (1964), and *Wilson: Campaigns for Progressivism and Peace,1916–1917* (1965), and the same author's *Wilson the Diplomatist* (1957 and 1963).

Special studies on this subject abound, and we will mention only a few of them: Karl E. Birnbaum, *Peace Moves and U-Boat Warfare* (1958), is one of the best monographs in modern diplomatic history; Joseph P. O'Grady (ed.), *The Immigrants' Influence on Wilson's Peace Policies* (1967), begins in the period 1914–1917; Laurence W. Martin, *Peace Without Victory: Woodrow Wilson and the British Liberals* (1958), is useful for the entire period 1914–1919; H. C. Peterson, *Propaganda for War* (1939), over-rates the influence of Allied propaganda; George S. Viereck, *Spreading Germs of Hate* (1930), is excellent for German propaganda in the United States; and Carl Wittke, *German-Americans and the World War* (1936).

Robert E. Osgood, *Ideals and Self-Interest in America's Foreign Relations* (1953), and John Milton Cooper, Jr., *The Vanity of Power: American Isolationism and the First World War* (1969), present incisive analyses of American reactions to the challenges of the war. For the preparedness controversy and the peace movements from 1914 to 1917, see Hermann Hagedorn, *The Bugle that Woke America* (1940), a study of Theodore Roosevelt and the preparedness crisis; Elting E. Morison, *Admiral Sims and the Modern American Navy* (1942); Hermann Hagedorn, *Leonard Wood* (2 vols., 1931); Peter Brock, *Pacifism in the United States* (1968); Charles Chatfield, *For Peace and Justice: Pacifism in America, 1914–1921* (1971); and Arthur S. Link, *Wilson: Confusions and Crises, 1915–1916* (1964).

Almost all the biographies and memoirs cited in preceding sections have chapters on the background of America's first intervention in Europe. To these should be added Robert Lansing, *War Memoirs of Robert Lansing* (1935); Burton J. Hendrick, *The Life and Letters of Walter H. Page* (3 vols., 1922–1926); Ross Gregory, *Walter Hines Page: Ambassador to the Court of St. James* (1970); and Stephen Gwynn (ed.), *Letters and Friendships of Sir Cecil Spring Rice* (2 vols., 1929).

E. *American Participation in the First World War*

Two recent general works are Edward M. Coffman, *The War to End All Wars: The American Military Experience in World War I* (1968), and Harvey A. DeWeerd, *President Wilson Fights His War: World War I and the American Intervention* (1968). The best summaries of military operations are John J. Pershing, *Final Report* (1919), and Leonard P. Ayres, *The War with Germany* (1919). John J. Pershing, *My Experiences in the World War* (2 vols., 1931), and James G. Harbord, *The American Army in France, 1917–1919* (1936), are candid memoirs by two American command-ers. On the American naval contribution, see Thomas G. Frothingham, *The Naval History of the World War* (3 vols., 1924–1926), and Elting E. Morison, *Admiral Sims and the Modern American Navy* (1942).

F. *The War, the Paris Peace Conference, and the Treaty Fight*

We are now beginning to have an excellent literature on American diplomacy during the First World War. Among the general works, Charles Seymour, *American Diplo-*

macy during the World War (1934), is strongly supplemented by W. B. Fowler, *British-American Relations 1917–1918: The Role of Sir William Wiseman* (1969); Arno J. Mayer, *Political Origins of the New Diplomacy, 1917–1918* (1959); Harry R. Rudin, *Armistice, 1918* (1944); Louis L. Gerson, *Woodrow Wilson and the Rebirth of Poland* (1953); Victor S. Mamatey, *The United States and East Central Europe, 1914–1918* (1957); George F. Kennan, *Russia Leaves the War* (1956), *The Decision to Intervene* (1958), and *Russia and the West under Lenin and Stalin* (1961); Betty Miller Unterberger, *America's Siberian Expedition, 1918–1920* (1956); Carl P. Parrini, *Heir to Empire: United States Economic Diplomacy, 1916–1923* (1969); and David F. Trask, *The United States in the Supreme War Council* (1961).

The early American movement for a League of Nations is related by Ruhl J. Bartlett, *The League to Enforce Peace* (1944). For background on the Paris Peace Conference, see Charles Seymour, *American Diplomacy during the World War* (1934), and Lawrence E. Gelfand, *The Inquiry: American Preparations for Peace, 1917–1919* (1963). R. S. Baker, *Woodrow Wilson and World Settlement* (3 vols., 1922), is a friendly account rich in source materials. Also sympathetic to Wilson are N. Gordon Levin, Jr., *Woodrow Wilson and World Politics: America's Response to War and Revolution* (1968); Paul Birdsall, *Versailles Twenty Years After* (1941); Herbert Hoover, *The Ordeal of Woodrow Wilson* (1958); and Seth P. Tillman, *Anglo-American Relations at the Paris Peace Conference* (1961).Thomas A. Bailey, *Woodrow Wilson and the Lost Peace* (1944), is more critical of Wilson. Arno J. Mayer, *The Politics and Diplomacy of Peacemaking: Containment and Counterrevolution at Versailles, 1918–1919* (1967), and John M. Thompson, *Russia, Bolshevism, and the Versailles Peace* (1966), highlight the Russian problem. Russell H. Fifield, *Woodrow Wilson and the Far East* (1952), relates Wilson's struggles with the Japanese at Paris.

The best accounts of the treaty fight in the United States are Ralph Stone, *The Irreconcilables: The Fight Against the League of Nations* (1970); Thomas A. Bailey, *Woodrow Wilson and the Great Betrayal* (1945); and Denna F. Fleming, *The United States and the League of Nations, 1918–1920* (1932). John M. Blum, *Joe Tumulty and the Wilson Era* (1951); John A. Garraty, *Henry Cabot Lodge* (1953); Arthur S. Link, *Wilson the Diplomatist* (1957 and 1963); Richard W. Leopold, *Elihu Root and the Conservative Tradition* (1954); and Charles Seymour (ed.), *The Intimate Papers of Colonel House* (4 vols., 1926–1928), have significant chapters on the treaty fight.

3. The American People and Their Economic Institutions, 1900–1920

A. *The American People: Demographic Changes and Wealth*

The handiest references for general economic and social data are Bureau of the Census, *Historical Statistics of the United States* (1960) and *Statistical Abstract of the United States* (published annually). Warren S. Thompson, *Population Problems* (1953), is an excellent survey. The best sources for decennial demographic changes are the summary volumes of the *Census*.

There are a number of excellent studies of wealth, income, and income distribution in the United States in the twentieth century. For discussions in the broad context of economic development, see Harold U. Faulkner, *The Decline of Laissez Faire, 1897–1917* (1951), and George Soule, *Prosperity Decade: From War to Depression, 1917–1929* (1947). Milton Friedman and Anna J. Schwartz, *A Monetary History of the United States, 1867–1960* (1963), is a monumental study. Robert F. Martin, *National Income in the United States, 1799–1938* (1939), is an excellent statistical summary. Charles B. Spahr, *An Essay on the Present Distribution of Wealth* (1896); Wilford I. King, *The Wealth and Income of the People of the United States* (1915); and Wesley C. Mitchell *et al., Income in the United States . . . 1909–1919* (2 vols., 1921–1922), discuss income distribution from the late 1890s to the 1920s. Simon Kuznets, *Capital in the American Economy* (1961), and Raymond W. Goldsmith, *The National Wealth of the United States* (1962), are general studies.

B. *The Problems of Labor*

There are brief discussions in Harold U. Faulkner, *Decline of Laissez Faire, 1897–1917* (1951); George Soule, *Prosperity Decade: From War to Depression, 1917–1929* (1947); Philip Taft, *Organized Labor in American History* (1964); and Henry Pelling, *American Labor* (1960). However, the third and fourth volumes of John R. Commons *et al., History of Labour in the United States (4vols.,1918–1935), and Philip Taft, The A. F. of L. in the Time of Gompers* (1957), are the best general works for the period.

For detailed and specialized studies of unionization, union politics, and labor struggles, see Melvyn Dubofsky, *When Workers Organize: New York City in the Progressive Era* (1968); Lewis L. Lorwin, *The American Federation of Labor* (1933); Leo Wolman, *The Growth of American Trade Unions, 1880–1923* (1924); Marguerite Green, *The National Civic Federation and the American Labor Movement, 1900–1925* (1956); David Brody, *Steelworkers in America: The Nonunion Era* (1960); and Marc Karson, *American Labor Unions and Politics, 1900–1918* (1958). See also Louis Adamic, *Dynamite, the Story of Class Violence in America* (1934); Samuel Yellen, *American Labor Struggles* (1936); Stanely Buder, *Pullman: An Experiment in Industrial Order and Community Planning, 1880–1930* (1967); and George S. McGovern and Leonard F. Guttridge, *The Great Coalfield War* (1972), on the Colorado coal strike of 1913–1914.

All the general and many of the special studies cited above include discussions of the development of public policy and judicial interpretation concerning labor unions. For judicial interpretation, the following monographs are excellent: Felix Frankfurter and N. Greene, *The Labor Injunction* (1930); Edward Berman, *Labor and the Sherman Act* (1930); Charles O. Gregory, *Labor and the Law* (1946); and Elias Lieberman, *Unions Before the Bar* (1950). Arthur S. Link, *Woodrow Wilson and the Progressive Era* (1954) and *Wilson: The New Freedom* (1956), discuss the labor policies of the Wilson administration, but for labor during the First World War, see Henry F. Pringle, *The Life and Times of William Howard Taft* (2 vols., 1939), and Alexander M. Bing, *War-time Strikes and Their Adjustment* (1921).

For specialized studies on wages, hours, working conditions, and the health of American workers, see Solomon Fabricant, *Employment in Manufacturing 1899–1939* (1942); Albert Rees, *Real Wages in Manufacturing, 1890–1914* (1961); and Robert M. Woodbury, *Workers' Health and Safety* (1927).

The history of the labor movement since 1900 is writ large in the memoirs and biographies of its leaders. Samuel Gompers, *Seventy Years of Life and Labor* (2 vols., 1925), is one of the great autobiographies in American literature. See also Bernard Mandel, *Samuel Gompers: A Biography* (1963). Elsie Glück, *John Mitchell, Miner* (1929), and Hyman Weintraub, *Andrew Furuseth: Emancipator of the Seamen* (1959), illuminate the careers of two wise leaders.

C. The Changing Tides of Immigration

Carl Wittke, *We Who Built America* (1939); George M. Stephenson, *History of American Immigration, 1820–1924* (1926); and Oscar Handlin, *The American People in the Twentieth Century* (1954), are the standard surveys, but John R. Commons, *Races and Immigrants in America* (1907), is still useful. Louis Adamic, *From Many Lands* (1940), and Oscar Handlin, *The Uprooted* (1951), highlight the impact of the uprooting upon the immigrants and their contributions to American life. Good specialized studies are Humbert S. Nelli, *The Italians in Chicago, 1880–1930* (1970); John M. Allswang, *A House for all Peoples: Ethnic Politics in Chicago, 1890–1936* (1970); Rowland T. Berthoff, *British Immigrants in Industrial America, 1790–1950* (1953); Theodore Saloutos, *They Remember America: The Story of the Repatriated Greek-American* (1956); and Carl Wittke, *The Irish in America* (1956). William I. Thomas and Florian Znaniecki, *The Polish Peasant in Europe and America* (2 vols., 1927), is a classic.

Most of the works on immigration policy reflect the controversial aspects of the issue, but Roy L. Garis, *Immigration Restriction* (1927), and William S. Bernard, *American Immigration Policy* (1950), are thorough and objective. John Higham, *Strangers in the Land, Patterns of American Nativism, 1860–1925* (1955), concentrates on nativism in the twentieth century. Roger Daniels, *The Politics of Prejudice: The Anti-Japanese Movement in California and the Struggle for Japanese Exclusion* (1962), is excellent.

D. American Industry and the Economy

Harold U. Faulkner, *Decline of Laissez Faire, 1897–1917* (1951); George Soule, *Prosperity Decade: From War to Depression, 1917–1929* (1947); and Harold F. Williamson (ed.), *The Growth of the American Economy* (1957), include chapters on the growth of industry from 1900 to 1920. Thomas C. Cochran, *The American Business System, 1900–1950* (1957), is a thoughtful analysis. Interesting also among the general studies are Alan R. Raucher, *Public Relations and Business, 1900–1929* (1968), and Morrell Heald, *The Social Responsibilities of Business: Company and Community, 1900–1960* (1970). The government's influence upon the economy is surveyed by Merle Fainsod and L. Gordon, *Government and the American Economy* (1959), and Gerald D. Nash, *United States Oil Policy, 1890–1964* (1968).

For general developments in the late nineteenth century and from 1900 to 1920, see also Thomas C. Cochran and W. Miller, *The Age of Enterprise* (1942); Edmund E. Day and W. Thomas, *The Growth of Manufactures, 1899 to 1923* (1928); Solomon Fabricant, *The Output of Manufacturing Industries, 1899–1937* (1940); and John W. Kendrick, *Productivity Trends in the United States* (1961).

For the growth of particular industries, see Harold F. Williamson and Arnold R. Daum, *The American Petroleum Industry, 1859–1899: The Age of Illumination* (1959); Harold F. Williamson *et al., The American Petroleum Industry: The Age of Energy, 1899–1959* (1963); Harless D. Wagoner, *The U. S. Machine Tool Industry from 1900 to 1950* (1968); Arthur M. Johnson, *The Development of American Petroleum Pipelines . . . 1862–1906* (1956) and *Petroleum Pipelines and Public Policy, 1906–1959* (1967); and Alfred S. Eichner, *The Emergence of Oligopoly: Sugar Refining as a Case Study* (1969).

The best survey of the concentration movement in American industry from 1870 to the 1920s is Henry R. Seager and C. A. Gulick, Jr., *Trust and Corporation Problems* (1929); but see also Arthur R. Burns, *The Decline of Competition* (1936); Ralph L. Nelson, *Merger Movements in American Industry, 1895–1956* (1959); and Adolf A. Berle, Jr., and G. C. Means, *The Modern Corporation and Private Property* (1932).

Frederick Lewis Allen's racy *The Lords of Creation* (1935), gives special attention to the financial leaders during this period. Indispensable general works for the serious student are George W. Edwards, *The Evolution of Finance Capitalism* (1938); Margaret G. Myers, *A Financial History of the United States* (1970); and Vincent P. Carosso, *Investment Banking in America: A History* (1970). For specialized studies, see C. A. E. Goodhart, *The New York Money Market and the Finance of Trade, 1900–1913* (1969); Cedric B. Cowing, *Populists, Plungers, and Progressives: A Social History of Stock and Commodity Speculation, 1890–1936* (1965); Louis D. Brandeis, *Other People's Money, and How the Bankers Use it* (1914), which summarizes the findings of the Pujo Committee in 1913; and Henry L. Staples and Alpheus T. Mason, *The Fall of a Railroad Empire* (1947), the story of Morgan and the New Haven Railroad.

Excellent surveys and special studies of the technological revolution are John W. Oliver, *History of American Technology* (1956); Leonard S. Silk, *The Research Revolution* (1960); and Harry Jerome, *Mechanization in Industry* (1934).

Biographies are often the most palatable form of economic history for the general reader. Frederick Lewis Allen, *The Great Pierpont Morgan* (1949), and Lewis Corey, *The House of Morgan* (1930), reveal different points of view about the great financier. Alan Nevins, *Study in Power: John D. Rockefeller, Industrialist and Philanthropist* (2 vols., 1953), is as much a history of the American oil industry as a biography of its master builder, just as his *Ford, the Times, the Man, the Company* (1954), tells the saga of the automobile industry. For the leaders in iron and steel, see Joseph Frazier Wall, *Andrew Carnegie* (1970), and Ida M. Tarbell, *The Life of Elbert H. Gary* (1925).

4. Social and Intellectual Main Currents in American Life, 1900–1920

A. Social Trends and Changes

Harold U. Faulkner, *The Quest for Social Justice, 1898–1914* (1931); Preston W. Slosson, *The Great Crusade and After, 1914–1928* (1930); Lloyd R. Morris, *Postcript to Yesterday* (1947); and Frederick Lewis Allen, *The Big Change: America Transforms Itself, 1900–1950* (1952), are excellent general surveys emphasizing manners and ideas. Mark Sullivan, *Our Times: The United States, 1900–1925* (6 vols., 1926–1935), contains a wealth of social history, as does Walter Lord, *The Good Years: From 1900 to the First World War* (1960). Most helpful for understanding prewar social and intellectual currents is Henry F. May, *The End of American Innocence: A Study of the First Years of Our Own Time, 1912–1917* (1959). See also Nathan G. Hale, Jr., *Freud Comes to America* (1971); John C. Burnham, *Psychoanalysis and American Medicine, 1894–1918* (1967); Dorothy Ross, *G. Stanley Hall: The Psychologist as Prophet* (1972); Richard Weiss, *The American Myth of Success: From Horatio Alger to Norman Vincent Peale* (1969); and James Harvey Young, *The Medical Messiahs: A Social History of Health Quackery in Twentieth-Century America* (1967).

B. Currents of American Thought

Herbert W. Schneider, *A History of American Philosophy* (1946); Merle Curti, *The Growth of American Thought* (1964); and Ralph H. Gabriel, *The Course of American Democratic Thought* (1956), discuss important developments since the 1890s. Henry S. Commager, *The American Mind* (1950), is also general in scope.

For specialized studies, see Morton White, *Social Thought in America* (1949); Joseph Dorfman, *The Economic Mind in American Civilization* (5 vols., 1946–1959); Sidney Hook, *John Dewey* (1939); Donald B. Meyer, *The Positive Thinkers* (1966); R. Wilson Jackson, *In Quest of Community: Social Philosophy in the United States, 1860–1920* (1968); and John Tipple, *The Capitalist Revolution: A History of American Social Thought 1890–1919* (1970).

C. American Education

Of all the major fields of American history, the history of education is most neglected. Among the general surveys, Ellwood P. Cubberly, *Public Education in the United States* (1934); Stuart G. Noble, *A History of American Education* (1938); and Edgar W. Knight, *Education in the United States* (1951), are the best. Isaac L. Kandel (ed.), *Twenty-Five Years of American Education* (1924), has excellent chapters on developments during the first two decades of this century, but see especially his thoughtful *American Education in the Twentieth Century* (1957). Lawrence A. Cremin, *The Transformation of the School: Progressivism in American Education, 1876–1957*

(1961), is excellent social history, while Laurence R. Vesey, *The Emergence of the American University* (1965), is superb.

D. *American Religious Institutions and Thought*

James W. Smith and A. Leland Jamison (eds.), *Religion in American Life* (4 vols., 1961), is the best introduction to the subject. The two bibliographical volumes in this series are particularly helpful. William W. Sweet, *The Story of Religion in America* (1939); Robert T. Handy, *A Christian America: Protestant Hopes and Historical Realities* (1971); Martin E. Marty, *Righteous Empire: The Protestant Experience in America* (1970); Jerald C. Brauer, *Protestantism in America* (1953); and Clifton E. Olmstead, *History of Religion in the United States* (1960), cover the period, but more detailed are Herbert W. Schneider, *Religion in 20th Century America* (1952), and Willard Sperry, *Religion in America* (1945). Other useful surveys are Thomas T. McAvoy, *A History of the Catholic Church in the United States* (1969); John T. Ellis, *American Catholicism* (1956); Will Herberg, *Protestant, Catholic, Jew* (1955); Nathan Glazer, *American Judaism* (1957); Winthrop S. Hudson, *American Protestantism* (1961); and Kenneth K. Bailey, *Southern White Protestantism in the Twentieth Century* (1964). William G. McLoughlin, Jr., *Modern Revivalism* (1959) and *Billy Sunday Was His Real Name* (1955), are superb on twentieth-century revivalism. Gerald B. Smith (ed.), *Religious Thought in the Last Quarter-Century* (1927), and Arnold S. Nash (ed.), *Protestant Thought in the Twentieth Century* (1951), are both very useful.

Excellent for the awakening of the church's social conscience in the progressive era are Charles H. Hopkins, *The Rise of the Social Gospel in American Protestantism, 1865–1915* (1940); Aaron I. Abell, *The Urban Impact on American Protestantism, 1865–1900* (1943); Henry F. May, *Protestant Churches and Industrial America* (1949); Aaron I. Abell, *American Catholicism and Social Action* (1960); Herbert A. Wisbey, Jr., *Soldiers without Swords: A History of the Salvation Army in the United States* (1955); Charles H. Hopkins, *History of the Y.M.C.A. in North America* (1951); Jacob Henry Dorn, *Washington Gladden: Prophet of the Social Gospel* (1967); and Dores R. Sharpe, *Walter Rauschenbusch* (1942).

E. *American Writing*

For significant work in fiction, poetry, and drama, see the relevant sections in this volume. The following list includes only general works and omits biographies and critical studies of individual writers.

The basic general history is Robert E. Spiller *et al., Literary History of the United States* (1963), which contains discussions of virtually every American writer worthy of mention, lengthy essays on major writers, and a good bibliography. For general works on fictional writing, see Leon Howard, *Literature and the American Tradition* (1960); Willard Thorp, *American Writing in the Twentieth Century* (1960); and Frederick J. Hoffman, *The Modern Novel in America, 1900–1950* (1951), all brief but incisive surveys. For more specialized studies, see Walter F. Taylor, *The Economic*

Novel in America (1942); Walter B. Rideout, *The Radical Novel in the United States, 1900–1954* (1956); Warner Berthoff, *The Ferment of Realism: American Literature, 1884–1919* (1965); Alfred Kazin, *On Native Grounds* (1942); and F. Garvin Davenport, Jr., *The Myth of Southern History: Historical Consciousness in Twentieth-Century Southern Literature* (1970). Alan S. Downer, *Fifty Years of American Drama, 1900–1950* (1951), and Louise Bogan, *Achievement in American Poetry, 1900–1950* (1951), cover the main currents in their respective fields.

F. American Blacks, 1900–1920

There is a rewarding, rich, and fast-growing literature in this field. The best guide is James M. McPherson *et al., Blacks in America: Bibliographical Essays* (1971). Rayford W. Logan, *The Negro in American Life and Thought: The Nadir, 1877–1901* (1954) and *The Betrayal of the Negro from Rutherford B. Hayes to Woodrow Wilson* (1965), and C. Vann Woodward, *The Strange Career of Jim Crow* (1966), provide background discussions for twentieth-century developments. General histories abound, but the best are John Hope Franklin, *From Slavery to Freedom: A History of American Negroes* (1967), and August Meier and E. M. Rudwick, *From Plantation to Ghetto: An Interpretive History of American Negroes* (1966). Other useful general volumes are Gunnar Myrdal, *An American Dilemma* (2 vols., 1944), a massive, penetrating study; Arnold M. Rose, *The Negro in America* (1948), an abridgement of Myrdal's volumes; E. Franklin Frazier, *The Negro Family in the United States* (1939); Charles S. Johnson, *Patterns of Negro Segregation* (1943); John Hope Franklin and Isidore Starr, *The Negro in Twentieth Century America: A Reader on the Struggle for Civil Rights* (1967); S. P. Fullinwider, *The Mind and Mood of Black America: 20th Century Thought* (1969); August Meier and E. M. Rudwick (eds.), *The Making of Black America* (2 vols., 1969); August Meier, *Negro Thought in America, 1880–1915* (1963); Francis L. Broderick and August Meier (eds.), *Negro Protest Thought in the Twentieth Century* (1970); and Talcott Parsons and Kenneth B. Clark (eds.), *The Negro American* (1966).

For black movements and militancy and the Negro in politics during the first two decades of the twentieth century, see Samuel R. Spencer, Jr., *Booker T. Washington* (1955); Charles F. Kellogg, *NAACP: A History, Volume I: 1909–1920* (1967); Robert L. Jack, *History of the National Association for the Advancement of Colored People* (1943); Arvarh E. Strickland, *History of the Chicago Urban League* (1966); W. E. B. Du Bois, *Dusk of Dawn* (1940) and *The Autobiography of W. E. B. Du Bois* (1968); Francis L. Broderick, *W. E. B. Du Bois: Negro Leader in a Time of Crisis* (1959); Shirley Graham Du Bois, *His Day Is Marching On: A Memoir of W. E. B. Du Bois* (1971); Stephen R. Fox, *The Guardian of Boston: William Monroe Trotter* (1970); and Margaret L. Callcott, *The Negro in Maryland Politics, 1870–1912* (1969). William B. Hixson, Jr., *Moorefield Stovey and the Abolitionist Tradition* (1972), is excellent on a white leader of the early civil rights movement.

The following is an incomplete list of specialized studies: Edwin S. Redkey, *Black Exodus: Black Nationalist and Back-to-Africa Movements, 1890–1910* (1969); John D. Weaver, *The Brownsville Raid* (1970); Gilbert Osofsky, *Harlem: The Making of a Ghetto* (1966); Seth M. Scheiner, *Negro Mecca: A History of the Negro in New York City, 1865–1920* (1965); Allan H. Spear, *Black Chicago: The Making of a Negro Ghetto, 1890–1920* (1967); Louis R. Harlan, *Separate and Unequal: Public School Campaigns and Racism in the Southern Seaboard States, 1901–1915* (1958); Claude H. Nolen, *The Negro's Image in the South: The Anatomy of White Supremacy* (1967); Thomas F. Gossett, *Race: The History of an Idea in America* (1963); I. A. Newby, *The Development of Segregationist Thought* (1969) and *Jim Crow's Defense: Anti-Negro Thought in America, 1900–1930* (1965); and David M. Reimers, *White Protestantism and the Negro* (1965). Louise V. Kennedy, *The Negro Peasant Turns Cityward* (1930), and Ira DeA. Reid, *The Negro Immigrant* (1939), are both excellent for the black migration from the South during and after the First World War. Walter White, *Rope & Faggot* (1929), and Arthur F. Raper, *The Tragedy of Lynching* (1933), are both good on lynching in the twentieth century.

Index

A NOTE ON THE TYPE

The text of this book was set on the computer. The type is based on the original Times Roman, designed by Stanley Morison for The Times of London, and first introduced by that newspaper in 1932.

Among typographers and designers of the twentieth century, Stanley Morison has had a strong influence. He was typographical advisor to the English Monotype Corporation, and director of two distinguished publishing houses, as well as a writer of sensibility, erudition, and keen practical sense.